METAL CASTING

Pouring gun-metal (bronze LG2) into moulds for Pelton turbine wheels, using the Roman technique of lost-wax casting

METAL CASTING

Appropriate technology in the small foundry

STEVE HURST

INTERMEDIATE TECHNOLOGY PUBLICATIONS 1996

Intermediate Technology Publications Ltd,
103-105 Southampton Row, London WC1B 4HH, UK

© Intermediate Technology Publications 1996

A CIP record for this book is available from the British Library

ISBN 1 85339 197 2

Typesetting by Diamond People, Bromyard
Printed in UK by SRP, Exeter

Contents

'The founder is always like a chimney sweep, covered with charcoal and distasteful sooty smoke, his clothing dusty and half burned by the fire, his hands and face plastered with soft muddy earth. To this is added the fact that for his work a violent and continuous straining of all a man's strength is required, which brings much harm to his body and holds many definite dangers to his life. In addition, this art holds the mind of the artificer in suspense and fear regarding its outcome and keeps the spirit disturbed and almost continuously anxious. For this reason they are called fanatics and are despised as fools. But, with all this, it is a profitable and skilful art and in large part delightful.'

From Biringuccios *De la Pyrotechnia*, Venice, 1559

Traditional Newar method of lost-wax casting using a clay-dung slurry investment

Preface

Dr E.F. Schumacher was one of the first economists to understand and consider the wisdom and skills which were cast aside or destroyed in the rush to develop higher and higher technology, and to have the wisdom to revitalize and record these skills. In *Small is Beautiful*, Dr Schumacher used the symbols of capital value to illustrate levels of technology: 'If effective help is to be brought to those who need it most, a technology is required that would range in some intermediate position between the £1 technology and the £1000 technology. Let us call it – symbolically speaking – a £100 technology'. He continued: 'Such a technology would be immensely more productive than the indigenous technology (which is often in a condition of decay), but it would also be immensely cheaper than the sophisticated highly capital-intensive technology of modern industry'.

If you look at the small investment casting foundries of India, South-East Asia and West Africa you find models of the type of technology that Dr Schumacher describes. Using the minimum capital, abundant skilled or semi-skilled labour, simple machinery and materials found locally, these traditional co-operatives and small family businesses manufacture objects of great precision. The objects that they make, usually religious or tourist sculpture, have sometimes blinded engineers and business advisers to the possibility of making other objects, such as irrigation, agricultural, micro-hydro-electric or medical items, which are within their wide range of skills.

The technique we now call sand casting, or green sand moulding, was developed much later than investment (or lost-wax) casting. The former is now common to cities and small towns all over the developing world. It was introduced in the nineteenth or early twentieth century, invariably for the repair or replacement of railway or river-boat engines, or the replacement of weapon or vehicle parts.

Investment casting, by contrast, is indigenous. Though it developed in all the early civilizations, it is now only found in its original form in a few places. Its grandchild, the ceramic shell technique, is to be found wherever there is an aerospace or weapons manufacturing industry.

If I concentrate on Nepal, South-East Asia, North and West Africa, it is because I observed and researched foundries in these areas. Another observer might have cited Sri Lanka, China or Indonesia. Although in the pre-Colombian civilizations South America possessed sophisticated and highly developed metal casting industries, these were destroyed, together with agricultural and irrigation systems. Today only small fragments of these technologies remain.

Acknowledgements

This book owes its existence to so many people that it is difficult to know where to start. Firstly, and most recently, to the staff and consultants of ITDG with whom I worked overseas during the last five years, particularly to David Poston whose energy and enthusiasm started the process of collecting and writing down the techniques needed to set up and run a small foundry.

To go back to my own early experience, my gratitude and thanks to the late, great bronze caster Albert Angeloni who taught me lost-wax investment casting at the foundry of the Royal College of Art (RCA), London; to the staff of the Midland Foundry Industries Training School, West Bromwich, who taught me the theory and basics of sand casting; to Ernie Nelson, Senior Lecturer in charge of the foundry, Belfast Technical College, Northern Ireland, for his experience of heavy industry and large iron castings, and for wise and tolerant advice.

For the important and rewarding task of 'taking technology off the back shelf', museums have been vital stopping places, and I should like to thank Janet Peatman, Peter Smithhurst and Nicola Moyle of the Abbeydale Industrial Museum and Kelham Island Museums, Sheffield. My thanks to Sir Eduardo Paolozzi, at the RCA, for encouraging my interest in traditional West African casting over many years.

Partner organizations form an essential part of the work of ITDG overseas, so I wish to thank Tony Wilce who worked for both GTZ and ITDG in Malawi; Rajan Tappah and the staff of the Agricultural Development Bank in Nepal; Bob Buckner, Engineer IC workshops, United Missions Nepal at Butwal, Nepal; Thomas Scheutzlich, Engineer of GTZ, Cuzco, Peru; the Director Jose Muniz and the staff of Asiacion Civil PROMIDHEC in Cuzco, Peru.

I shall not forget, nor cease to be grateful for, the help given me by colleagues in ITDG: David Poston, Rod Edwards, Greg Wishart and Godfrey Cromwell, all based in Rugby; Bikash Pandy in Kathmandu; Teodoro Sanchez, Jorge Segura and Edgardo Rojas in Peru. Dr John Burton of Reading University gave valuable advice on the first castings of Pelton wheels that we made for ITDG.

In the foundry business, by tradition trade secrets are well guarded, and so I am especially grateful to my colleagues in the industry for letting me look around their foundries, both in the UK and overseas. My thanks to Frank Soko of Engineering Services Foundry, Lilongwe, Malawi; to Chris Stevens of Dedza pottery, Malawi, for making ITDG's first crucible; to Shakya Sahib of Nepal Dhalout Udyog Foundry, Patan, Nepal, for showing me the traditional Newar technique of casting; to Gopal Mital Sahib of National Structures Foundry, also in Patan; Vijay Shrestha Sahib of Shrestha Engineering, Bhairawa, Nepal; to Professor Justo Aparichio, Fundicion Ocupacional, Cuzco, Peru; and to Professor Mauricio O'Fallon of the Engineering

Faculty, University of Bogota. Thanks to the Caballero propellor foundry, Callao; EURQIA propellor foundry, Pucalpa; Carena foundry, Cuzco; Arnie Vince, Buena Fortuna Engineering, Callao; and Alberto Colmanarez Electrical Engineering, Lima, all in Peru.

My thanks to the many engineers, foundries and bronze and aluminium casters in Europe, who gave me practical experience, or who helped with my research; to John Payne of F.J. Payne Engineering, Oxford for common-sense advice in both business and engineering; to Rungwe and Claude Kingdon of Pangolin Editions Foundry for a fruitful association which has lasted many years; to Tissa Ranasinghe at the RCA for invaluable advice on the Indian clay slurry process; to Ray and Dave Arnatt, neighbours and colleagues.

Thanks to David Reed of Red Bronze Foundry, London; Monsanto Chemicals; British China Clay Co.; and to Rolls Royce Aero Engines, Bristol, UK for information about the ceramic shell process.

Thanks also to Herman Noak Bildgeiserie, Berlin, for showing me the German method of lost-wax casting, and to Peter Gray of Bristol University for help in setting up my business.

Many people helped me before and during my research into the West African method of casting in Cameroon. At the British Museum Dr Paul Craddock gave me advice on alloying and simple metallurgy. My thanks to Dr Nigel Barley at the British Museum for his advice on where to start; Julian Paxton of the Shell Company, London; Lucien Ngoundo Black and Aboubakir Michirain of the Shell Company in Douala; and the British Council in Yaounde. In Foumban, West Cameroon, my thanks to El Hadj Mustapha Rengou without whose aid I would never have got to know the bronze casters of Le village des artisans, Abdou Ngou and Monta Oumarou, and Artisans Fondeurs de Foumban who were both hospitable and helpful.

Sadly, I must thank my father posthumously, Harold Hurst, physicist and hydrological engineer, who spent his life working in the service of the people of Egypt and Sudan; who, when I was a small child, first introduced me to the drama, heat and smell of a brass foundry at the Department of Nile Control, Cairo.

What impressed me then, and stays with me now, is the sheer drama of molten metal: the wonder at first seeing the brilliant dangerous liquid poured at great heat into the black sand; the sight of the golden metal changing to scarlet, to dull red and then to black, being allowed to cool and congeal, then being dragged from the sand transformed into curiously shaped lumps, to be refined by lathe and milling machine into pumps or parts for excavators or other pieces of irrigation machinery.

Last, but certainly not least, thanks to my wife Sylvie, and two daughters, Sophie and Emma, without whose encouragement, help and labour over a hot furnace my small foundry would not function.

Steve Hurst

Rubber moulds and wax components for a Pelton turbine

Wooden assembly jig and Pelton wheel at the wax pattern stage after it has been assembled in the jig

1. Introduction

The handbook is written for the artisan, metal caster or entrepreneur with more ingenuity than capital. It is aimed at small industries with limited resources. An engineer in a university, or a metallurgist in a large steel works, could pick out many processes that are not described in detail. There is not the space to cover the most recent developments, or processes demanding high capital outlay, important though these developments are. Where appropriate these processes are mentioned in outline.

Simple guidelines in the first section are followed by examples. Using the examples and Contents list, you should have no difficulty finding the process suited to the object you wish to manufacture. For quick reference there is a Glossary covering the different processes and materials in alphabetical order.

Finally, only a fool insists that there is one way, and one way only, to approach a practical problem. Thre are many useful methods; the difficulty lies in selecting the method most appropriate to the job, bearing in mind the financial and supply problems of the workshop.

Making a choice of production method

The alternatives to casting

Where resources are limited, casting is unlikely to be the first choice when manufacturing metal objects. For this reason it is sensible to look at the alternatives before describing those open to the caster.

These alternatives are:

- o Forging
- o Pressing
- o Fabricating
- o Metal joining.

Forging
This is the method most used for tools which demand high tensile strength; for example, agricultural tools – forks, spades, hoes, and all edged tools – knives, machetes, axes, and for most replacement parts for vehicles where tensile strength is important.

Pressing
Dished objects can be pressed or spun, using inexpensive fly presses or simple lathes.

1

Fabricating

Combined with a method of joining metal this is a relatively cheap method of producing a prototype or small numbers of the same object.

Metal joining

This term covers a range of techniques, including:

- o Riveting
- o Pop-riveting
- o Turned and pressed sheet metal seams
- o Lead soldering
- o Silver soldering
- o Brazing
- o Forge welding
- o Oxy-acetylene welding
- o Manual arc welding
- o Inert gas shielded arc welding (MIG or TIG welding).

The experienced blacksmith will make use of a combination of these processes. He or she might, for example, press or spin a dished form then weld or braze it onto a forged lever or arm. In both East and West Africa hoes and machetes are forged out of good quality steel (vehicle leaf springs, for example) and then welded to a length of mild steel pipe.

Blacksmiths in Nepal once produced water-wheels, used for grinding rice and grain, by beating out the buckets from sheet steel and attaching them to a forged boss with rivets. Later, as oxy-acetylene welding became more widely used, the rivets were replaced by welds.

The advantages of casting

If none of the methods mentioned above offers any particular advantage then the answer to your problem probably lies in casting. The advantage of casting is that it enables the production of many identical objects cheaply. A secondary advantage is that it enables the forming of precision objects that cannot be produced by any other method.

The choice of casting method is governed by:

- o The size of the pattern (the original object to be cast)
- o Surface finish required
- o Detail, undercuts or internal forms
- o Number of castings in a production run
- o Acceptable cost.

For the vast majority of casting jobs the choice is simple: low cost + large quantity of castings = sand.

A small number of small, precision castings are more likely to be produced using lost wax. Cost is usually the factor that rules out more specialized forms of casting.

Small, mass-produced articles are most likely to be made in sand. Large, or very large, castings can *only* be formed by the sand process, usually by the floor-moulding (also known as pit-moulding) technique.

Common processes in outline

Sand casting

This is a metal casting process in which a natural sand, containing a proportion of clay to bind the grains of sand together, or a pure silica sand with an artificial binder added to it, is contained in a flask (the name given to a pair of matching moulding boxes) and compressed by hand, or mechanical ramming, around a pattern.

A parting powder prevents the sand in the two halves of the flask from sticking together. When these are parted and the pattern and the dowels forming the sprue system are removed, a negative mould shape is left in the sand. The molten metal is poured into this cavity. See Chapter 9 for details of melting and pouring.

There are a number of different sand casting techniques which can be used.

1. Green sand moulding

This process uses sand which contains a small percentage of clay when in its natural state. When a measured quantity of water is added and the sand is thoroughly mixed and conditioned with rollers, the clay and water act as a binder enclosing and holding together the sand grains. When it is compressed (rammed) round the pattern, the sand becomes solid. This state is called its 'green strength'.

2. Dry sand

This is a sand mixture rich in clay, more commonly used in iron casting. An advantage of this process is that the sand can be rammed more tightly, but it must be well vented using a venting rod. Before molten metal is poured into the mould, the sand is dried either in a kiln or using surface flame.

3. Carbon dioxide–silica sand

In many foundries this process has superseded the green sand process. Sand is bound together using sodium silicate which is hardened by gassing with carbon dioxide (CO_2).

4. Synthetically bonded sands

These are silica sands using one of many synthetic resins as a binder. The resins may be air set, thermoset, or set off with a catalyst.

5. Floor moulding

This is usually used for large, one-off castings. See Chapter 5 for a detailed description of sand processes.

3

6. Loam moulding

A different process used for large one-off castings, as above (see Appendix E).

Note that, where oil is mentioned in a process, as in 'oil-bonded sand', this invariably means a vegetable oil which is used for its oxidizing (drying) qualities.

Lost-wax casting

A wax pattern is formed by hand, or by painting or injecting wax into a mould or die. The wax pattern is invested (coated and contained) in a liquid refractory (heat resisting) mixture known as a 'slurry'. Coats of slurry are built up into a block, or poured around the wax which is in a flask. Alternatively, the wax is dipped in a refractory slurry and then dusted with even grains of dry refractory (known as 'stucco').

Once the refractory, in block or thin shell form, has set and hardened, the wax is removed by heating. Methods of de-waxing vary, but the principle remains the same. Unlike the sand processes where the parts of the mould are opened to allow the removal of the pattern, in the lost-wax process the investment (sometimes called the 'mantle') remains united and the wax pattern is removed by melting it through the sprue system and filling funnel (known as the 'cup'). Finally, the empty mould is removed from the kiln while still hot, inverted and reinforced (unless it is already contained in a flask) and the metal is poured into the mould cavity through the cup.

Die casting

A dic is a reusable mould, usually made of steel, for the mass production of small parts in low melting point alloys – usually zinc or aluminium alloys.

For mass production of small parts which have no undercuts, the durability and excellent surface quality of the die, added to the saving in labour costs, make the expense of producing the die worthwhile. (See Chapter 8 on die making.)

Advantages and disadvantages of each process

For more detailed descriptions, see the relevant chapters on each process.

Sand casting

Green sand moulding

Advantages

- Versatile
- Low cost
- Materials available worldwide
- Suitable for long production runs
- Sand is reusable

Disadvantages

o Simple patterns only – limited range of undercuts possible

o Not a perfect surface, needs machining

o Craft based, demands highly skilled moulders.

Dry sand moulding

Possesses most of the advantages and disadvantages mentioned above, with the following exceptions:

Advantages

o For larger, heavier castings (usually, though not exclusively, in iron) a closer, fine-grained sand with a higher clay content which holds together in its dry (baked) state where a green sand mixture would become weak and friable

o Being dry, there is less gassing and porosity and greater dimensional accuracy

Disadvantages

o Sand requires careful blending and preparation

o Denser sand demands plentiful and thorough venting

o Moulds have to be baked, which needs a kiln and fuel.

CO_2–silica sand

Advantages

o Versatile

o Good surface

o Less distortion

o Suitable for use by semi-skilled labour

o Long production runs

Disadvantages

o Expensive

o Materials harder to obtain

o Needs thorough mixing, usually mechanically

o A common fault is poor surface due to over-gassing

o Sand cannot be reused unless processed through a sand reclamation plant.

Floor moulding

Advantages

- o Suitable for large (and very large) castings
- o Materials readily available

Disadvantages

- o Limited application
- o Demands very experienced, skilled moulders.

Loam (or loom) moulding

Advantages

- o An excellent technique for a single casting or a small number of large castings
- o It is usually, though not exclusively, used for casting cylindrical, conical or domed forms, for example, bells, flywheels and large motor casings
- o The moulder uses a strickle instead of a large, expensive pattern

Disadvantages

- o Loam moulding is a highly specialized, craft-based technique that has almost died out, except in bell foundries
- o It is not suitable for large production runs.

Die casting

Advantages

- o Precise, excellent surface
- o Suitable for mass production
- o Assuming a long production run, unit costs are low
- o Unskilled or semi-skilled labour

Disadvantages

- o High initial cost of making die
- o Limited in size
- o Limited to low melting point metal of casting (zinc based, or aluminium alloys)
- o No undercuts.

Lost-wax casting

Advantages

- o Versatile
- o Materials available worldwide
- o Material reusable (in the traditional processes)
- o Very precise. Good surface and precise details
- o Undercuts present no problems
- o Process can cast thin, complex forms where details, or internal passages, cannot be machined

Disadvantages

- o High cost
- o Requires a skilled labour force
- o Limited production run
- o Requires a more complicated foundry layout compared with sand casting (sophisticated processes demand a controlled environment for the investment area).

Other investment processes

Lost mercury (or 'mercast') process
Too specialized and expensive to be appropriate for this handbook.

Lost expanded polystyrene (backyard technique)

Advantages

- o Low cost
- o Materials found worldwide
- o Simple to use with semi-skilled labour
- o Useful for rapid production of a prototype or one-off piece to be machined or modified

Disadvantages

- o In its basic form it has a very limited application
- o Suitable for one, or very small number of castings
- o Imprecise, very poor surface
- o Unpredictable, liable to distortion
- o Only suitable for aluminium (this limitation applies only to the basic process: the high-tech version casts any metal).

7

High-tech polystyrene method

This is an automated production line process and is too specialized to be appropriate for this handbook.

Examples

1. Pelton wheels (for hydro-electricity production)

The earliest examples (over one hundred years old) were made by blacksmiths. The buckets were forged to shape and fixed onto a central boss.

More recently these large wheels (also called runners) were cast in iron. The cups were welded, riveted or bolted onto the centre. Examples of these can be seen all over the world.

Recent examples

o   Medium-sized Pelton: 350mm PCD (pitch centre diameter). Both boss and cups were sand cast in bronze. Larger sizes were in cast iron. The cups were held in a jig and welded or bolted onto the boss.

o   Small Peltons: 175mm and 150mm PCD. These were formed in wax and then cast entire by the lost-wax process.

Choice of metal

For very large Peltons, cast iron or steel is superior. Gun-metal (bronze) alloy types LG2 or LG3 or admiralty brass are excellent for the medium or small Peltons. Aluminium is a good substitute but will not last as long as bronze. However, aluminium is still vastly superior to cheap imported plastic Pelton wheels. In the Himalayas these last less than a year.

2. Pulley wheels

These are used in all rural areas for agricultural machinery of all kinds. They wear out and need to be replaced.

Size of casting – medium, 150–300mm (6–12in)
Metal – aluminium
Surface finish – to be turned
Detail: undercuts or internal forms – none
Number of castings – one or small number
Cost – low
Answer – simple sand casting, without core.

3. Agricultural sprinkler head

These are small, semi-precise parts and there is a continuous demand for them.
Size of casting – small, no more than 100mm (4in)

Metal – aluminium or zinc alloy

Surface finish – good

Detail: inside surfaces must be smooth and accurate – this can be achieved by casting the sprinkler in two halves and fitting them together

Number of castings – many

Cost – low

Answer – die casting.

4. Impeller for water pump

Small volume of production but very precise finish

Size of casting – medium, 100–200mm (4–8in)

Metal – gun-metal LG2 or phosphor bronze

Surface finish – good

Detail – fine internal surface is essential

Number of castings – few

Cost – high for a precision machine

Answer – lost-wax casting.

2. Setting up the workshop

Only the metal caster or workshop manager can make the final decision on the layout of the workshop. The choices made depend on climate, location and cost, and rules sensible for one region do not apply in another. Therefore it is possible only to give general guidelines, or to suggest points that should be considered, rather than to provide answers. This chapter does not include building kilns and furnaces – see Chapter 11.

The most useful advice (based on painful experience) is to start simply, within your means, and expand the business organically. In other words, re-equip with more expensive, sophisticated machinery only as your business grows.

A conventional and established foundry is divided into four areas:

1. Pattern making
2. Moulding and core making
3. Melting and casting
4. Fettling.

A large foundry will have a fifth area, for testing and inspection, but this is rarely found in small businesses.

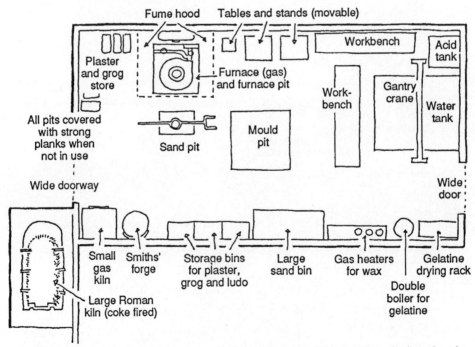

Figure 1. Plan of the Italian foundry at the Royal College of Art, London, designed and built by Albert Angeloni

The small workshop or sand foundry

A rural foundry, or one starting from small beginnings, may well have to follow a different pattern. Many foundry businesses in Africa, Asia and South America run very successfully with a minimum of equipment but an abundance of skilled labour.

The equipment required to start a foundry is not expensive or sophisticated. Certain things, however, are essential. Water and hot metal do not mix, or not without violent consequences, and for this reason you need a roof, no matter how basic. The simplest foundries in Africa and South-East Asia are roofed with sheets of corrugated iron. Walls are not, in most cases, necessary.

In a city, on the other hand, some kind of secure fence or storage area is equally essential. Non-ferrous metals are valuable and must be protected against thieves.

The furnace can range in type from the most expensive electric induction furnace to a hole in the ground. (See Chapter 11.) A furnace pit or a 40 gallon oil drum lined with bricks and refractory clay both serve well.

Furnace fans or blowers are expensive, but they can be made by a competent blacksmith. They range from the simplest hand-powered bellows or cycle-powered blower to bellows driven by an electric motor. Fuels range from charcoal and coke to waste engine oil, kerosene or bottled gas, though gas is usually expensive.

Most craftsman hold to the sound belief that apprentices should be trained in the skilled use of hand-tools before they use power tools, and much fine work has been done with hand-tools, over many centuries. Power tools save time, labour and effort. They do not of themselves make better work. Indeed sometimes the reverse is true: a grinder in the hands of an inexperienced fettler can ruin the best casting in a second.

The following is a list of basic requirements for setting up a foundry.

o Roof

o Security wall or fence (or a secure store)

o Simple vice or clamp fixed to the floor, or a workbench with vice attached (there is no hard and fast rule; different people prefer to work in different positions)

o Furnace pit (or drum)

o Simple, low-temperature oven for baking cores

o Air blower

o Fuel store

o Moulding boxes (or flasks) which can be made from either wood or steel

o Furnace irons and crucible lifting tongs (if you have a welder you can make these yourself out of steel scrap)

o Sand-moulding tools (these too can be made out of hardwood and scrap steel; old kitchen knives and spoons are useful, so are tins or old containers for measuring volume)

o Metal finishing tools.

There are many advantages in sharing power tools with a blacksmith. An oxy-acetylene or electric arc welder is an expensive item of capital equipment, but pays for itself, in time, many times over. The same can apply to a power drill and a power grinder.

Hand-tools such as fettling chisels can be made out of good quality tool steel. In many countries good quality files and hacksaw blades are either difficult to obtain or extremely expensive. For many jobs a sharp chisel will do instead, but in some cases a good sharp file is essential.

The workshop for a lost-wax foundry

The roots and traditions of lost-wax (investment casting) foundries are quite different, and usually much older, than sand foundries. In many cultures lost-wax casting was indigenous, whereas sand foundries were attached to railway, mining or irrigation workshops introduced in colonial times. For this reason, as well as practical reasons, the lost-wax foundry is quite different in appearance from the sand foundry.

Most traditional and modern lost-wax foundries separate the workshops into three areas (even if there is no physical division between them, as in West Africa).

1. Wax working shop
2. Furnace and kiln area
3. Metal finishing and welding area.

A fourth area is the metal store or strong room. Power tools, the electric blower, finished castings and other valuables are kept in the strong room. In some foundries the strong room and the wax working shop are combined.

1. Wax working shop

For this area you will require the following:

- o Either low tables or benches (according to which working position you prefer)
- o Small charcoal stove, gas burner or electric heating unit to melt wax and also to heat the wax working irons
- o Old buckets, metal pots or large tins to contain liquid wax
- o Brushes of various sizes
- o Vegetable oil
- o Plaster of Paris
- o If using flexible moulds, a clean area should be set aside for making the plaster cases and accurately measuring and mixing the rubber moulding compound.

2. Furnace and kiln area

This is described in detail in Chapter 11. A cardinal rule is to allow plenty of space around the furnace. Cramped conditions make lifting and pouring the crucible awkward, and accidents more likely. Having said that, sometimes you have no choice and must do the best you can with what space you have.

The first foundry that the author rebuilt and took charge of was in an old cellar. It was very cramped, with low headroom and poor ventilation. There was nowhere to run in the event of an accident. Fortunately we did not have an accident. After I left, for a better job in a larger foundry, this tunnel foundry was condemned by a safety inspector.

Metal melting arrangements are the same for either a sand foundry or a lost-wax or die casting foundry (though sand casters usually melt larger quantities). But remember that when setting up a lost-wax foundry you will need a de-waxing kiln or burn-out furnace as well as a crucible or reverberatory furnace.

3. Metal finishing and welding area

This is always separated from the wax working shop, and usually separated from the furnace area. There are exceptions, however. If space is limited, or the furnace is used infrequently, foundry and metal finishing areas can be combined. Whereas in a sand foundry, moulding, metal melting and fettling continue in parallel (making separate shops necessary), lost-wax casting is usually cyclical and so the same space can be used for different parts of the process.

Examples of foundry designs

In a typical Italian lost-wax foundry, where space is limited, the furnace is set below ground. This has many advantages, not least that it can be covered over with heavy timbers when not in use. The foundry sand pit is covered in the same way. The Italians usually place the kiln in a nearby, but separate, building. In the author's foundry (modelled on the Italian layout) the kiln is outside, covered with a lean-to shed, but the main doors open into the foundry so that the hot moulds can be lifted directly into the sand pit ready for filling with molten metal.

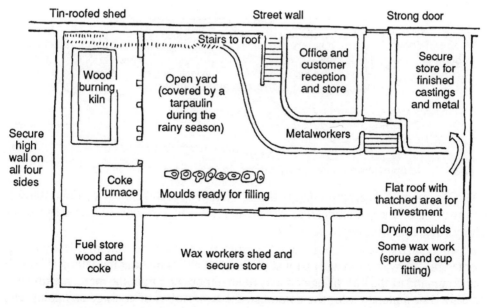

Figure 2. The Newar foundry (belonging to the Shakya family), Patan, Nepal

13

This is the usual practice in a city, or anywhere where floor space is expensive. Where the foundry is located in a village, or in farming country where space is less of a problem, the different phases of the process can be separated.

Although the layout and casting processes varied in Nepal and western Cameroon (though less than one might expect), the foundries that the author has visited in each country have many similarities. Each workshop for each process was separate, and in each the different parts of the process were carried out by different groups.

In Patan, Nepal, the Newar foundry is protected by a high wall which contains one main building and several outbuildings which house the various workshops.

In Foumban, western Cameroon, the store house, or strong room, is the only solid structure, and the kiln and furnace room are built onto it as a lean-to. Thatched roofs radiate out from this central point to protect the artisans from sun and rain. A night-watchman and a pack of dogs protect this foundry, *Le village des artisans,* at night.

The Newar (Nepal) foundry has electricity, though supply is intermittent, and they own a petrol driven generator as a back-up.

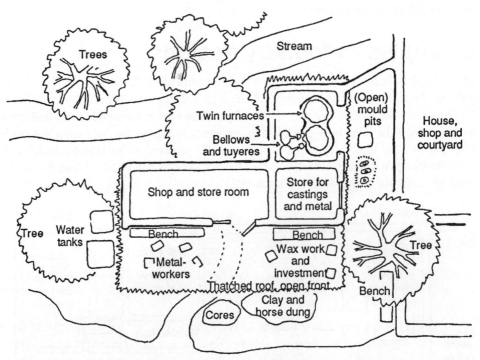

Figure 3. Co-operative foundry, *Le village des artisans*, Foumban, Cameroon

The Bamoum (Cameroon) foundry has no electricity and therefore no motor blower or power tools. The Bamoum artisans were all male, and they were surprised by photos of my daughters working in our foundry.

However, in the Newar family foundry, women play an important role. The younger women run the wax room and do most (though not all) of the wax modelling. The aunt had command of the kiln firing and played an important part in the metal melting and pouring. For a metal caster she combined the two virtues of courage and calm. Her serenity, even under the most dangerous conditions, calmed everyone around her.

3. Pattern making

Casting bears some resemblance to letter press printing. Each is a reproductive process which requires a particular mental agility in the artisan: the skill and experience to move from positive to negative and back to positive again.

A print requires a block (or letter) which is made in negative; a casting requires a negative form which is called the mould. Moulds are made of many materials, but all need a positive form from which they are constructed.

This original positive form is called the pattern. It is the model from which the final casting is made. It is the image of the casting in every respect, except one, and that is size. The reason why the pattern has to be made over-size, and the method the pattern maker uses to arrive at that size, are explained later.

Though patterns vary widely in size, complexity and material, these few basic principles remain the same. There is, however, one major difference between a pattern made for sand casting and a pattern made for lost-wax investment casting: the former is designed to withdraw from the mould and so has no undercuts or heavily textured surfaces that might drag, or distort the sand, while the latter is not withdrawn, but is melted or 'lost' in the mould. Though a complex, or undercut, surface is not impossible in sand casting, it presents a major problem for the sand moulder, and can only be undertaken by a moulder of great skill and long experience. On the other hand, undercuts present no problem in lost-wax casting, and this is one of its major advantages.

Materials

An industrial pattern for sand casting may be made from aluminium, brass, epoxy resin or hard plaster, but the most usual pattern seen in racks in a pattern maker's shop is made from a close-grained hardwood.

A mould for lost-wax casting may be made from any of the above materials. There is one very important exception to this rule. In the Asian, West African and South American tradition of lost-wax casting, the artist or artisan forms the pattern directly in wax, omitting the intermediate process (making a mould) which is a part of the Roman–Italian tradition.

This feature of craft tradition may appear to rule out the former methods for use by engineers. In practice this is not a problem. The engineers must make the mould and produce the wax pattern(s) to their own specification and then hand over the wax pattern to the local foundry for casting. (See Appendices A and B.)

There is no doubt that metal patterns, followed closely by epoxy resin, last longer than those made of any other material. But both metal and resin are expensive. A hard plaster or cement makes an efficient pattern, if you need only a small number of castings. Many foundries dislike plaster patterns and resist using them, but in practice a hard plaster, though it will not last as long as wood, will not break up when the sand is rammed and will make several excellent castings.

Wooden patterns

The first thing to be considered is which type of wood to use. It is difficult to lay down hard-and-fast rules about woods because often you have to use whatever is available.

The wood must be well-seasoned so that it does not warp or shrink, and it must have an even grain and be free from knots. Traditionally in the UK, pattern makers used yellow pine imported from Scandinavia. Today the Malay wood jellatong is the most common. Other woods in general use include obeche and various types of African mahogany. Balsa is rather soft for pattern making but can be used if necessary, provided you harden the final surface with shellac or varnish. Some books on pattern making recommend teak because of its water resisting qualities. In India, Burma (Myanmar) and Thailand, teak has the advantage of being readily available, but personally I find it rather too gritty. Edged tools are blunted and have to be sharpened frequently when working teak. As a general rule, patterns for only a few castings should be made out of softwood, and those that will be used many times from a hardwood such as mahogany. This is the ideal, but often you have to use whatever you can find.

Laminated or processed woods

These are more stable than natural woods, and many pattern makers prefer them. They are, however, difficult to obtain in many countries.

If plywood is used, then it must be good quality ply of several thicknesses, and the best is birch ply. Laminating the wood using a strong synthetic glue makes the pattern strong and resistant to warping. The other advantage is thrift. Using up small pieces is a lot more economical than carving the entire pattern out of one large chunk. When you glue the wooden pieces to make up the laminate, make sure that they are clamped in several places, or use heavy weights to press the parts together.

Compressed wood laminates

Thin sheets of wood have been glued and pressed together so that the grains of alternate laminated sheets run across each other. They are stronger and denser than natural woods and can be bought in any thickness from 12 to 50mm (0.5 to 2in).

Laminated wood impregnates

The wood laminate may be impregnated with resins to fill the cell cavities, or both impregnated and compressed to increase the density of the material – for example, WPC (wood plastic combination).

Another stable but expensive wood substitute is a resin and wood flour composition which is used by pattern makers in the car and truck industry.

Old castings

These are frequently used in the developing world as a substitute for a wooden pattern. To allow for contraction, machining allowance and draught allowance or taper (see p18), the casting must be lagged with wooden strips, leather, or resin filler paste to obtain the correct pattern size. Provided this is done accurately there is no reason why you should not get good castings by this method. Unfortunately the foundry I saw using old castings in East Africa did not make allowance for contraction. No doubt the puzzled customer wondered why the replacement part, which looked the same as the original part for his old Landrover, would not fit.

Resin patterns

Since wooden patterns have a limited life, and must be cut and worked from solid blocks by hand-tools or machine, it can be useful to make rubber moulds from which to make resin patterns. Plastic, castable pattern materials (including hard plasters) can then be cast in the rubber moulds. The strongest and most commonly used resin is epoxy.

Epoxy resin

This comes in two liquids the consistency of honey. Mixed together the resin becomes solid in a predictable time. Hardeners of different setting speeds can be bought from the manufacturer. Epoxy has good machining qualities and can be repaired with an epoxy filler such as that used for car body repairs.

If the resin pattern is cast in a plaster mould this will need a thin coat of a release agent. Silicone rubber moulds, however, do not need this (see Chapter 4 on mould making for lost-wax casting).

Polyester resins

These are about half the price of epoxy. They are normally used with glass fibre reinforcement. Polyester patterns can be hollow, or filled. In either case the process starts with a surface coat resin known as the gel coat. Once the mould has been prepared with a separator, or release agent, two or three layers of gel coat are laid on and allowed to set, but not cure completely. Laminating resin is used over the top of the gel coats to hold and impregnate the layers of glass fibre reinforcement.

Casting resin

Fillers are usually added to this form of resin to increase its strength and reduce cost. Talc, slate powder, fine sand, and even wood flour are all used as fillers. Casting resin can be used with or without the glass fibre and laminating layer.

Most polyester resins take about 24 hours to cure, or set, completely. Polyester and glass fibre, in all forms, are common materials in any area of the world where modern boats are built or repaired. (Expanded polystyrene, another useful foundry material, is also common in these areas.) You should seek the maker's advice on which setting speed is most suitable for the job you have in mind. In some cases you can speed up the cure by adding an accelerator. Heat also accelerates the curing process. However, be careful: too fast a setting time can be quite spectacular. A bowl of resin smoking and catching fire, while the pattern maker dances round it or throws it out of the door, provides great amusement for idle bystanders but much less for the pattern maker. *Be very careful if you use aluminium powder as a filler.* Aluminium is itself an accelerator when mixed with some resins.

Skills

Pattern makers almost always come from a woodcarving background. All the developing countries I have visited have an abundance of woodcarvers whose skill inspires awe and admiration. These artisans work by eye and touch and have no need for any theoretical knowledge.

However, pattern making is a trade in its own right, and one demanding a high degree of both technical knowledge and experience. It deserves a book to itself. Having said that, the small-scale founder has to manage as well as possible with the best resources available. Some skill with wood-tools is essential, but measurement, accuracy and the ability to read drawings are more important than formal woodworking training (though I would be the last person to deny the usefulness of a skilled cabinet maker, if you are lucky enough to know one living near your foundry).

Finding a craftsman (I have not seen any women carvers) who can read drawings is a major problem for the owner of a small foundry. You may have to train a pattern maker from a group of bright apprentices. Another solution might be to pair an experienced woodcarver with someone less experienced and less skilled, but who has the advantage of some technical training, including the reading of engineering drawings.

Training a good pattern maker deserves your attention, because the accuracy of the castings depends on it. If the surface where the metal meets the sand is crucial, then it is the surface of the original pattern which forms the sand surface. One of the basic causes of bad castings is badly made, or inaccurate, patterns, although modern glues and fillers (polyvinylacetate – PVA – based glues seem to be obtainable all over the world) do make it easier to construct, or modify, a pattern that will do the job.

The pattern maker has to think several moves ahead. As has already been mentioned, much of metal casting resembles printing in that it involves thinking in reverse. The facility to move mentally from positive to negative comes with practice. Teaching students flexible mould making, I found that some grasped it at once, others took much longer.

Designing the pattern

Taper or draught allowance

The first thing to remember in making a pattern is that it must come out of the sand cleanly. There must be no undercuts or awkward corners which will bind on the sand and hold it. No matter how finely made the pattern, or how cleverly designed, if the sand does not release from it, leaving a clean crisp impression, then the pattern is useless.

Every pattern must have a draught allowance, or taper. Without this taper the sides of the pattern will bind in the sand and will not come out cleanly. Taper varies from about 1–3 degrees. The greater the taper, the easier it is to draw the pattern out of the sand.

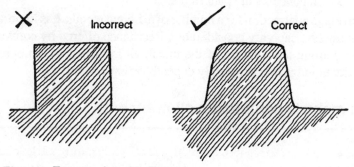

Figure 4. Taper or draught allowance

The important surface is the sand; that is what forms the metal. The pattern is only a tool to this end.

To give an example, a cylinder pattern is easy: you make the split line along the axis. You must, however, be sure to incline the ends; they too must taper. A sausage shape, or cylinder with hemispherical (evenly rounded) ends, is easier still. A cube is not difficult; you split the mould on the diagonal. But once again, you must incline the two ends. If, for some reason, you have to cast the cube square on, you must incline the sides. An example of this would be a box with a flange around one edge. I will return to the design of the pattern later.

Contraction allowance

Another important consideration is the problem of shrinkage. The final casting is made of metal, but all metals expand on being heated (melting) and contract on freezing (solidifying). Therefore the negative, or mould, must be sufficiently oversize to allow for this shrinkage. To carry this still further, the mould is formed by ramming sand around the positive. The positive is the pattern. The pattern must be larger than the final casting. The obvious question is how much larger?

Since different metals have different rates of contraction this might seem like an immense difficulty. However, it is not. Plans and drawings always state the dimensions of the final casting and the metal in which it will be cast. To avoid much complicated mathematics (and many wasted castings) a simple tool was invented, called a pattern maker's rule.

The rule is calibrated along one edge in normal measure in inches or millimetres. On one edge of the reverse side is a calibration allowing for the contraction in brass, and on the other edge for aluminium.

There are three stages of volume change between pouring the molten metal and retrieving the casting from the mould:

1. Liquid changes which take place during the fall in temperature from pouring to freezing or solidification.

2. Shrinkage during freezing (solidification).

3. Solid shrinkage, or contraction, in the solidified casting as it cools to atmospheric temperature.

It is the third factor which concerns the pattern maker.

Table 1 shows the average contraction for a number of different metals. It is important to remember that contraction can vary considerably. Resistance offered by cores and moulds, and also the pouring temperature of the metal, all influence the amount of contraction. The ability to judge this accurately depends on experience.

Table 1. Pattern maker's contraction allowance

Cast iron	0.9–1.3%
Brass	1.3%
Gun-metal	1.0–1.6%
Phosphor bronze	1.0–1.6%
Aluminium alloys (e.g. LM6)	1.3%
Zinc and zinc alloys	2.6%

Machining allowance

This allowance is added to the pattern over and above the contraction allowance so that when the surface of the casting has been removed by a lathe or other machine tool to give the desired finish, the product will be the correct size. It varies according to the type and size of pattern and the metal being used to produce the casting. Although typical allowances vary between 2 and 6mm, in exceptional cases it can be as high as 25mm.

Colour code for patterns

Pattern makers use a colour code so that it is clear to the metal caster which surfaces are which. This is as follows:

- o 'As cast' surfaces which are to be left unmachined – red or orange
- o Surfaces which are to be machined – yellow
- o Core prints (see below) for unmachined openings and end prints – black
- o Core prints for machined openings – yellow stripes on black
- o Seats for loose pieces and loose core prints – green.

(British Standards Institute, publication no. 467).

Core prints and core boxes

The core print is the extra piece on the pattern which leaves a cavity (or print) into which the end of the core fits, in order to hold the core in place. The core box is the negative shape, usually made of wood in which the core is formed.

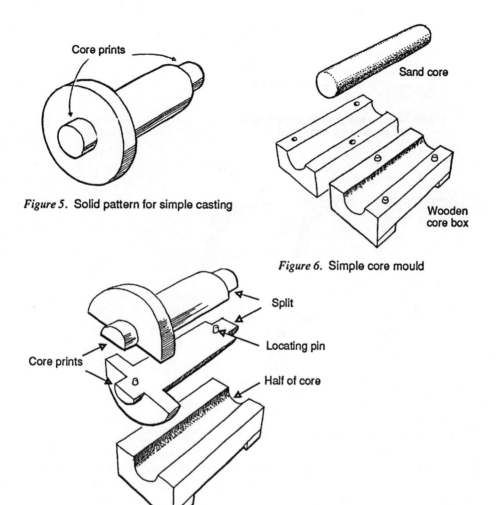

Figure 5. Solid pattern for simple casting

Figure 6. Simple core mould

Figure 7. Simple wooden split pattern

Chucking spigot

This is an extra piece on the pattern which looks very similar to a core print. It is used to grip the casting in the chuck during turning on a lathe.

Design for casting

Like pattern making, design for casting is a specialized trade. But, once again, the founder has to be both designer and pattern maker so it is essential to grasp some of the essentials of design. (See also Chapter 9 on melting metal, and Chapter 10 on the flow and solidification of metals.)

The most efficient form for a piece of machinery may not be the best from the casting viewpoint. The design engineer and the pattern maker may have to reach a compromise. Certain factors make for bad castings, particularly sudden changes from thick to thin

21

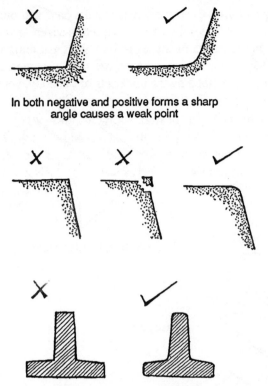

In both negative and positive forms a sharp
angle causes a weak point

Bad   Good

Figure 8. Good and bad pattern design

sections, sharp angles, or long thin stretches where the metal has to flow horizontally. If a thin section is flanked by two thick sections, the thin section will tend to freeze first, and it will then be drawn, or crack, as the thick pieces freeze and contract.

This can be best illustrated by the contrast between a simple and a complex form, both from the caster's point of view. If a hollow hemisphere with an even wall thickness is one of the simplest forms to cast, a model horse is one of the most difficult. This is a problem for the art caster; an engineer will be able to think of many shapes that suffer from the same difficulties.

Artists have made drawings and models of horses, symbols of both wealth and power, from the earliest times. Neither stone nor clay possess the tensile strength of metal, so the legs were formalized or, in other words, thickened. The first metal casters did not know how to make a core, so they had to cast their horses solid. On encountering the problem of shrinkage in the thick section they formalized the design still further, making the body of the horse flatter and thinner.

As the skill of the foundries increased, reaching a peak in France and Italy in the nineteenth century, so the demand for realistic art castings increased. The resulting bronze says far more for the caster's virtuosity than the sculptor's taste. The case of the spindly-legged racehorse provides a useful lesson in how not to design a good casting.

The body is large, the legs long and thin. Even if he detaches the base and pins the feet in place later (which is the usual practice) the caster encounters severe problems with contraction along the thin, complex form of the legs. Also, the great majority of these model horses are above miniature size and well below life size. This means that these models have an enclosed core, demanded by the thickness of the body, yet there is no natural vent to take the gases to the surface of the mould.

The Chinese avoided this problem by intelligent design. The model horse was adorned with a saddle blanket. This was not mere adornment, the blanket hid the belly of the horse which was left open forming a natural vent for the gases. Thus the Chinese founder sidestepped the enclosed core problem. The Newar casters of Nepal found another solution. A model of a god, demon or dancing girl also has an enclosed core. The Newar added a decorative belt, even on a nude figure, or sometimes bracelets around the arms and legs. They cut the figure in two, using the belt to hide the join.

The moral of this story is that the intelligent designer works with the nature of the material, not against it, and avoids the problem of thick sections adjacent to thin sections and the problem of the enclosed core if he can do so.

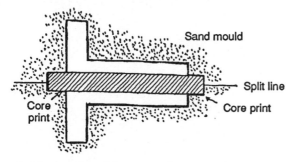

Figure 9. The location of the core using core prints

Another problem which can be solved by compromise and intelligent design is the right-angled bend. Faced with a sharp corner, molten metal behaves badly. Its flow is governed by those same laws that apply to any other liquid. A sharp change in direction causes turbulence. In a sand mould the flowing metal can break off the sharp corners of the mould leading to extra metal on the casting and sand inclusion. Last but not least sharp corners cause cracks or weak points in the finished casting (see Chapter 10 on metallurgy).

The ideal design ought to have sections that are uniform, but this is an ideal rather than a practical possibility; any change should take place gradually.

Storing patterns

Metal patterns present few storage problems. Wood, on the other hand, is a problem, especially in a country with a tropical climate. Nearly all wooden patterns are made up of small pieces of timber, or plywood, and this is often glued cross-grained to add to the strength. If pieces are glued cross-ply the pattern is less likely to crack or distort.

Unfortunately, the glues in common use, most of which are based on polyvinyl acetate, are not completely water-resistant, though they are much better than the old-fashioned 'hide and hooves' type of carpenter's glue. Extreme heat may cause the timbers to move about and to warp. For this reason storage is a problem in countries like Malaysia, Cameroon or Nigeria which experience both great heat and high rainfall. The answer is to store the patterns which you believe you will use again away from the sun and the damp and somewhere where air can circulate around them. However, when workshop space is limited this is more easily said than done.

The Intermediate Technology team in Nepal found that epoxy patterns, which we thought were stable, became flabby and unreliable in the heat. Epoxy, thought to be the new super material, was in fact less reliable than wood. It is worth casting a pattern which is going to be used over and over again, such as a Pelton bucket, in aluminium.

4. Flexible moulds for the mass-production of wax patterns

There are several different methods of making moulds for forming waxes:

1. Press mould for simple shallow forms

2. Rigid piece mould, made of plaster of Paris, plastic (e.g. glass fibre resin), metal, or even wood

3. Gelatine

4. Hot-melt rubber

5. Polysulphide rubber RTV (room temperature vulcanizing)

6. Silicone rubber RTV.

The method you choose depends on the type of form you are making. A simple shallow form can be press-moulded. A deeper form can be moulded using a piece mould. A more complicated, undercut, or heavily textured form demands a flexible mould made from one of the materials 3 to 6 listed above.

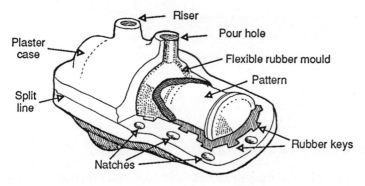

Figure 10. Cut-away view of flexible mould with pattern

The advantage of a flexible mould is that it can be peeled away from the undercut form without damaging the wax or itself. However, once the original pattern, or the wax, is removed the rubber cannot, by its very nature, accurately hold its shape. To prevent this loss of shape it must have a rigid backing. This backing is called a 'case', and the case has to be made first.

The surface of the flexible mould material is a negative impression of the original pattern in every detail. This flexible skin must be backed up with a rigid case, which must come off the flexible layer without sticking. To put it another way, the *outside* of the flexible layer must have no undercuts, or impediments, to prevent the easy removal of the case.

To make a case that follows the surface of the pattern closely, yet has no undercuts, you need an intermediate stage. This will create a case that can be easily removed from the flexible inner layer, which in turn can be peeled away from the pattern. The flexible material is always replaced in its case, and so keeps its shape. In fact it should be stored not only in its case but also, if possible, with the pattern inside it.

The most convenient and most easily obtained material to form the intermediate layer is clay.

The stages that follow are common to making a case for all flexible materials. The difference lies in the thickness of the flexible mould. A gelatine or hot-melt rubber mould is always thicker than an RTV mould. The thickness of the RTV varies according to the tear strength of the rubber. All RTV rubbers are expensive, so there is no point in using more than you have to.

Making the case for a flexible mould

1. Decide on the split line on the pattern, just as you would decide on the parting line for a sand cast.

2. Embed the pattern up to the split line in clay (or build clay up around it) to resemble Figure 11.

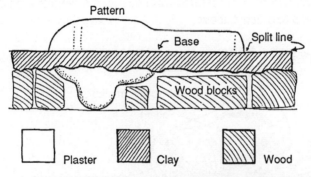

Figure 11. Making the clay base (following the split line)

3. Protect the exposed half of the pattern with thin paper (or thin plastic; cling film is ideal if it is available).

4. Place an even layer of clay over the exposed half of the pattern. There are two ways of making an even layer. Either flatten the clay out, like making pastry, or roll out coils, like making a coil pot. The thickness of the clay layer depends on

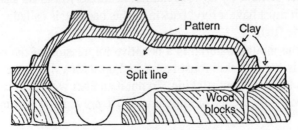

Figure 12. Building the clay intermediate layer

the material which will eventually form the flexible mould. For hot-melt rubber or gelatine it should be approximately 12.5mm (0.5in), but thicker for a pattern larger than 230mm (9in) long or 75mm (3in) from the split line. For polysulphide rubber use a thickness of about 65mm (2.5in). Silicone rubber needs a thinner layer of about 32mm (1.25in).

5. When the rubber is introduced it must be retained in place in the mould. There are two ways of ensuring this: use a flange, or use keys (wedges) – see Figure 13.

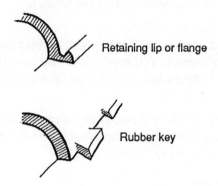

Figure 13. Two methods of holding the rubber in place aginst the plaster case

6. Cover the clay in plaster. There are several ways of doing this. The easiest way is to make a clay, or thin metal, retaining wall around the clay form, then simply pour plaster into it to make a solid block; however, this can be wasteful of plaster. The method less wasteful of plaster, and less heavy, is to flick the plaster on with your hands to the thickness of a finger, and finish off the surface with a metal spatula. The edge is the weakest point, so make it stronger and thicker. For larger moulds, reinforce the plaster with scrim. For very large moulds, use batten or steel rod or pipe, or whatever you have at hand, held with scrim and plaster, to reinforce the mould. (For notes on the mixing of plaster, see page 35.) When the plaster has set, turn the whole thing over and start on the other side.

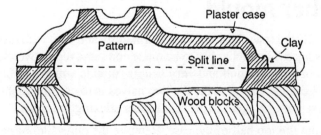

Figure 14. Forming the plaster case (first half) on the clay layer

7. The top half of the plaster case must fit precisely onto the bottom half. To do this use 'natches' (cone shaped holes) or keyways cut into the edge of the case (see Figure 15). Remove a layer of clay to leave a void, and fill this with liquid rubber. When the rubber sets, repeat the process on the other side.

27

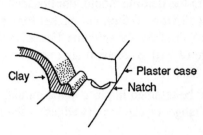

Clay → | ← Plaster case
| ← Natch

Figure 15. Use 'natches' in the plaster case to ensure that the two halves fit together accurately

8. Cut a pour hole in the highest point of the case. For hot-melt rubbers this needs to be wide (about the size of your thumb). You must also make two, three, or more risers, according to the size of the mould. For silicone, make several pour holes of smaller size.

9. To make the second half of the case turn the pattern, firmly holding it in its case. Cut the natches into the rim of the plaster. Repeat the process you followed for the first half. When the plaster is set, the case is completed.

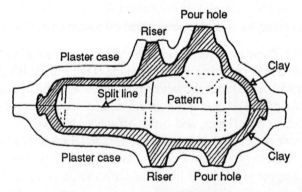

Figure 16. Both clay layers in place and both halves of the case formed in plaster

Making a rubber mould

1. You now have to empty the space between case and pattern, and fill it with rubber. You do this in two stages. The rubber has to be made and removed in two pieces (with the exception of certain small and very simple moulds which can be slit along one side). The easiest way to make the two halves is to cast the rubber in two stages, using a separating agent to prevent rubber sticking to rubber.

2. Remove the clay from the top half of the case. Remove the cling film or paper. Take great care to clean the pattern so that no trace of clay or paper sticks to it. Finally, use a fine spatula of wood, bone or plastic to level the clay along the split line. This will take care and patience. You must avoid holes or gaps, and also avoid any protrusions, lumps or smears of clay on the pattern. The more accurately you smooth this split line the less of a seam line you will find on your wax casting, and the less time you will need to spend cleaning up the wax.

28

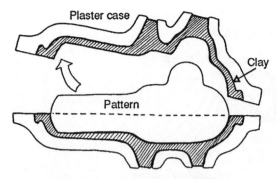

Figure 17. Lift the first side of the case and remove the clay layer

3. Clean up the inside of the top half of the case. Some rubbers stick so you must smear a parting agent onto both pattern and case. With other rubbers this is not necessary. Polysulphide tends to stick to any material, including itself, so you must use a refined grease such as petroleum jelly (e.g. Vaseline). Silicone sticks to very few things, except for certain plastics, and it will not stick to itself. But be very careful; because of its penetrating qualities (so valuable in a moulding material) it will cling to porous material. If in doubt make a small test. To avoid this problem, seal the surface of the case with shellac or varnish and smear it lightly with petroleum jelly.

4. When you have checked that the inside of the mould is spotless, and the seam line as accurate as you can make it, close up the mould.

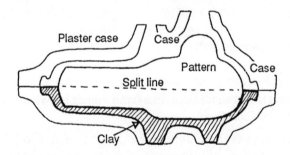

Figure 18. When the clay layer has been removed, replace the plaster case

5. Next, seal the joint. To avoid wasting expensive material, make the pour holes as small as possible. You will have to judge their diameter according to the sluggish movement of the rubber. Whatever the type of flexible material even the largest of the holes will be too small to pour into accurately. To increase the size of the cup, use wax paper cones or, better still, small tins. Be careful to seal round the mould joint with clay (or on a larger mould it is worth backing up this clay layer with scrim and plaster).

    The odd thing about silicone is its sluggish movement. Despite its penetrating qualities it takes time to flow into the mould, and during this time it is beginning to thicken (though it will not actually cure for several hours). To save a lot of sweat and worry on a large mould it is worth assembling a team to help you.

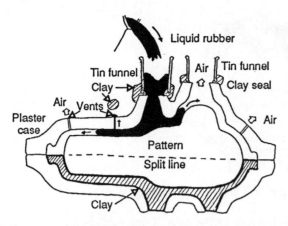

Figure 19. Removing the clay leaves a void: rubber is poured into this void

Instead of mixing one large batch of rubber with its catalyst, three people mix up the rubber in small quantities. You then pour simultaneously into three holes.

Silicone collects more air than other rubbers, so you need many small riser holes (sometimes called whistlers) in the case (make these with a small drill). Have an extra person standing by with small pellets of clay, ready to stop these holes as the air escapes and the rubber rises in the case. These extra air vents are not necessary for hot-melt rubber or gelatine.

To mix RTV rubbers, follow the maker's instructions. Unlike gelatine, mixing RTVs is a matter of common sense. The only necessary word of warning is that accuracy is vital. You need to obtain a set of accurate scales, particularly for the catalyst. The catalyst is only a small percentage of the total (usually about 5–10%) so a small error in measuring the catalyst can have a large effect. This is particularly marked in the case of silicone rubbers. Black polysulphide is less critical but needs great care because the catalyst is lead-based and, therefore, *highly poisonous*. This calls for particular care in a family business where young children may wander into the foundry.

6.   Leave the rubber to cure (or, in the case of hot-melt or gelatine, to cool). Most rubbers take about six hours to cure. This varies according to the type of catalyst you use and the air temperature. The simplest procedure is to leave it overnight.

It is good working practice to stay close to the mould for the first hour. Find some other useful job to do, and keep an eye on the mould, keeping some clay near at hand to stop leaks. If there is a leak, and you fail to notice it, the silicone will find its way onto the foundry floor and you will waste time and expensive rubber.

7.   Repeat the rubber filling process on the other side. Do not forget to grease the exposed surface of the rubber (first half) if you are using polysulphide rubber, though this is not necessary for silicone.

8.   A small or medium sized mould is usually easy enough to open. A larger, deeper or more complex mould can present problems and you can easily ruin the case if you are clumsy or rush at opening it without thinking about the best approach.

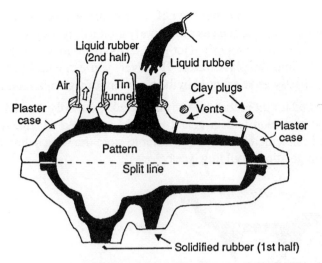

Figure 20. Repeat the process, filling the second half with rubber

If the mould sticks, do not rush at it, take your time. Then have another good look at the case. First make sure that it is strong enough to take a moderate amount of force. If you judge that it is not, reinforce the rim with scrim and plaster and leave it to set hard. Do not fiddle with it, go away and work on something else. Mould making demands a patient and methodical frame of mind. The experienced moulder has several jobs going. When he has to leave one, he picks up where he left off the previous task.

When the repaired case is set hard, take a set of small wooden wedges and separate the two halves of the case with care. Do this methodically, easing the split open gently but firmly all round. Take a smooth-ended dowel or hammer handle and push down on the rubber through the pour holes. This will displace the rubber inside the case, and help to push up the plaster. Keep easing the wedges and pushing down on the dowel until the case comes free of the rubber. Remove the top half of the case.

9.   Finally, peel the rubber from the pattern and replace the two rubber halves, each in its plaster half case.

At this point, and all subsequent replacements, it is essential to make sure that the rubber is fitted accurately in its case. If, for example, one of the rubber keys, or the round cylinder that fits into the pour hole is not properly located the rubber will distort. This will create a protuberance in the mould which, in turn, will cause an inaccuracy (a depression, or 'flat') in the wax casting.

If you are storing the mould for longer than a few days, keep the pattern inside it. By doing this you will make sure that the rubber part of the mould will keep its shape.

Stored in this way silicone moulds will keep for a very long time without changing their shape or nature in any way. Polysulphide keeps slightly less well. Over a period of years it begins to sweat and grow sticky. Dusting the surface of

31

the rubber with powdered chalk, known in the UK as 'talc' or french chalk, helps to prevent this. Hot-melt should be seen as a temporary mould only, though once again, it will keep well if stored properly. Hot-melt tends to shrink as the oil in this oily material soaks into the plaster case. However, you can avoid this by shellacking the case, exactly as you would in the treatment of a gelatine mould.

Gelatine cannot be stored for more than two or three weeks, and only then under ideal conditions. The best plan with a gelatine mould is to take all the wax impressions you need immediately. It is a lot easier to store the waxes than the gelatine. (For notes on gelatine moulding, see below.)

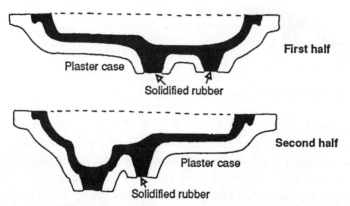

Figure 21. Remove the pattern and open the case to receive the wax

10. Once the mould is complete you can paint or slush cast the wax into it. This varies according to the size and shape of the mould. The different types of rubber make no difference to the temperature of the wax. Gelatine, however, has to be treated with much more care.

Melting, painting and pouring wax into moulds is covered in Chapter 6.

Gelatine moulding

Unlike the rubbers, gelatine moulding is a craft with several stages, and it is not an easy craft to master. In the hands of a skilful moulder, a gelatine mould gives detail as fine and accurate as any of the silicones. Its great advantage is its low cost. Its disadvantage is the small number of impressions you can take from the mould, and its rapid deterioration. Unlike silicone, gelatine is subject to shrinkage.

To prepare, melt and store gelatine you need a space in the wax-working area of the foundry, and extra equipment, as follows:

1. A double boiler to melt the gelatine

2. A small stove, gas cooker or charcoal burner

3. Large, flat, metal trays (these can be similar to the type bakers use to bake small cakes or biscuits in; they are not hard to make, but they must be free from leaks)

4. Wire drying racks (chicken wire on a wooden frame does the job well).

Preparing the gelatine

No doubt you could make up your own gelatine using waste products from your local abattoir, if you have a strong stomach, or you may prefer to buy it in the form of flakes which generally come in 12kg sacks.

Soak the flakes or hard gelatine overnight. In the morning throw away the water that has not been absorbed.

Heat the soaked gelatine in the double boiler, stirring until all the lumps are absorbed and the mixture is the consistency of thick soup, or cream. New gelatine has quite a pleasant smell, whereas gelatine which has gone off does not.

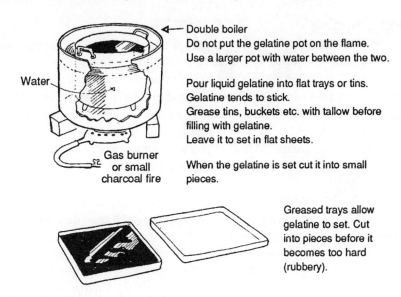

Double boiler
Do not put the gelatine pot on the flame.
Use a larger pot with water between the two.

Water

Pour liquid gelatine into flat trays or tins.
Gelatine tends to stick.
Grease tins, buckets etc. with tallow before filling with gelatine.
Leave it to set in flat sheets.

Gas burner or small charcoal fire

When the gelatine is set cut it into small pieces.

Greased trays allow gelatine to set. Cut into pieces before it becomes too hard (rubbery).

Figure 22. Preparing the gelatine

If your foundry is making moulds all the time it is worth having a large double boiler. You can then heat up the boiler by day and leave it at night. The material will remain in a flexible state and you can melt it again in the morning.

When you have to leave it, for example at the time of a holiday, pour the liquid into the shallow trays, well greased with tallow to prevent the gelatine sticking. Then, once it has changed to a rubbery consistency, cut the gelatine into small cubes and spread it on drying racks. In the case of a used mould, simply cut it up and spread it out to dry. Once it is dry, gelatine keeps indefinitely. In its liquid or flexible state the mixture breaks down because of bacteria. A few drops of strong disinfectant in the liquid will slow down this attack (for example, a 5% solution of Topane). If you are unlucky, or careless, and the gelatine does go mouldy, clean off all the mould with kerosene before remelting. Take care that none of the mould gets into the melting pot.

During hot weather gelatine takes about four hours to melt and about four hours to cool. In cold weather it cools in about an hour.

Making the plaster case

The procedure is exactly the same as described earlier for rubber. For small or medium moulds the thickness of the clay intermediate layer should be about the thickness of your finger, thicker for a large mould. This can be adjusted by trial and error.

There is a difference in procedure once the case is made. A case for gelatine moulding has to be sealed and greased. The Italian method is to use shellac for this purpose because it dries quickly. If your original pattern is porous (plaster or wood) you will need to seal this too in the same way. Some pattern makers use polyurethane boat varnish because it is so much harder than shellac.

Sealing and greasing

Assuming that your pattern is embedded up to the split line in one half of the case, with its clay intermediate lining in place; first make sure that your split line (parting line) is accurate and that the clay is pressed neatly against the side of the pattern. Next shellac the clay, trying not to splash extra shellac onto the pattern. Oil the pattern and the clay split line lightly with vegetable oil. Grease the top side of the case. Be very particular about this as gelatine sticks. Also grease the pouring cup (an old tin with the bottom cut out) and do not forget to grease the bucket you will use to transfer the gelatine from the double boiler to the mould. (For grease recipe see page 35.)

Making the gelatine mould

Close up the case, seal round the edges and round the tin cup. Remember that gelatine penetrates, despite its sluggish movement, and will find any holes. For this reason, have an apprentice standing by with several small balls of clay ready to stop any leaks.

The correct pouring temperature is blood heat. The simplest way to test the temperature is with your finger; when you feel neither hot nor cold, the gelatine is ready. Pour it steadily into the mould cup without any breaks in the flow. Check it periodically during the next fifteen minutes, and top up the level of the cups as the liquid settles.

Later that day, if possible, or the following morning, ease off the case and dust the outside of the gelatine to prevent sticking, then replace the case and start to prepare the other side. (This is another difference from the procedure used for making a rubber mould.)

To make the second side of the mould, follow these steps:

1. Ease off the case and dust the first gelatine side with powdered chalk. Replace the case. Do not remove the gelatine from the pattern.

2. Expose the clay side. Dust the exposed gelatine around the pattern with powdered chalk to remove grease.

3. Paint the exposed gelatine with alum solution. Do not use too much water because this weakens the gelatine.

4. Lightly oil both the gelatine and the pattern.

5. Replace the second side of the case and fill it with liquid gelatine. Use exactly the same procedure as for the first side.

Making the wax form in a gelatine mould also needs care and skill, and is described in Chapter 6. The key phrase in preparing the surface of the mould is 'light touch'. Powdered chalk degreases the surface of the gelatine. Alum hardens the surface. Oil helps to remove the wax from the gelatine without damaging either. But remember this. A build-up of these materials on the surface of the mould creates a positive in the mould which means a negative on the wax. In other words, you lose small sharp details on the wax. Lack of attention to detail throughout the entire process leads to a blurring or inaccuracies in the final casting. In taking the process through from the original pattern to the finished casting, some deterioration is inevitable; but the conscientious craftsman or craftswoman tries to keep this change to a minimum.

Oiled and stored with care, the gelatine mould should last for two or three weeks. That gives ample time to make a number of waxes.

In very hot weather, or if the gelatine deteriorates and more waxes have to be made, paint the surface with formalin. Only use this as a last resort; the formalin spoils the gelatine so that it cannot be melted down and used again.

Gelatine gradually loses its elasticity. To make it supple, add glycerine. Good gelatine should last several years provided you care for it in the way outlined. However, eventually it will lose its elasticity altogether and have to be thrown away.

Making the grease for gelatine mould cases
Equal quantities of:
  Tallow (sheep fat)
  Olive oil (or any vegetable oil which is available locally)
  Powdered chalk.
  If the mixture is too thin and runny, add more powdered chalk. If it is too thick, add more oil.

Mixing plaster

Plaster is a form of fine white cement made from gypsum. Gypsum is a common and widespread mineral and is the crystallized form of hydrated sulphate of lime. Its chemical formula is $CaSO_4\ 2H_2O$.

Gypsum is a solid crystalline material which is calcined; that is to say, heated in a kiln to dehydrate and de-crystallize it, and then crushed and ground fine to make plaster. Powdered plaster, mixed with the right quantity of water, re-crystallizes and returns to its original hard, gypsum state.

Different plasters have different strengths and hardnesses, and different setting times.

When plaster is fired in a kiln it is re-calcined. This offers a great advantage to the lost-wax caster as it means the plaster can be used again. The recycled refractory is called 'ludo' by Italian casters (see Chapter 6).

There are two ways of mixing plaster, the correct way and the slapdash way. Most casters find the latter good enough, but there is no doubt that potters make more beautiful moulds.

1. The correct way, favoured by potters. Weigh out the plaster and water, and mix them very carefully in a rubber mixing bowl.

2. The way favoured by everyone else. Estimate the total volume of liquid plaster you need. Half this volume will give you the quantity of water to use. For example, let us suppose that you need a bucket full of plaster. Half fill the bucket with water. Next sprinkle on top of the water handfuls of plaster until it reaches the surface, forming little islands. Leave it to settle for a few minutes. By leaving it alone and not mixing it at once you allow the water to permeate the plaster, and the air to escape. This way is less likely to form lumps.

Tips for successful plaster mixing

Do not use hot water. Heat accelerates the chemical action, thus speeding up the setting time. (Quite obviously you should not carry this to a ridiculous extreme. If the water is near freezing temperature bring it up to a bearable level.)

Do not add more plaster after you have mixed the original amount of plaster and water as this too will accelerate the setting time and also form lumps.

If mixing a lot of plaster, wear a mask. Like any other fine powder, it is harmful to your lungs. You may find that you need to protect your hands: plaster is not toxic but, in time, it has a drying effect and can cause dermatitis. Rape-seed oil is a very effective barrier on the skin.

Summary

1. Solid moulds

For most of the component parts for engineering products metal moulds are the most practical. Plaster moulds are an excellent substitute though, obviously enough, they do not last and you have to renew them. In both Nepal and Peru we used moulds made of ordinary builders' plaster.

2. Flexible moulds

(i)   Gelatine. An economical and versatile material. Problems with storage make this more suitable for a foundry with a large volume of production and a larger labour force. Gelatine is especially appropriate in a country where RTV rubbers are expensive or hard to obtain, and where labour is plentiful.

(ii) Silicone RTV. Without doubt the best in every way. Silicone makes a mould which is accurate, stable, and will last for many years. In fact it has all the advantages except one – and that is its price. It is extremely expensive.

(iii) Polysulphide RTV. A good substitute for silicone. Costs about half the price and is efficient for most jobs. The major disadvantage is that it is *poisonous*, messy, smelly and unpleasant to use.

(iv) Hot-melt rubber. Less accurate than any of the above; no good on porous materials such as wood, nor will it work well on many plastics. Obviously you cannot take an impression of anything that will melt below 200°C. It is said to be *carcinogenic*, though the manufacturers claim to have modified the rubber to make it safe. Considering all these disadvantages it may come as a surprise to learn that I use it as a substitute for gelatine. Hot-melt rubber comes into its own in a small research foundry where you do not have a high volume of production, nor a pool of semi-skilled labour to care for the gelatine. Hot-melt is useful where you are taking a one-off cast, or are going to modify the pattern. It takes a good impression off any metal and is excellent off damp clay or plaster. You can save money by melting the rubber, modifying the pattern and taking another impression. There are no storage headaches, and you can use the rubber over and over again. *However, despite the makers' assurances, I take care in my foundry that I am the only person to use it, and I do not breathe in the fumes.*

5. Sand casting

Sand casting, at its most basic, is both cheap and easy to understand. For this reason it is often used in schools as an introduction to metalworking technology.

A visit to a foundry exhibition, or trade fair, anywhere in the world shows how sophisticated, specialized and complex the industry has become. Attractive though such displays are, few of the products have any relevance to the small jobbing foundry. They are aimed at the specialized, high-tech, high-capital foundry which has superseded the small family business in Europe and America. In the developing world, by contrast, the small to medium sized foundry is still alive and healthy.

European and North American textbooks give priority to the latest discoveries in technique and materials. However, in a foundry (or a society) where there is abundant skilled labour, but where foreign imports are expensive, the latest novelty is not necessarily the most appropriate.

For this reason I have reversed the order favoured by most foundry books and have concentrated first on those methods used worldwide. The more complex and expensive processes are described later.

The oldest and most basic form of sand casting is green sand moulding. Good quality moulding sand may be any colour from yellow to red, and after a few days' use it turns

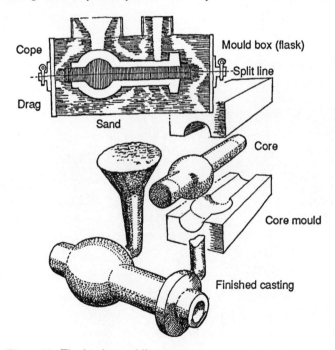

Figure 23. The basic moulding process

38

black or grey, not green. So green sand does not refer to colour. Green, in this sense, means its natural binding qualities, using no artificial binders, additives or catalysts. There is only one additive needed, and that is water. The correct water content, or dampness, of sand is one of the most important factors in sand casting. You will find more information about green sand on page 56.

Casting solid forms by the green sand method is not complicated, nor does it involve complex equipment. The tools to make simple aluminium casts, such as pulley wheels or cooking pots can be put together by anyone with average manual skill.

Essential moulding equipment

○ A pattern for each product (either solid or split pattern).

○ Moulding boxes, known as flasks. The best of these are made of cast iron, or welded out of steel, but satisfactory boxes have been made out of wood for many hundreds of years.

○ Parting powder. This prevents the sand in the two sides of the mould from sticking together. Brick dust powdered and sieved fine is excellent for this purpose. Fine chalk or talc is used to prevent the sand from sticking to the wooden pattern.

○ Sand moulding tools. You can improvise these out of old knives, spoons or strips of steel. You will need to make a wooden rammer and some wooden dowels or short pieces of pipe to form runners and risers. A skewer, or strong piece of wire, is used to vent the mould. Discarded fish tins, or any flat round tins, will serve very well as cups, lined with sand into which you pour the metal, or to put an extra head of metal on the riser.

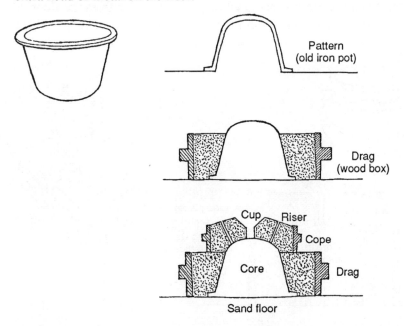

Figure 24. Aluminium cauldron: simple tapered pattern with no undercut (Douala, Cameroon)

○ To recondition the sand you will need a sieve or riddle. These can be bought in almost any market. A coarse riddle can be made by banging nail holes through sheet tin. Use metal insect netting for the fine sieve. A roller is also an important item for conditioning the sand. A cylinder of solid iron or steel is best, but a large-diameter pipe filled with concrete will do very well.

Making a simple, solid casting

To make a simple, solid casting there are various techniques, as follows.

Floor moulding

This is the conventional way of producing large or very large castings. It is also a useful and direct method of producing castings that do not require a surface finish on the upper face. Foundries in many parts of Africa and India make castings by this method. Examples of products are: drain covers, weights, mould boxes, manhole covers, floor plates and gratings and cooking pots.

The technique is simple. The mould cavity is prepared in the floor and the molten metal poured directly into it. There is no runner or sprue system to carry the molten metal into the mould.

A simple casting where the top surface is important can also be moulded in the floor using a technique called 'one-box moulding'. Examples are: covers of slightly greater complexity, symmetrical pieces, or the iron balls for crushers. One side of a flask (see 'two-box moulding' below) is placed on top of the floor mould. This acts as a cope (see below) and carries the sprue and risers.

Large moulds demand extra vents to allow gases to escape from the floor. Make a bed of coke ash and line the sides with fire bricks. Vent pipes can be embedded in the floor beneath the coke. The gases will escape through the porous material.

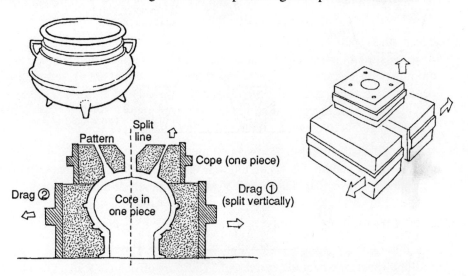

Figure 25. Aluminium 'marmite' cooking pot: complicated French pattern using a split pattern and three mould boxes (Douala, Cameroon)

40

Two-box moulding

Next to floor moulding, this is the technique most commonly used for one-off jobs, such as forming a replacement part for a vehicle or agricultural machine. Therefore it is the method encountered in rural areas or small jobbing foundries on the edge of cities. There are two techniques of two-box moulding, the simpler of the two known as 'flat-back moulding'. This is similar to floor moulding in principle, but a raised box of sand provides a smooth surface rather than the sand floor (see Figure 26).

A pair of matching moulding boxes is used, known as a 'flask'. The upper part is known as the 'cope', the lower the 'drag'. The two halves of the flask are located and clamped together accurately.

Clamps, or weights, are necessary to prevent the molten metal lifting the cope as it flows in, and locating pins are essential to prevent the cope and drag getting out of alignment. The cope has protruding pins. The drag has sockets to receive the pins (they could be called male and female boxes). See page 48 for more details about the cope and drag.

The first box to be filled is the drag because this has no protruding pins and so it can be placed face down on the turnover board (also called the moulding board). A smooth, even face can be achieved by ramming the face edge against the board.

Sequence of operations

1   The drag is inverted and placed face down on the turnover board. After the board is dusted with parting powder it is covered in facing sand which is pressed in place and then covered with backing sand (floor sand). This is rammed into place, then more sand is added, rammed and strickled (levelled).

2   The drag is turned right way up. The flat side of the pattern is placed on the smooth surface, and parting sand dusted on. The runner tube and header tube (if necessary) are held in place. Facing sand is placed over the pattern and around the dowels. Then backing sand is rammed in place as described above.

3   The mould is parted (cope lifted off the drag) and the pattern removed. The gate or sprue system, which conducts the molten metal from the runner tube into the mould cavity, is cut in the sand. Both sides of the mould are vented with wire venting rods, the edges of the mould are made good, any fallen sand removed, and the mould put together. Finally the cope is weighted, or clamped to the drag, and the mould is filled with molten metal.

A more complicated variant of the two-box method is 'odd-side moulding'. This is the only way that a pattern can be moulded if it does not have a flat back (in other words, a cylinder or irregular shape). See page 44 for details of this technique.

Three-box moulding

This is used to make a casting with a flange or similar complication. An example is a simple pulley wheel, or wheel for a drive-belt. These are difficult to form in two boxes, but can be done easily with three. The middle box is called the 'cheek' (see Figure 27).

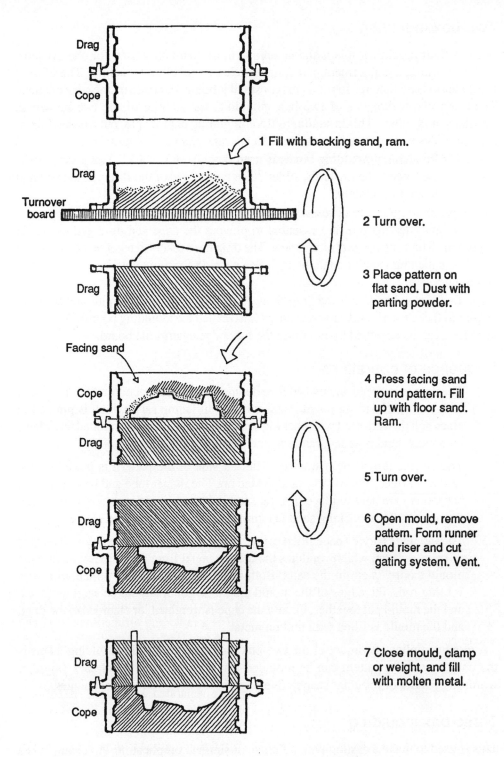

Drag

Cope

1 Fill with backing sand, ram.

Drag

Turnover
board

2 Turn over.

Drag

3 Place pattern on
   flat sand. Dust with
   parting powder.

Facing sand

Cope

Drag

4 Press facing sand
   round pattern. Fill
   up with floor sand.
   Ram.

5 Turn over.

Drag

Cope

6 Open mould, remove
   pattern. Form runner
   and riser and cut
   gating system. Vent.

Drag

Cope

7 Close mould, clamp
   or weight, and fill
   with molten metal.

Figure 26. Flat-back moulding

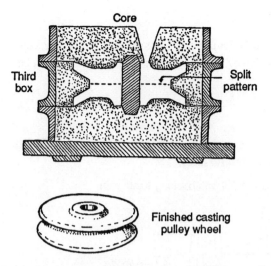

Figure 27. An example of three-box moulding: a pulley wheel, using a split pattern

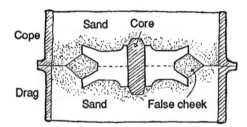

Figure 28. An alternative method of casting a pulley wheel, using a 'false cheek'

Moulding with a false cheek

An alternative technique uses two boxes, with inserts similar to core pieces (see Figure 28).

Plate moulding

For steady repeat-order castings (for example, simple parts for vehicles or gas cooking stoves) the split pattern and flat plate technique is a rapid and efficient method. The pattern is divided in half and the two halves (usually made of metal or plastic) are fixed accurately on either side of a board (known as the plate).

The first side is moulded in the drag. Then, the whole is turned over and the second side is moulded in the cope. The two boxes are separated and board and pattern removed. When the boxes are reassembled the two sides match up and the flask can be clamped and filled with molten metal.

In a large production line foundry the plate moulding method is done by machines, with sand ramming, pattern lifting and rolling all done mechanically.

Stack moulding

A large number of small castings, each having one flat surface, can be stacked using a series of boxes with one common runner. By this means several pieces can be cast in one pouring operation.

Odd-side moulding

This is not difficult once you have grasped the basic principle of the 'odd side', and the two halves of the flask, the cope and the drag.

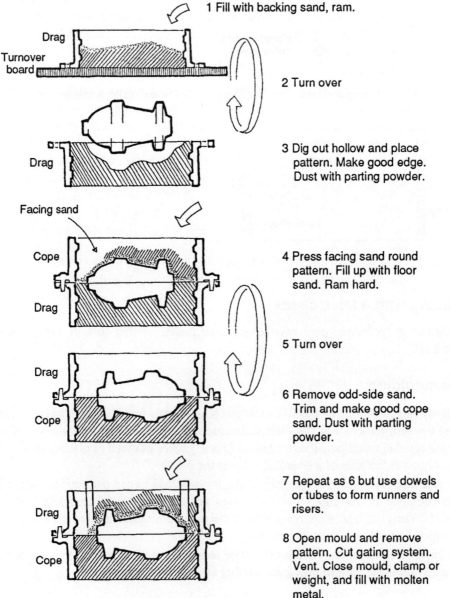

1 Fill with backing sand, ram.

2 Turn over

3 Dig out hollow and place pattern. Make good edge. Dust with parting powder.

4 Press facing sand round pattern. Fill up with floor sand. Ram hard.

5 Turn over

6 Remove odd-side sand. Trim and make good cope sand. Dust with parting powder.

7 Repeat as 6 but use dowels or tubes to form runners and risers.

8 Open mould and remove pattern. Cut gating system. Vent. Close mould, clamp or weight, and fill with molten metal.

Figure 29. Odd-side moulding

1. Fill the drag with sand. This can be sand straight off the foundry floor, but it should be sieved to remove stones, nails or pieces of metal. Using a ruler, or a straight edged piece of steel, strickle (level) the surface of the sand, using the edges of the drag as guides.

2. Assuming that you have decided and drawn the split line (sometimes called the parting line) on the pattern, scoop out enough sand from the odd side to allow the pattern to rest in it, up to the parting line. With a small trowel or knife make good the edge around the pattern, up to the line. Strickle, or smooth the sand. The odd side is now completed.

3. A muslin bag filled with sieved brick dust will produce an even layer of parting powder. Use this to dust the surface of the odd side. Dust the pattern itself with talc. Blow off any surplus powder or any loose grains of sand. Position the cope on the drag, using locating pins.

4. Scatter a layer of facing sand on the surface of the pattern and make sure that you press it into every detail firmly but gently. The most usual mixture for facing sand is 50% new sand and 50% floor sand. There are some excellent made up facing sands on the market but these are expensive. However, if you can obtain one of these sands and want a very fine, clean surface, the extra cost is worthwhile. Next, scatter into the flask the backing sand, which is usually floor sand. Ram this sand in and then scatter in more floor sand. Ram and then strickle

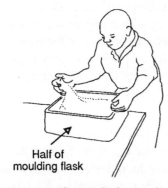

Half of
moulding flask

Figure 30. Scatter in the sand

Rammer

Scoop

Figure 31. Ram the sand

Strickle

Figure 32. Smooth the surface with
the strickle and remove surplus sand

Figure 33. Turn the flask (cope and
drag) when it has been filled with
sand and rammed tight

45

off the surface, fill in any hollows with sand and strickle again until the sand layer is even and level with the edges of the flask. (You will find more information about floor and facing sand on page 56.)

5. The cope is now full and completed. Bolt, wire or clamp the cope and drag together to make sure that they do not slip, and then turn the whole flask over. This is the moment of truth. If you have rammed the sand correctly and the sand has the right quantity of water, it will stay in place. If not the sand will fall out and you will have to start again.

    Assuming that it is correct, and all is well, the odd side is now on top. Unclamp the two halves of the flask and, carefully remove the odd side (which is, of course, the drag). Put the odd-side sand to one side; you can use it as backing sand. You now have the other side of the pattern exposed and set in the cope. Clean the surface very carefully and make good any irregularities along the edge of the pattern, at the parting line. Dust on the parting powder and dust the surface of the pattern, as you did before, and blow off any surplus. Clean and replace the drag. Next place the dowel which will form the runner and the thinner dowels which form the risers. Finally place the facing sand, followed by the backing sand, and ram the sand up, exactly as you did for the first side, or cope.

6. Tap the dowels very gently and withdraw them. They should leave clean channels. Unclamp and lift the drag off the cope. It should lift free of the pattern without disturbing the facing sand. Lay the two halves of the flask side by side, pattern, or mould side up. Make good the edges with a fine trowel or knife all round the pattern. Using a soft paintbrush paint the edges next to the pattern with a little water. This will strengthen the sand edge and help it to stay in place as you remove the pattern. Gently tap the pattern and ease it out of the sand. Finally, cut the feeder and the riser channels from the cavity left by the pattern to the round holes left by the dowels.

7. The inner surface of the mould is now complete. You can pour the metal into the mould in this condition, or you can coat the surface to aid the flow of the metal and improve the surface. There are many types of mould coats on the market. A simple old-fashioned recipe is powdered graphite in methylated spirits. (As much graphite as will stay in suspension in the alcohol.) Spray this into the mould using a simple mouth spraying device (the mouth tube ending at right angles to the down tube which is immersed in the liquid: blowing raises the liquid and transforms it into a fine spray).

    Place the two halves of the flask together and bind or clamp them. Vent the mould by making fine holes through the sand, using either a skewer or a venting wire, being careful not to pierce the sand too close to the pattern.

    The last thing you have to do is to make the pouring cup, and the header, if this is necessary. Either weld up some steel cylinders, or cut the bottoms out of some round shallow tins (fish tins do well). Pick up a handful of sand and push it into the tins, then press and hollow a cone shape to fit onto the runner tube. Either spray this with mould coat, or dust it with talc. The thickness of the cone and the runner is dictated by the size of the casting. This is obvious enough. What is less obvious is the relative thickness dictated by the type of metal. Aluminium demands a much larger runner than either brass or bronze.

8. The completed flasks are laid out in lines on the sand floor of the foundry. Aluminium is unlikely to lift the top flask provided it is clamped, but bronze, and particularly cast iron, exert considerable pressure on the upper part of the mould. The sight of the mould opening and red-hot molten metal pouring out is not uncommon, so be certain that the flask is well wired or weighted down.

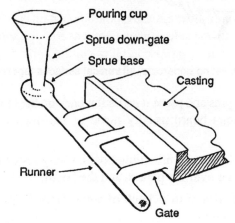

Figure 34. Gating system

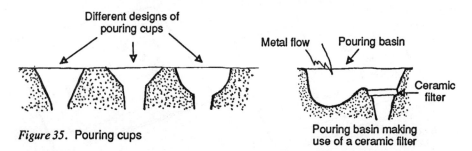

Figure 35. Pouring cups

Pouring basin making use of a ceramic filter

Making a simple casting using a split pattern

The procedure described above is satisfactory for a one-off, or a few castings. For a production run, or periodically-repeated castings, either a permanent odd side (usually made in plaster or glass fibre) or else a split pattern will save the sand moulder much time (and therefore money). A split pattern is, of course, more complicated to make, but it is easier to use.

The mould box or flask is usually made of two halves; less usually, the mould can be made up of several flasks, as in stack moulding.

The convention is to name the two parts the 'drag' and the 'cope', as described below.

Drag

1. The pattern is constructed in two halves. These are located together accurately with small dowels or brass studs.

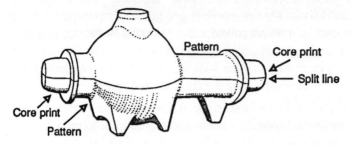

Figure 36. A split pattern with core prints: no undercuts, all vertical surfaces tapered

2. Take the side without the dowel pins and place it on its flat back on the moulding board or base board, a flat, clean board usually made of half-inch (10mm) plywood.

3. Position the drag side of the flask over the moulding board. Using a muslin bag, dust a fine layer of parting powder over the pattern and the board.

4. Riddle the facing sand over the pattern to a depth of about 6mm (0.25in). By hand, tuck the sand around the pattern.

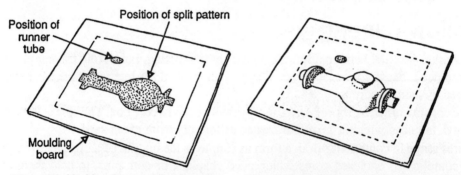

Figure 37. Marking the moulding board to position the first half of the split pattern

Figure 38. Half of the split pattern located on the moulding board

5. Shovel backing sand into the drag to a depth of about 100mm, ram the sand firmly and then shovel in more sand. Repeat this until the flask is full.

6. Strickle the sand level with the flask edges, fill and level any irregularities and then strickle again. Finally vent the sand, exactly as you would if you were using an odd-side moulding.

Cope

1. Turn the drag side over and remove the bottom board, clean up any small faults on the mould surface and position the second half of the pattern, using the locating pins.

48

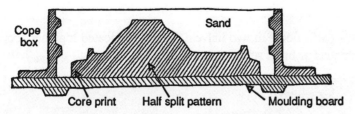

Figure 39. The cope or first half of the split pattern

2. The cope is located on the drag, using the flask locating pins.

3. The runner and risers are located exactly as described in the previous method. Parting powder is scattered over the pattern and mould joint as before.

4. The cope is rammed up with sand and the top strickled as before.

5. The dowels forming the runner and risers are gently pulled out of the sand.

6. The two halves of the flask are separated, each side of the split pattern is removed using a spike or a ramming bar (once again it is wise to damp the edges around the pattern before removing it). Any damage to the edge of the mould is repaired and any sand which has fallen into the mould is dusted or blown out. A very small pair of bellows is a useful tool for this and is not difficult to make.

7. The cope is replaced on the drag, the two halves of the flask are clamped together, the cup placed in position and the mould made ready to fill with molten metal.

Hollow casting

The flasks, described above, form the outside of the casting. For a solid casting this is all you need, but if your casting needs to be hollow then the interior of the casting is formed by using a core.

The core is formed in a core mould, more usually called a core box. The core is formed of sand, but sand which is mixed or treated differently from green sand.

Cores range in complexity from a form as simple as the interior of a cylinder to large and complicated enclosed cores which need chaplets, or core pins, to hold them in place.

The technology used in forming the cylinder block of a petrol engine, for example, with its water-cooling passages, is extremely sophisticated. Different types of core sands, binders, and methods of forming these complex cores are contributory factors in both a large and competitive industry. Cores can be made by hand or by machine. Core-making machinery is expensive. There is one exception to this rule and that is the carbon dioxide (CO_2)–silica sand process. This way of casting has become common practice all over the world, particularly for making cores.

The CO_2–silica sand process is described in Appendix E. In core making much of the procedure is similar to that using oil-bonded sands – except that the former process is much easier.

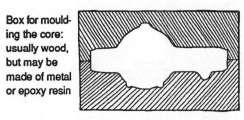

Box for mould-
ing the core:
usually wood,
but may be
made of metal
or epoxy resin

Figure 40. Section through the core box

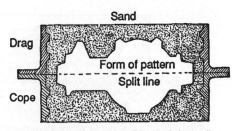

Figure 41. The second half of the split
pattern

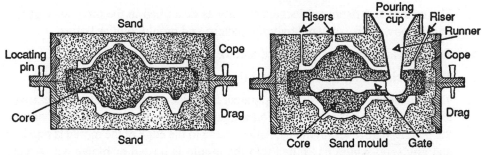

Figure 42. Assembled mould with core in
place

Figure 43. Mould ready for metal pour showing core, runner, risers and gating system

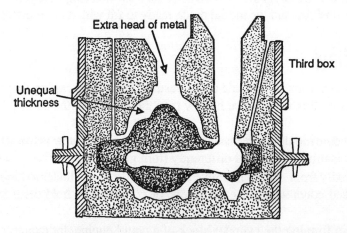

Figure 44. If the pattern is complicated with an area of casting having unequal thickness
of walls, a third box provides an extra 'head' or volume of metal to feed the thicker parts

Core box and pattern

Core making starts at the pattern stage because practically all moulds require a core
print to hold the core in the mould. A colour code painted on the pattern indicates which
part forms the core print and which the mould (see page 20). The core box is usually
made of wood using exactly the same methods of construction as the pattern.

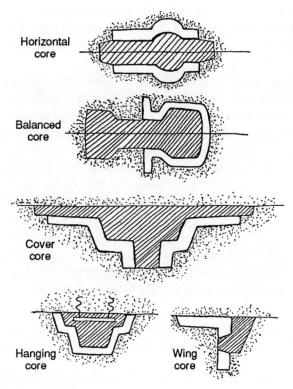

Figure 45. Types of core

Core sands

Binders

A sand core has to be tough enough to stay in place while the metal flows round it, and yet permeable enough for the gases to escape through it. While moulding sands are simple to mix and use, core sands are more complicated and difficult. In European foundries CO_2–silica sand or resin-bonded sands are most often used. If these materials are not available or too expensive you can make your own core sand in one of two ways. You can increase the green strength by adding binders (see below). The second way is to add a vegetable oil and bake the core.

Binders in common use include: dextrine, starch, molasses, and sulphite lye.

DEXTRINE: an intermediate product in the degradation of starch. Dextrine is a more effective binder than starch. Add from 1 to 2% to green sand.

STARCH: a common product of corn, maize, potatoes or cassava. The proportion of starch to sand is from 1.5 to 2% by volume. Unlike the other binders starch needs more water in the mixture. The others require 1% or less while starch needs a 2 to 4% addition of water.

MOLASSES: a viscous solution of sugar. Add from 2 to 4%.

SULPHITE LYE: a waste product of the paper making industry, it can be bought as either a powder or a liquid. Add from 2 to 4%.

Core sand which uses vegetable oil is usually called dry bond, or dry strength. The core has a modest green strength, but it only reaches its full strength as it dries. For this reason it is supported on a core drier and baked in a moderate oven. An ordinary domestic cooker will do well.

Dry silica sand will not hold together, so an oxidizing oil is added. The most usual is linseed oil, but most vegetable oils will do. During mixing each grain of sand becomes coated with oil which oxidizes when heated, holding the sand rigid while allowing air and other gases to pass between the grains. This is known as 'permeability'. Permeability is assisted by the use of core vents. These are passages made with either wire pins, or wax or plastic rods which melt out in the baking oven as the sand hardens (see Core venting).

Oil-bonded sand

The most usual mix for oil-bonded sand is pure silica sand and linseed oil. However, linseed oil is not always obtainable. As a guide, any vegetable oil that hardens as it oxidizes can be used to make a core sand. As with most foundry difficulties, improvization and trial and error based on common sense usually solve the problem.

I have used avocado oil, and I have no doubt that olive oil or groundnut oil would work equally well. Here one comes up against a problem to which I have no answer. In some countries there are regulations to prevent the use of any food product in industrial processes.

One final warning about oils: it is the oxidization of the oil that binds the sand. Most vegetable oils oxidize, whereas mineral oils such as motor oil are lubricants and have the opposite effect.

Silica sand, as was pointed out earlier, has no green strength, nor does the oil add to this. The binder holds the sand together in its green state, and the oil bonds it very efficiently when it is baked in a low oven, or core drier. The oil encloses each grain of sand and, as it oxidizes, it glues the grains into a solid mass. For this reason the core has to be well vented, because the oil-sand mass is much less porous than the green sand mass.

Examples of oil-bonded sands

The following are a rough guide, not exact formulae:

1. Silica sand   50kg
   Starch   1kg
   Vegetable oil   2kg
   Water   0.5 litre (or less)

2. Silica sand (dry) 60kg
   Water   1 litre
   Dextrin   1kg
   Linseed oil   0.5 litre

The consistency of the sand should be similar to brown sugar; squeezed in the hand, it should retain its shape without feeling sticky. It should not crumble or fall apart.

Make the core by ramming the oil-bonded sand into the core box after dusting the surface of the box with parting powder or powdered chalk. Place the batch of cores on a core rest on a metal tray and place them in a core-baking oven. You can either use specially constructed metal core rests, or, if you only need a few cores, make the rests out of floor sand. Remember that the cores are not strong until they are baked. Heat the core oven up to approximately 200°C.

Core venting

Any hole in a mould or a core which allows gases to escape freely is called a vent. Venting wire is suitable for making vent holes in simple straight cores. The most common form of core vent is waxed string. Venting wax can be bent into shape and inserted into complicated cores. Nylon or polystyrene vents do the same thing. Perforated tube vents are used in large cores with intricate sand sections which have to be both vented and supported.

The other main property required of a core is described as 'collapsibility'. It is obvious that the core must be removed from the inside of the casting. The core must be strong enough to hold together without distortion while the molten metal flows round it (no mean feat in itself) and yet not be so strong that it cannot be removed. During 'knock-out' (the removal of the sand once the metal has cooled) the core sand must collapse and flow out easily from intricate hollows.

Randupson process

This method was popular in Europe and the USA forty years ago because it avoids the use of a core-baking oven. In many foundries it has been superseded by the CO_2 process.

The process uses a mixture of silica sand with between 9% and 12% Portland cement and water.

The mixture is rammed into the core box and removed when hard. This takes about an hour. The sand is then left in core rests to cure for 24 hours, before being placed in the mould flask.

Ashland process

The bulk of the mixture used in this process is dry silica sand using resin as a binder. In precision foundries using aluminium alloys, aluminium bronze or magnesium alloys (for example, those which cast parts for the aircraft industry) this process has superseded the processes described above. Dry silica sand is mixed with resin automatically in a hopper and a catalyst is added (either in liquid or gas form) as the mixture drops into the mould (or is blown into the core box). This produces a very hard, accurate mould which is easily moved and handled. After the mould is filled, the metal cooled, and the sand broken off, the sand can be reclaimed by using a specially designed recycling furnace to burn off the resin and restore the silica sand to its original state.

The nature of moulding sand

Sand is a much more complicated material than one might suppose. On the one hand, casting sand is less complicated in practice than many textbooks would have us believe. The caster needs to have sufficient knowledge to select a sand which suits his purpose. That is the ideal: in practice, however, he has to make the best job he can with whatever material is at hand. In many countries transport is more of a problem than finding the material; sand is not a light material and transporting it is expensive.

First we must differentiate between natural sands and synthetic sands. In a sense all sands are natural, but in casting terms natural sand means a sand which is suitable for mould making in the state in which it is dug out of the earth. (Obviously it has to be sieved to remove impurities and checked for the right moisture content.)

On the other hand, a synthetic sand is one which cannot be used in the form that it comes out of the ground, but makes a usable casting sand when it is mixed with other materials. Silica sand is the basis for synthetic sand and it is found all over the world. It often costs nothing except for the hire of a cart or truck to carry the sand to the foundry.

Very often the craftsman has to search for the sand and dig it himself. To do this he needs to know what sand will provide him with the properties he needs.

Mineral composite of sand

Silica is one of the earth's commonest raw materials. Silica is quartz.

Quartz grains originally derive from disintegrated igneous or metamorphic rocks. These are deposited to form either sand or sandstone and later may be carried away to form a new deposit when the first is eroded. Other minerals which occur as sand grains are less durable, for example feldspar which changes more rapidly than quartz. Most sands contain a proportion of other minerals, including tourmaline, garnet, apatite, zircon, rutile, magnetite, or ilmenite. All these have a density above that of quartz and feldspar. The grains of quartz and feldspar tend to be uniform in size; the grains of the heavier minerals are usually smaller. Silica withstands high temperatures. Feldspar and mica are tolerable in small quantities, but they fuse at very high temperatures. This is not a major problem when pouring non-ferrous metals, but it may become a problem with iron casting. Too much feldspar, or other impurities, may cause scabbing or cracking on the surface of the mould. Another material found with quartz and feldspar is zircon. This is particularly useful in the foundry industry because of its refractory qualities and its fine grain size.

Choosing the right type of sand

The term 'sand' means a natural deposit consisting of grains of average size. Sand grains are classified by sieve sizes and, generally speaking, grains of the same average mass tend to be concentrated in the same deposit. This is a useful thing to bear in mind if looking for a particular sand type.

Sand deposits are found in various places, according to how they were made. Many were formed in river valleys and estuaries, lakes and shallow seas. Sand dunes are formed in desert areas and are the result of the decay of exposed rocks. Glacial sands were carried by the melt waters and deposited in roughly graded masses. Glacial sands have sharp, angular grains, while wind-blown sands are rounder and smoother.

Sand is used according to its specific properties. For example, sand used for glass consists almost entirely of quartz with a little feldspar and the smallest possible iron content. The presence of iron adds colour to the glass.

'Sharp' sand, used in the building trade, binds together well and so makes a good strong mortar when mixed with cement. The shape of the grains makes it less porous and so not so good for casting.

Porous sand, suitable for casting, has round grains of a uniform size and has a sufficient quantity of fine material (clay) to bind the mass together.

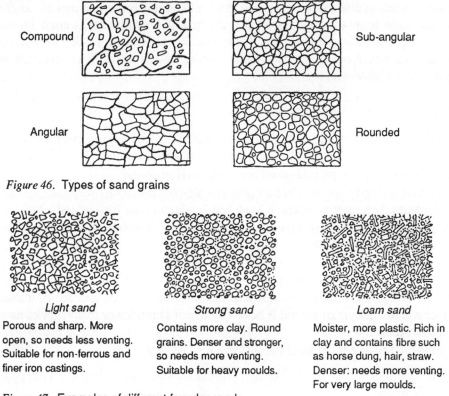

Figure 46. Types of sand grains

Light sand	Strong sand	Loam sand
Porous and sharp. More open, so needs less venting. Suitable for non-ferrous and finer iron castings.	Contains more clay. Round grains. Denser and stronger, so needs more venting. Suitable for heavy moulds.	Moister, more plastic. Rich in clay and contains fibre such as horse dung, hair, straw. Denser: needs more venting. For very large moulds.

Figure 47. Examples of different foundry sands

Finding sand – examples from the field

In East Africa we could not find any natural sand, but were lucky enough to find natural seams of pure white silica sand. A woman potter showed us the source of a fine clay of the kaolin type. We dried the clay, ground and sieved it and then added it to the sand by measure, starting with 5% (by volume) dry powdered clay added to the dry sand. Then we added water until the mixture was damp, but not too wet.

According to the textbooks, clay content ranges from 5% to 12%. We went on adding and testing, and could not get the sand to bind well until we reached 20%. This is theoretically incorrect, but it worked and made a satisfactory casting sand.

In both Nepal and Peru we found silica sand on the bends of rivers, or in beds that had once been oxbow lakes. In each case the quality was adequate once the sand was washed, dried and sieved. We found the simplest way of obtaining clay was to buy it from potters. Some other additives cause problems. These problems are not technical or logistical, but man-made.

If the foundry lies within transporting distance of the coast, another useful source of silica sand is the dunes. Dunes are composed of the finer grains of beach sand blown by the wind, mixed with small particles of shell. Dune sand should be washed to remove traces of salt.

Ant heap sand is found all over Africa. The termite mounds are formed by white ants which excrete a form of silica which mixes with the sand.

Textbooks tell us that a mixture of sand, clay, and termite excreta makes an excellent sand. I have no doubt that this is true. It is also true that termite sand varies. The type that we tried in Malawi was adequate, but coarse. For aluminium casting the synthetic sand that we mixed ourselves gave better results, once we had discovered the best proportion of clay to use.

Natural sands

As has been said before, the term 'green sand moulding' has nothing to do with colour. It means a mould which holds together in its 'green' or natural state. Unlike silica sand, which is white or grey, natural sands are red or buff in colour.

Floor sand is simply casting and facing sand which has been used over and over again. This becomes dark grey, or black, if coal dust is added to the facing sand.

Facing sand is made up of new sand and floor sand, carefully sieved to get rid of impurities and rubbish from the foundry floor.

Green sand contains somewhere between 4% and 12% clay. Water is added, to about 4–6%. A simple test for water content is to squeeze a handful of sand. The sample should hold together and give a clear impression of the lines of your hand. It should not feel wet or sticky, nor should it be so dry that it crumbles or disintegrates as you open your hand.

A good quality moulding sand should have several properties:

○ It should hold together and keep a faithful surface impression when the pattern is removed.

○ It should be sufficiently porous to allow gases to escape. Too high a proportion of clay will cut down porosity.

○ When rammed up with care the sand should resist the pressure of the metal. It should not distort, either when the liquid metal flows into the mould, or as the metal is cooling and solidifying.

○ The sand should have good refractory qualities.

Mixing and conditioning green sand

Repeated use makes sand less plastic and more impure. The first step is to sieve the sand to remove nails, lumps and small pieces of scrap metal. Apart from reducing the casting qualities of the sand, these can injure the moulders' hands. Natural sands are processed by heavy roller mills, turning in a circular drum. The rollers break up the lumps of clay and increase the natural bond between sand grains. Lighter rolling mills are more suitable for silica sand. The blacksmith in Malawi could not afford a mechanical mill so his assistant rolled a large steel cylinder, found as scrap near a sugar mill, backwards and forwards across the foundry floor. This method, though slow, was as good as any other.

To increase the plasticity and refractory qualities of natural sand, the most common additives are:

o   Fireclays. Coarse, refractory clays found near coal seams.

o   Bentonite. Smooth and very plastic. It feels like soap. Bentonite is quarried in areas of volcanic activity: most bentonite comes from the USA, but it is also found in parts of India and Africa.

Figure 48. Sand mixer, Nepal

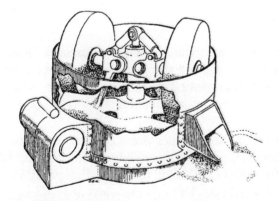

Figure 49. Sand mill, Peru

Other additives

Coal dust is added to the facing sand for iron castings. As the molten metal enters the mould, the coal dust produces a fine film of gas. This gas forms a cushion preventing the molten iron burning and penetrating the mould face. This undermining is one of the causes of scabbing on the surface of the casting.

A second cause of scabbing is the sand cracking or buckling. To prevent this by allowing thermal expansion of the sand, small quantities of peat, wood flour, cereal flour or iron oxide are added to the facing sand.

Other sand processes

Loam moulding and rigid sand processes are both useful in certain circumstances and are covered in more detail in Appendix E.

Loam moulding

This is often known as loom moulding.

Clay binds the sand, but at the same time it makes the sand less porous. It can also affect the refractory qualities of the mixture so that the mould cracks as the molten metal pours into it through the sprue system. Loam, being rich in clay, needs plenty of fibrous material to increase its porosity.

The best known example of loam casting is found in a bell foundry.

To make a bell the moulders do not use a pattern, but shape both the exterior mould and the core with large scrapers, known as strickles. Green sand would not stay in place and keep the form, so the moulders use loam, a soft plastic material made from a blend of natural sands and fibrous material, such as peat, chopped straw or animal hair, hops, and not forgetting that most useful of chopped fibres, horse dung.

Bell casting is a highly specialized business. Not only does the casting have to be strong and look right, but, most important of all, it has to sound right. Obviously, a crack during the cooling of the metal, or porosity or sand inclusions, make the casting useless.

The rigid sand processes

The basis of all these artificial, or chemically bound, sands is silica sand. Generally speaking, they are efficient and labour saving, and also expensive. In Europe and the USA these sands have largely superseded green sand moulding. In a country where the cost of foundry chemicals is high and the cost of labour cheap, the advantage is much less.

Rigid sand is based on silica sand used with a binder which coats the grains of sand and is hardened by chemical action. The type most commonly used is the CO_2–silica sand process. Indeed you will find this used in any small foundry in Europe. Silica sand is mixed with 2% or 3% liquid sodium silicate. This mixture reacts and hardens when exposed to carbon dioxide forming a hard mass, very like sandstone. Up to that point, the procedure is similar to green sand moulding. The sand is rammed into the moulding flasks, then carbon dioxide is injected through gassing holes. Gassing time is about 50 to 60 seconds. The mould can be filled with molten metal immediately. Unlike the resin-bonded sands there is no unpleasant smell or chemical fumes.

Some types of resin depend on heat to harden and bond them, other types set when a catalyst is added.

The advantage of these processes in mass production is obvious. Their use does not demand the skill or training required by green sand moulding. Casting can be done by unskilled labourers (see Appendix E).

Sand testing

This is essential in a large, production line foundry. A large foundry has both a metallurgy laboratory, for testing the quality of the metal, and a sand laboratory for testing moisture content, permeability and compression strength. For this reason all textbooks have large sections on testing. Neither the foundries I visited in developing countries nor the foundries in which I worked in the UK could afford sophisticated equipment. For this reason I have placed notes on testing equipment in the appendix (see Appendix D).

6. Lost-wax casting

The earliest illustrated descriptions of lost-wax casting were French, or Italian. One of the best known and most beautiful is the description of the casting of the giant equestrian statue of Louis XIV, written by the Royal Architect, Bosrand, and illustrated by the engraver, Bernard.

Sculpture.
Fonte des Statues Équestres, Figure Équestre de Cire, avec les Jets, les Events et les égouts des Cires.

Figure 50. Casting of Louis XIV, showing the runners and risers

In the sixteenth century the process was commonly called 'cire perdu' or 'cira perdida'. All these terms mean the same thing.

Since 1940 there has been great change in the nature of the industry, and the process has been renamed investment casting. Up until the World War II, the process was used to make sculpture, and to some extent for ornamental or architectural purposes. During the Renaissance, for example, cannon and bells were cast in sand, but the ornament and lettering on them by lost wax.

Since the World War II the lost-wax process has become varied, complex and precise. To understand how it works we have to go back to simple beginnings.

In its simplest form, the craftsman – or, more frequently, craftswoman – takes natural waxes blended to make the right mixture, and models or press-moulds a shape. To this shape she attaches wax rods. The larger of these come together at a cup, or cone shape, also made of wax. These rods are called 'runners'; thinner wax rods known as 'risers' are placed to the side of the cup.

The cup, runners and risers are together known as the 'sprue system'. In order to form the mould, and lose the wax, the wax model is coated with a liquid refractory mixture which sets, or drys. This is called by a variety of names: investment, coating, mantel, shell, or slurry. Investment is the most usual. Materials vary (and are described later). Refractory simply means a material which does not change its nature when heated to red heat.

The refractory material is mixed in water so that it can be painted or splashed onto the wax, or the wax dipped into it. Liquids other than water are used in some sophisticated variants of the process (alcohol, for example). Water is the most common. The refractory is held together by a binder; once again the binder used varies in different parts of the world. The investment is allowed to dry and then heated. The finished moulds are placed in an oven, or kiln, and the wax melted out. Traditionally, for many hundreds of years, the wax was burnt out. This is still the method most commonly used, but the more sophisticated foundries (those in the aircraft industry, for example) remove the wax using an autoclave. In the final stage the mould still has to be baked in a kiln, but the autoclave avoids the smoke and fumes of the burning wax, and has the added advantage of saving most of the wax.

When the refractory mould is cleaned of every trace of wax and wax gas, in other words when the mould is in its negative state, it is removed from the heat, inverted, and filled with molten metal. The metal is poured into the cup and flows quickly through the runners which are designed to carry molten metal to every extremity. Air escapes through the risers until these too fill with metal. Risers are sometimes called vents, because they allow the air to vent out of the mould.

The sight of bright molten metal venting out of the risers delights the caster because this shows that every part of the mould has now filled with metal. Blocked risers, or gas bubbles spitting out of the cup, provoke a sombre mood. Though these signs do not invariably indicate a spoilt casting, the results are likely to be less good, and may be no good at all.

Whether the moulds are cooled rapidly, or left to cool naturally, depends on the alloy used, and the thickness and complexity of the casting. Hot or cold, the investment is broken away and the casting is cleaned, either by hand or by chemical means. Finally the sprue system, runners, risers and cup, are removed with care and the casting fettled and finished.

This is a very crude outline of a complex process; there are many variations and complexities, some of which will be described in detail later. Today the wax is rarely modelled by hand. Most casting is reproductive; the craftswoman takes a pattern, usually made by a specialist pattern maker, takes an intermediate mould from this pattern, and makes the wax from this mould.

There is a danger of some confusion here. Many people confuse the refractory mould (the mould from which the wax is burnt out and into which the metal is poured) with the preliminary mould in which the wax is formed. In the precision investment industry this is usually a metal die into which the wax is injected while pressure is maintained until the wax has set, to minimize contraction. By using a specific wax, with a known rate of contraction, the investment foundry workers know exactly how much to enlarge the original pattern to allow for shrinkage, both in the wax and in the metal.

For prototypes, or other one-off jobs (or short runs, as in art casting) flexible moulds are more usual, though plaster piece moulds are also a common way of forming the wax pattern.

Broadly speaking, the investment casting industry in Europe and the United States divides between thick and thin, between ceramic shell and the block investment method known as the 'Shaw process'. Both were developed during the 1940s to form precise parts for aircraft engines, too complex to be cast and machined in the usual way.

The Shaw process was based on the ancient Roman method, and developed in the USA. The ceramic shell method was invented and pioneered by Rolls Royce in the UK. It is the descendant and distant cousin of the dung and clay shell method used in India, Africa, and South America since the earliest times.

The eccentric millionaire can play with any technique that he chooses and buy any material or technology that excites his interest. Most of the rest of us are not in that happy position. A craftsman setting up a business has to compromise: technical efficiency and good workmanship are vital qualities, but not the only factors in the survival of his business. If he makes the best castings in the world but cannot find a market for them, he will soon have no business. The market, the cost of materials, overheads, and selling price, are all-important factors. Lost-wax casting is the only way certain parts can be manufactured (micro-hydro-electric turbines, for example). It enables the engineer, artist or skilled artisan to produce precise, efficient and often beautiful objects. Perfection is never cheap.

Waxes

Waxes are a sub-group of true fats, comprising the esters of higher alcohols with fatty acids. They are distinguished from the fats by being non-greasy to the touch, and are generally solid.

A mixture of the most unlikely looking waxes will make a good casting, provided you know what qualities are essential and how to achieve them.

The necessary qualities are:

○ Toughness – not brittleness.

○ High melting point – there is a danger that waxes will sag or distort, especially in hot climates.

- Stability – the least shrinkage possible. Waxes vary a great deal in their relative shrinkage.
- Flexibility – waxes should bend rather than snap.

Waxes in Europe and the USA are refined and purified. Working on a casting project in Nepal we discovered that we could refine a very impure and dirty beeswax by melting and then sieving it through a fine wire mesh, sold for agricultural use. We then refined it still further by sieving it again through muslin. Though shrinkage was unpredictable, one batch relative to another, the results were good enough to use, for example, to cast the Pelton turbines for micro-hydro-electricity generation.

Qualities of different waxes

Microcrystalline waxes
These are now generally the most common of the more refined waxes in countries which have a petroleum refining industry. Microcrystallines are a by-product of petrol, and as such they are also known as synthetic waxes. They range from very soft to waxes so hard that they can be turned on a lathe. By experiment, mixing hard with soft, one can find a suitable blend of wax. You must allow some time for experiment as you need to try out the mixture in a mould to find out how it performs.

Earth wax (known in Germany as montan wax)
This is now hard to find. At one time it was, literally, dug out of the earth. The material sold as earth wax today is more often than not a crude microcrystalline type.

Paraffin wax
Probably the most useful and easiest to find of all the waxes, especially as it is widely used for candles, it is also the cheapest. Paraffin wax makes a good base for casting wax, although on its own it is too brittle and 'short' to be useful. It is, rather, a body of wax to which other types must be added to give it the right quality.

Tree resin (also known as rosin)
Resin is used in the papermaking industry. It is well known to musicians for waxing violin bows. In Nepal it is called 'sal-dup' or juice of the pine tree. Resin raises the melting temperature of the wax mix. It adds toughness and hardness. It is an essential ingredient and luckily not difficult to obtain. Caution must be used in mixing, as too great a proportion will make the casting wax brittle.

Beeswax
This wax is so good and so pleasant to use that the Italian casters of old treated it almost with veneration. It softens the mix, making it more flexible, and generally refines the quality.

Vegetable waxes

There are several excellent vegetable waxes, such as Carnauba and Ouricouri, both palm waxes, and Candellila, made from a Mexican weed. All these waxes are used to make high quality furniture polishes. Generally speaking these are far too expensive to use for lost-wax casting. But there might be a situation in a tropical country where one of these waxes is a local product and therefore cheaper, and more appropriate, than microcrystalline wax.

Useful styrenes and plastics in common use

Styrene wax has a remarkable effect on the toughness and flexibility of the wax. Polyethylene adds flexibility. This is found in thick, flexible, clear plastic bags (not polystyrene, from which thin cheap crackly bags are made). Polypropylene adds hardness. This is often used for making ropes.

Making wax mixtures – various recipes

In practice, you use whatever there is to hand, but it may be useful to have a few examples, as guides rather than rules.

Roman wax. This was used throughout Europe, in the Near East, and in Central America after the Spanish conquest, up until the microcrystallines came into common use.

2 parts paraffin wax

2 parts genuine earth wax

1 part tree resin.

To control the malleability of the wax, more resin was added in summer and less in winter, thus raising or lowering the melting temperature to suit the ambient temperature.

Newar mixture. This mixture is common to many parts of Asia and Africa.

2 parts unrefined beeswax.

1 part 'sal-dup' tree resin.

The mixture is melted and blended together, then cleaned through a fine metal sieve. The pieces of twig, leaf and dead bees are picked out. It is next remelted and refined again through muslin. Finally it is hand modelled into flat plates, the size of chapattis, and stored. One thing that is noticeable about this mixture is that the more one handles it the more malleable and plastic it becomes.

Wax mixture Cuzco, Peru. Because of the altitude (11,000 feet) we encountered a special problem with wax. The extreme change from daytime to night-time temperature caused the expansion and contraction of the wax, thereby cracking the shell. This was one of several factors which made us decide to use the Roman method of casting in Cuzco, rather than the ceramic shell method (see Chapter 7 and Appendix F).

We managed to blend a satisfactory wax without beeswax, using paraffin wax mixed with resin, softening it by adding Vaseline (commercial petroleum jelly). Having blended various mixtures in the technical college in Cuzco, in the end we used this one:

3 parts paraffin wax

2 parts tree resin

0.5–1 part Vaseline

'Bogota university recipe'. We tried this mixture later in the course; it was an improvement on the earlier mix.

12 parts paraffin wax

3 parts resin

1 part polyethylene

Moulding the wax

Having blended a suitable wax, it must be formed into the shape you want to cast into metal. There are many ways of doing this. It is necessary to work out which of them is the simplest and least expensive for your purpose.

The simplest way is the Newar method; this is, hand rolling and modelling wax sheets or making simple press moulds. This is a very beautiful way of working and well-adapted to certain markets, but it is extremely laborious and not accurate, nor is it intended to be. One of the Newar selling points is that no two castings are the same. In order to produce many parts which are interchangeable, that is to say each part being the same as the last one, a mould is essential.

Metal moulds

The best is a metal mould with some type of device to inject wax into it under pressure. This is not only rapid and accurate but the pressure, maintained as the wax cools, prevents major shrinkage.

This is ideal if you are producing a large number of parts in continuous production. But if production is varied and irregular the toolmaking necessary to produce the mould is too expensive.

Plaster moulds

Plaster has to be damped to prevent the wax sticking, and this shortens the useable life of the mould. Plaster and metal present problems, but on the whole a plaster mould is one of the easiest, and certainly the cheapest, ways of solving the mould problem.

Flexible moulds

Of the range of flexible moulds, rubber moulds present fewest problems as far as temperature is concerned. You are unlikely to damage the surface of the mould even if the wax is too hot. Nor will you get cold flow lines when the wax is too cold. The only major problem you come across with rubber is a tendency for the first coat of wax (painted in) to be melted off the high points. You can overcome this by making a mastic of a resin-rich (high melting point) wax and building up these high points while the mastic is in a putty-like state. These high points will hold when you pour in the back-up coat of wax and resin. You should also reinforce the point in the mould where the flow of hot wax first strikes the inside of the mould, using a mastic in the same way.

A wax injector is not hard to build, you can make one out of an old pressure cooker, or any robust metal container, using a car foot pump to maintain the pressure. The alternative is either pouring the liquid wax into the mould (called 'slush casting') or painting it in, reinforcing the wax shell and then backing it up by pouring in and draining out a layer of secondary wax, poured at a temperature too low to melt the primary layer.

Slush casting

Quite simply, you pour the wax into the mould and leave it, assuming a solid wax is required. If you intend your wax to be 'cored', because you need a hollow casting, then you pour the wax into the mould and then out again. (Both the reason for coring and the procedure by which you produce a hollow casting, will be explained later.)

Experience, trial and error, and knowledge of the temperature of the wax will help you determine the thickness of the wax shell. The cooler you pour the wax, the less it will contract (though it is obvious that the wax will not flow at all if it is too cold). Rubber moulds allow a greater range of temperature, which is one of their advantages. With either metal or plaster moulds you will encounter a problem with ripples on the surface of the wax, if poured too cold. These are called 'cold flow lines'. Wax behaves very like metal when changing from its liquid to its solid state. The hotter the wax, the more it expands, so it follows that it has to contract more to regain its solid state. Pouring wax too hot increases contraction. A temperature chart does not help very much. The examples I have already given show how wax mixtures vary in different parts of the world. In my experience the basic ingredients supplied by even the most reputable wax refineries vary.

Painting in the wax

This has been briefly mentioned already. It is rarely, if ever, used in the engineering industry. This book is not really concerned with art or jewellery casting where this technique is used most. On the other hand, there are occasions where only this technique is appropriate. Open the mould into its two halves. Take a small quantity of wax in a small saucepan and heat it gently. When the wax is liquid, but not too hot, wash it into the mould quickly using a small paintbrush, flopping the wax into the mould so that it flows, rather than is brushed in. Try to avoid brushing over the areas that you have covered. By the time the two sides of the mould are covered the wax will have cooled (in practice I use two small saucepans, one containing wax at a slightly higher temperature then the other). With the cooler wax, brush over the first coat, roughening the wax as you go. This 'scumbling', as painters call it, puts a texture onto the wax for the back-up coat to stick to. Next, reinforce the high points, as described earlier, and close up the mould. Take a small quantity of hot wax and pour it into the mould to seal up the seams. By this time the resin-rich back-up wax should have cooled enough to pour into the mould.

There is an old Italian trick to estimate the thickness of this final layer. You need enough backup wax in the bucket to more than fill the mould. Leave it to cool until there is a film or skin on the surface. Check the chilled layer at the side of the bucket. When this is the thickness you need in the mould, pour the wax. Invert the mould and drain the excess wax back into the bucket immediately, swilling the mould round in a cylindrical motion as you do so, to distribute the wax film evenly on the surface.

Pouring wax into a gelatine mould

Gelatine, because of its comparatively low melting point, demands much greater skill and control over the temperature of the wax than when using the rubber moulds. Pouring wax at too high a temperature will distort or melt the mould surface.

To check the temperature of the wax, paint a thin layer of wax onto a greased surface (the edge of the opened mould case will do well). Pick up the film of wax with a spatula or knife point and float it on the molten wax. It should melt on the count of ten (approximately ten seconds). If it takes longer then the wax is too cold; if it melts more rapidly then it is too hot and will damage the gelatine.

Flow the first coat into the mould with a well-loaded brush and do not go over the same surface twice. The procedure is the same as for a rubber mould (described above). The difference lies in the care needed to check the wax temperature.

To repeat: gelatine moulds can only be stored for a very limited period. The wise course is to take all the wax impressions you need at once and store them in water (or a refrigerator). Cut up the gelatine and dry it out on the drying rack, before storing it in a dry place. Last, but not least, number and store the pattern and case carefully. If you need more waxes make another gelatine as before. (This was the procedure in Italian art foundries up until the invention of RTV moulding rubbers.)

Storing wax patterns

This presents no problem in a cold climate: waxes can be stored on any surface that does not stick to or mark the wax surface. Thin plastic on a bed of newspaper is ideal. In a hot climate the waxes should be kept in a refrigerator. Failing that, do as the Romans did and float the waxes in a tray full of cold water. If you leave them too long you may find a film of mould on the wax, but this is not serious and can be removed with alcohol.

Shelf life

Wax is one of those magic materials that does not change its state (with the obvious exception of applied heat). Anatomical models made from wax can be seen in the Victoria and Albert Museum in London. They may or may not be by the great sculptor Michelangelo, but were certainly made in the fifteenth century.

The block investment process

Within the block investment process there are two methods, the older Italian investment and the Shaw process. I will take the older method first.

The Italian method

As far as we know, the Romans were the first craftsmen to reproduce castings by a form of mass production. They certainly used plaster piece moulds, and probably invented the technique of gelatine moulding (described in Chapter 4). Wax and waxworking is also described above. Degreasing is common to all methods.

The remains of moulds on Roman foundry sites prove that the Romans used a brick dust and plaster investment. There are other forms of ground fired clay (known as 'grog') but brick dust was, and is, the most common form, and the cheapest. It was used in Britain from Roman times until the mid-1950s, when its use was banned because of the danger of silicosis (a lung disease).

Today most foundries use grog, as supplied to the pottery industry. I have experimented with various refractories, and in the end settled for silica sand. Silica sand with a plaster binder on its own is not ideal. The sand grains have little thixotropic quality. This makes the technique used in the Shaw process (which is used in making Pelton wheels) particularly difficult. The grains of silica sand are heavy and need some form of colloid to hold them in suspension: some fine, light material to enclose the larger sand grains and keep them from settling. Grog mixed with the sand sets off the plaster binder prematurely.

In Nepal the answer proved to be brick dust. The ideal combination is silica sand, brick dust and plaster in equal measure. But in the UK one cannot buy brick dust, so I I use a substitute, slate powder. No doubt there are other refractories that would do the job as well, or better; zircon, for example. The problem is always the same, balancing efficiency against the cost of materials. Slate dust does the job well enough, it helps to suspend the sand, and has no ill effects either during the firing process or on the mould surface. Very precise castings can result from using this mixture, free from either bubbles (called 'potati' – potatoes – by the Italians) or flashing (known as 'feathers').

Proportions and mixing

The Italian method uses brick dust and plaster, in the proportions two of brick dust to one of plaster, for the first coat only. The second coat is a mixture called 'one, one and one', explained below, and the third coat is made of ludo or 'luto'.

The first and second coat must be creamy in consistency, not too thick or the plaster will set too fast. The first coat is brushed on, backing this up by flicking or pouring the mixture on to the area where you are working. It is a good idea in theory to cover the whole wax with the first coat, but not always practical on a large or complex job with rich surface texture which may trap bubbles of air.

Before we come to ludo, one word of warning about the cup and sprue system. The cup is the first receptacle for the molten metal. The purpose of that elaborate system of cup and runners is to allow the metal to flow evenly to every part of the wax model, in turn to let the metal solidify in a logical and progressive order. Once the investment is on and the wax burned out, this sprue system will become a series of conduits for the rapid transmission of the metal. Thus it should be obvious that the surfaces of cup and runners are as important as the wax model. I do not use the first coat on the cup but usually paint and flick the second coat of 'one, one and one' onto the cup, because of its superior refractory qualities.

Ludo derives from *lodo*, which means 'mud' in both Italian and Spanish. Ludo is the refractory mixture (plaster with brick dust, or silica sand, or whatever refractory is being used) ground down after it has been fired and the molten metal poured into it. In other words the moulds are recycled. Once the castings are cooled, the apprentices break open the moulds, taking care not to damage the surface detail of the cast. The casts are put on one side while the mould material is broken up.

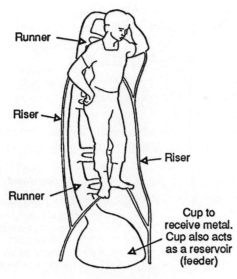

Figure 51. Wax model with sprue system (runners and risers) attached

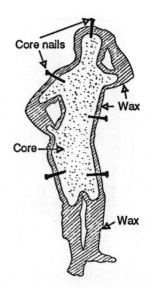

Figure 52. The core is held in place by iron core nails or, in very small models, copper pins

Figure 53. The first coat of the investment is painted onto the wax: take care to remove all air bubbles

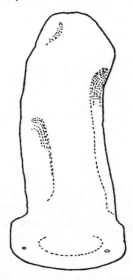

Figure 54. The second coat of the investment is laid on over the first (painted) coat

The moulds should be a pinkish or buff colour, free from smell. If a mould is underfired and some of the wax gas remains in the refractory it will be useless as ludo because it accelerates the plaster setting time. This is only one of the problems with an under-fired mould. Wax gas is the most common cause of faults in casting by the Italian method. Correct and meticulous firing is essential. Under-fired ludo has some distinctive characteristics. Not only is it grey in colour, but it gives off an unpleasant sulphurous smell, which is mildly nauseating. Separate out this underfired material from the usable ludo and throw it away. Good ludo is marvellous stuff: recycling means

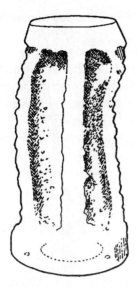

Figure 55. The main body of the invest-ment is put on in blocks (avoiding the weakness of 'onion skin' layers)

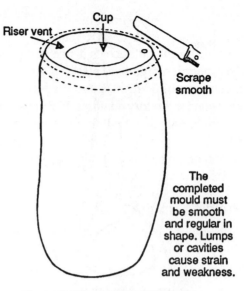

Figure 56. The completed mould is inverted, cup and riser vents are scraped clean, and the base is smoothed

The completed mould must be smooth and regular in shape. Lumps or cavities cause strain and weakness.

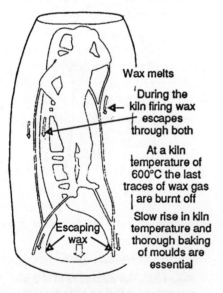

Wax melts

During the kiln firing wax escapes through both

At a kiln temperature of 600°C the last traces of wax gas are burnt off

Slow rise in kiln temperature and thorough baking of moulds are essential

Escaping wax

Figure 57. X-ray view of the mould at the moment of kiln firing (de-waxing)

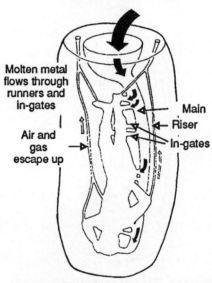

Molten metal flows through runners and in-gates

Air and gas escape up

Main

Riser

In-gates

Figure 58. X-ray view of the mould as molten metal is poured into it

that you get it for nothing (apart from the labour of grinding and sieving it); the steady baking in the kiln recalcinates the plaster – in other words, restores it to its original condition. The brick dust and sand are, of course, not affected by the heat. Ludo becomes, if anything, tougher than its original components.

Ludo is far more durable than the first coat. Trial and error proved that the mixture does not bond perfectly with the first coat unless there is an intermediate layer; during the firing process one coat opens away from the other, causing flashing on the casting.

This problem is overcome by a layer of 'one, one and one' (one part of plaster, one part of silica sand, or whatever refractory you are using, and one part of ludo). The preferred mixture for the outer coats is one part plaster to two parts ludo, but you can increase the proportion of ludo to plaster if you are short of the latter. In Nepal we used a very rough form of builders' plaster, which looked terrible, but in practice proved to have very good refractory qualities. In Europe and the USA there are various plasters on the market known as refractory plasters. These work well for casting aluminium or zinc alloys. The melting point of bronze or brass is too high for these plasters, but there is at least one type made for silversmiths which will also cast bronze and brasses. These plasters are all excellent for their intended purpose; their major disadvantage is cost.

Building up the mould

When building up the mould, avoid 'onion skin' layers. Once the first layer is brushed, poured or flicked on to the wax, then put on your second coat, flicking or pouring it over the first coat. Before this coat sets, roughen the surface with your finger tips to aid the bond. When you come to the next coat, put the ludo on in blocks rather than layers (see Figure 55). Where one block joins another keep the joint rough or irregular. This applies to the first two layers too. A rough surface always makes a better bond. Do not smooth the surface until the final coat, which does need to be smooth and regular.

Leave the moulds for around twenty-four hours for the ludo to harden. Unlike pottery, the moulds should not be dried before they go into the kiln. If you have to leave them once the initial setting time is past and before loading the kiln, wrap them in plastic. If the moulds do dry out, damp them down before the kiln firing. This is necessary because water in the mould turns to steam during the firing and helps to expel the wax gases which lodge in the refractory. The water present in the ludo adds to the weight of the moulds before firing. They are fragile, so you must take care handling them, and even more care when you take them out of the kiln, when they will be much lighter, but also more fragile. This is covered in detail later in this chapter under kiln firing.

Moulds that have been fired in a kiln for fifteen hours or more at red heat are bound to be fragile. At this temperature the plaster bond has partially broken down. This is not enough to impair the quality of the casting, but enough to make the mould brittle and easily broken. Medium and large-sized moulds need to be reinforced with woven jute scrim and plaster jackets immediately before filling with metal. Timing is a matter of experience, the later you can leave the scrimming the better. If you scrim up too early there is a danger of damp creeping through the hot, dry investment. On the other hand, if you leave it too late then you risk overheating, or 'stewing' the metal waiting to be poured. Very large or tall, thin moulds may need strengthening with metal or wood. Pieces of scrap steel pipe or angle iron are the best. The safest practice is to scrim up in the kiln to avoid unnecessary disturbance, but this depends on the design of the kiln. It is not always possible when using a fixed kiln, by which I mean a kiln which cannot be dismantled. Some foundries rely on the plaster and scrim jacket alone, others bury the moulds, at least partially, in the sand pit.

The Shaw process

This is an off-shoot of the Italian method which suited the earlier casters because of its flexibility, and it is used today in art bronze foundries for the same reason. The main difference between the two processes is the use of a flask. The Shaw process uses a flask, the Italian method does not. In foundry terms, a flask simply means a metal container for the refractory, whether this is small scale jewellery casting using a centrifuge, or a very large green sand casting.

When the work coming into the foundry varies and is mostly one-off pieces, there is no point in having a collection of tailor-made flasks for special jobs, when you will probably use the flask only once. On the other hand, when one is faced with a production line, or semi-production line, the situation alters. Take as an example the production

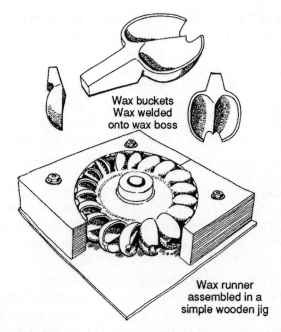

Wax buckets
Wax welded
onto wax boss

Wax runner
assembled in a
simple wooden jig

Figure 59. Assembling the wax pattern buckets for a Pelton wheel

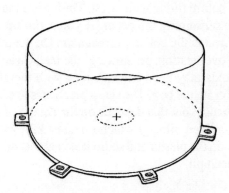

Figure 60. For the investment process a metal flask is attached to a metal base-plate

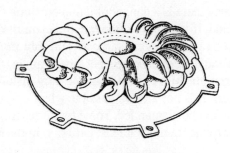

Figure 61. The assembled wax pattern is attached to the base-plate

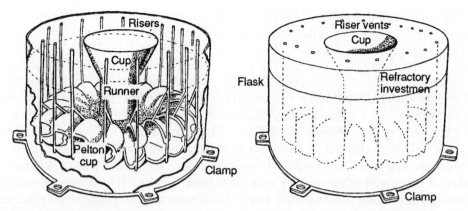

Figure 62. The sprue system: wax runners and risers are wax-welded to the wax pattern; the cup and heavy runner act as a reservoir, assisting progressive solidification

Figure 63. The filled 'Shaw' block investment mould ready for de-waxing

of small Pelton wheels for micro-hydro-electric generators. Leaving aside the larger Pelton wheels, which can be cast in many pieces by traditional sand casting methods, the range narrows down to two types of flask, or at the most three. The waxes are made in a jig, so castings will not vary in size. Once past the prototype stage (when one-off treatment is appropriate) you need to make your waxes and coat them with refractory with the minimum of effort and complication. Like ceramic shell, and unlike the Italian method, the Shaw process can be carried out by semi-skilled labour.

In theory the process is very simple. The flask is merely a large can of sheet steel. The diameter of the flask is the size of the outside of the mould (see Figures 60 to 63). The wax sits in the middle of the flask (or is suspended in the middle). The refractory is poured around the wax and left to set with the wax cup and risers either fixed to the base plate, or protruding from the top. The flask is placed in the kiln cup downward, and fired out in exactly the same way as the Italian method.

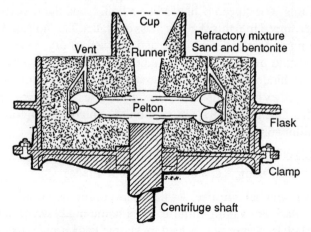

Figure 64. Pelton wheel mould clamped to the centrifuge *after* the wax has been baked out and *before* filling with molten aluminium

73

The main problem with the Shaw process lies in making sure that all the air bubbles are released from the wax, particularly the under surfaces. One sophisticated version uses a vacuum pump to suck out the air, while the slurry is liquid. This is very effective but demands special equipment. The second way is to fix the wax to a plate at the bottom of the flask, fill the flask with slurry and then agitate the flask to make the air rise to the surface. A third way is to keep the wax separate from the flask, for the initial coat. Paint and flick a first coat onto the wax. As soon as this has set, fix the wax to the flask, and then fill up the rest of the flask with a ludo slurry. This works well, though it is a little more laborious. One firm the author worked with used this technique combined with a ceramic shell first coat. The reason, they said, was to maintain the heat in the mould while making sure of a good surface. They achieved excellent castings, but I think the results are just as good using a tough plaster with silica sand

---

Case study

A small investment casting foundry near Sheffield, producing small, precise parts for aircraft turbines, using a wide variety of low and intermediate-level methods.

Process 1

Ceramic shell. This is the normal ceramic shell process. The only oddity, and of especial interest to me, was the equipment. All of it was home made.

- ○ *Slurry.* The slurry mixer was a 40 gallon oil drum, plastic lined. A 1/4 hp motor turned a paddle, made of stainless steel. This mechanism was kept running all the time and was only removed for dipping the waxes. Its major advantage was simplicity and relative cheapness.

- ○ *Stuccoeing.* The liquifying air bed was also made from a 40 gallon drum. There was an air chamber at the bottom of the drum with a filter made of calico and heavy metal mesh. Air at only a few p.s.i. rose from the air chamber through the filter to the main body of the fluidizer separating the grains of stucco and pushing them upwards. The stucco behaved like a liquid, and the wax coated with wet slurry, was dipped into this floating mass of grains. The stuccoed wax was then hung up on a stainless steel hook and allowed to dry. One of the partners of the firm told me, with great frankness, that they used a normal colloidal silica for the binder mixed with fine grade molochite to form a slurry in the normal way, but they had tried various fine refractories for the first stucco coat. These included silica, alumina, chromic oxide, magnesia, zircon, calcined china clay, sillimanite, mullite, and fireclay grog.

- ○ *Later coats.* The first coat was repeated, using fine stucco (60-80 grade). Then followed four more coats using a coarse stucco (16-30 grade).

- ○ *De-waxing.* This was another surprise. Against convention they used neither an autoclave, nor a flash de-waxing furnace, but a home-made water tank of thick stainless steel plate. Water was heated by simple gas burners under the tank. The shells were dipped into the tank just long enough for the bulk of the wax to melt out. The wax was skimmed off the surface of the water and

for the first coat, backed up with a ludo slurry. (See the normal refractory mixture and a variety of refractories in the following case study.)

In Colombia a variant of this method was used which included a centrifuge to force the molten metal into the extremities of the mould. The Colombian engineers used an investment quite different from the Italian. This included no plaster, but silica sand using Bentonite as a binder.

A major advantage of the Shaw process over the Italian is the ease with which the flasks can be carried straight from the kiln to the foundry floor. There is no need either to wrap the moulds in a protective layer of scrim and plaster or to bury them up to the neck in sand as a precaution against bursting. The steel flask protects against this type of accident.

recycled. This treatment had no ill effect on the shells. I expected cracks in the shells caused by the comparatively slow rate of heating, but I saw none.

o *Kiln firing*. The shells passed through a home-made tunnel kiln to bake the ceramic and remove the last traces of wax gas. The kiln was gas-fired and rose to a very high temperature estimated to be about 900°C.

o *Casting*. The shells were placed in buckets of hot sand while still pink hot, and filled with metal immediately.

o *Shell removal*. Most of the investment dropped off as the metal cooled. The core, I was told, took longer and had to be removed in boiling caustic soda.

Processes 2 and 3

These were both variants of the Shaw process. The unusual feature in each one was using ceramic shell for the first coat.

2. The wax was dipped and stuccoed in the usual way. The wax cup was then fixed to the base plate of the flask, the barrel of the flask fitted round it. The backing, or secondary investment, was then poured round the shell, and the flask agitated to consolidate the investment. The flask was placed in a low temperature oven (150°C) and the wax melted out through a hole in the base plate where it was trapped and recovered under the oven. Next the flask was removed and the entire mould baked in a high temperature kiln. The ceramics technician told me that the temperature was 1000° and that the back-up investment was made up of grog and plaster. This I found hard to believe, because plaster breaks down well below that temperature.

3. This was an even odder variant. The wax was invested with several coats of ceramic shell in the conventional way. The wax was removed in the water boiler. The dewaxed shell was then secured, cup downwards, in the flask and a mixture of fine silica sand and liquid sodium silicate poured round it and rammed gently in place. This was gassed with carbon dioxide. Once the silica sand was set, the flask was removed and the mould baked in the kiln. Once again it was filled when it was very hot.

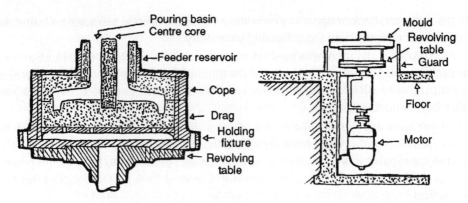

Figure 65. Vertical centrifugal casting machine of the type used to cast small Pelton turbine runners at the University of Colombia at Bogota

The flask

The flask is used repeatedly. Making it out of stainless steel is expensive, but will pay for itself several times over in the long run. The heat of the kiln oxidizes a mild steel flask very rapidly.

Refractories

The most common refractory slurry is brick dust and plaster. Today brick dust has been replaced to a large extent by grog (fired clay). The proportion is one of plaster to two of grog. The simplest method of investing is to degrease the wax, then fill up the flask with refractory. While this is still liquid, dip the wax into it, blow any bubbles off the surface, dip it again and finally immerse the wax in the refractory slurry.

Grog is now available which sets off the plaster very quickly. If this fast setting prevents the dipping and immersion method there is another way of doing it. Make a simple jig or frame so that you can rotate the wax while pouring on the first coat, or get someone to hold and rotate it on a metal shaft. Blow off any bubbles, or use a paint brush to remove them. Fix the wax cup to the base plate and, finally, fill up the flask with a back-up coat of ludo.

Kiln firing (de-waxing)

Firing procedure for block investment is the direct opposite to the ceramic shell flash de-waxing (Chapter 7; see also Chapter 11). For block moulds, firing is the same as for ceramic pots – heat is built up slowly to 200°C. At this point the liquid wax has melted out, but the wax gas takes far longer. From 200° you can increase the heat more rapidly to between 700° and 800°C, which is to say cherry red heat. If you are lucky enough to own a pyrometer keep it at 740°C. I use segar cones to check the temperature and also judge by colour, and this works well. If the temperature rises above 800° the plaster will break down and the moulds weaken and collapse. Recently I saw a display of lost-wax casting in a Paris museum where the firing temperature was given as 650°C.

The kiln must be built in such a way that you can see the bottom edge of the moulds, preferably the cups. The traditional wood-fired Roman kiln had a channel under the mould cups, this was partly to catch some of the liquid wax, and partly to view the cups. Whatever type of kiln you use the rule remains the same. You can only judge the final hours of the firing by watching the cups. Experience with a particular kiln over a long period will give you a rough idea of the time the firing will take, but this can never be exact. Other factors, particularly the ambient temperature, but also wind direction, size of moulds, or how recent (meaning how wet) they are, all affect the time of firing.

You must watch the final stage of the firing. This will tell you when the last vestiges of wax gas have gone. Early on in the firing the wax melts and burns, giving off a lot of smoke and steam. There is a strong smell of wax, which if you use a certain amount of beeswax, is not unpleasant. The kiln at this stage is 'black hot'. Looking through one of the observation holes, you can see the first signs of reddening on the kiln bricks and the moulds themselves. As the temperature increases and the inside of the kiln becomes incandescent, so the smoke and steam dies away until there is no discernible waste product coming out of the chimney. At red heat, turn off some of your burners (or level out the solid fuel) and keep the kiln stable at that temperature. You now have several hours when you can relax, so long as you check the kiln from time to time to see that the temperature had not changed. Towards the end of the burnout you will see small lazy flames curling out of the cups. These are the last vestiges of wax gas escaping.

I cannot over-stress the importance of these flames. They are an infallible guide to something that is invisible to your eye; that is, the condition of the refractory inside the mould. The flames are unmistakable: they seem to dance slowly, telling you that the mould is baked through to the core. Or, to be exact, the core is baked when those little flames cease. At this point you can ease down on the heat. Turn off a burner, or decrease the fuel, but do not turn off the heat source completely, sometimes the flames tease you, they appear to have finished only to return when you do not expect them. If there is no sign of a flame after 30 minutes, then you can shut off the gas, or oil burners, and close the damper and air vents. In the case of a solid fuel or wood burning kiln, keep it stoked up for an hour, then stop up all holes with bricks and mud.

A rough guide to firing times

ROMAN KILN (coke fired)

6 medium sized moulds, approximately 30in high × 12in wide (765 × 300mm) = 24 hours

4 large moulds, approximately 50in × 20in (1275 × 510mm) = 36 hours

GAS KILN (conventional front-loading)

6 moulds for Pelton wheels, approximately 12in high × 24in wide (300 × 600mm) = 15 hours

OIL-FIRED KILN (two kerosene burners; brickwork based on Roman pattern; very little insulation)

15 hours was not enough for 6 moulds for Pelton wheels

It may seem that I make too much of something which is a simple operation. It is simple – if you do it right. I cannot stress too forcibly the importance of correct and patient kiln firing. The Roman method is forgiving in many ways, but the moulds have to be correctly and thoroughly fired or several weeks' work will be wasted. In business terms this means a considerable financial loss.

To conclude, there are many minor factors that contribute to the quality of a casting made by the lost-wax method. There are three vital factors that make or spoil the final product. The first is the kiln firing; the second the temperature of the mould when it is filled with metal; and the third is the temperature and quality of the metal as it enters the mould.

The clay slurry investment method

The clay slurry investment method is used in many parts of the world, without any apparent connection between them. I have seen it used by casters in Bamoum, western Cameroon, and by Newar craftspeople in Nepal.

Below is an outline description of the basic technique and some of the differences in detail between the ways in which I have witnessed it being used.

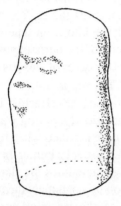

Figure 66. Clay slurry technique: the core is formed from a mixture of clay, straw and horse dung

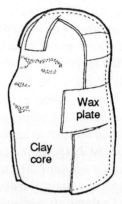

Figure 67. Wax strips or plates are warmed in the sunlight and placed over the core

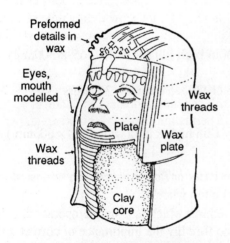

Preformed details in wax

Eyes, mouth modelled

Plate

Wax threads

Wax plate

Wax threads

Clay core

Figure 68. The detail, in the form of wax threads or wax press-moulded decoration, is laid over the wax plates

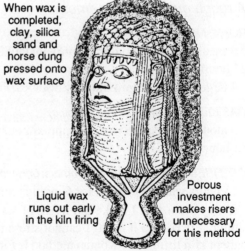

When wax is completed, clay, silica sand and horse dung pressed onto wax surface

Liquid wax runs out early in the kiln firing

Porous investment makes risers unnecessary for this method

Figure 69. Completed clay slurry mould with wax runners and cup attached

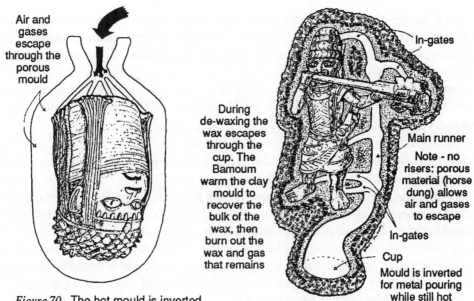

Air and gases escape through the porous mould

During de-waxing the wax escapes through the cup. The Bamoum warm the clay mould to recover the bulk of the wax, then burn out the wax and gas that remains

In-gates

Main runner

Note - no risers: porous material (horse dung) allows air and gases to escape

In-gates

Cup

Mould is inverted for metal pouring while still hot

Figure 70. The hot mould is inverted and molten metal is poured into the cup and down the runners

Figure 71. Clay slurry process: a more complex figure

The essential difference between the Italian block and the Indian and African clay slurry methods is that the latter, in the words of the Bamoum casters who use the method in western Cameroon, 'se respire': in other words, it breathes, allowing air and gases to escape. This rather startling statement means that the clay shell or investment is thin, lightweight and porous, the latter being one of its major advantages as it eliminates the need for risers. The thinner, lighter mould also requires less firing time for an equivalent wax object – as little as one third with a corresponding saving in fuel.

The third advantage is the cheapness of the investment material, consisting of materials found locally – clay and dung – prompting an obvious question: if the method is so marvellous, why did the Romans, and later Italian casters, not adopt the same method? The answer lies in its one major disadvantage, the slow drying time of each coat. Roman technicians must have heard of the method in common use in the Middle East and India, but the Roman foundries were situated in a colder part of the world.

Where the investing time for an Italian block mould is half a day, and it can be loaded into the kiln the following day while still damp, clay slurry will take seven to ten days to dry, depending on the weather. Since the shell depends upon the circulation of warm air to set and dry, the drying time depends on whether the atmosphere is warm and dry, or rainy and humid. So you will understand why, like my Newar hosts, I watched with such attention as huge clouds swelled and built up over the Himalayas as the process of investing our Pelton wheels using the clay slurry method got under way.

The differences between the Newar and Bamoum technicians lie in detail, rather than principle. Variations lie in kiln and furnace technology, in the use or not of a core, and the thickness and constituents of the clay-dung slurry.

As for the core, the Bamoum pre-form it, while the Newar, like the later Benin casters, avoid using a core by making any wax object to be cast into an open form – usually a cylinder – and welding, or more usually jointing the open forms together.

As for the investment differences, the Newar casters apply a liquid slurry as a first and second coat whereas the Bamoum press a sticky mud mixture into the details. Thus one depends on painting and dipping, the other on finger pressure to expel air bubbles. Both methods work efficiently.

The Newar method of casting has survived in Nepal with remarkably little foreign influence. Unlike the casters of Benin and Ife, Asante and Dahome, the craft tradition was never broken by war or conquest.

Today, lost-wax casting flourishes in Nigeria and, on a smaller scale, in Ghana and Cameroon. The technique seems similar to that used by their ancestors, but we cannot be certain.

In Nepal and West Africa there is no division between the sculptor and the caster, unlike the tradition in Europe where the division is almost complete (even extending to social status). In Nepal and West Africa the artist who makes the wax sculpture also melts and pours the metal, so that he understands the process from beginning to end and inside out. If the work is a team effort (any large sculpture is bound by its nature to be carried out by a team) the process is under the control of a master ('maestro' in Italian, or 'odumfwo' in the Akan language).

The Newar technique is described here in detail because this method has been successfully used to cast accurate Pelton turbine wheels for micro-hydro-electricity generation.

To recap: there are no risers, only runners (or 'in-gates'). Thus almost half the sprue system (and half the wax worker's labour) is avoided.

In designing the sprue system, Mr Shakya who, with his family, runs the foundry, provided a good head of metal and a generous size of 'dhwaya', or reservoir, above it. From the dhwaya the bulk of the metal flowed straight down three main in-gates (see Figure 72). Four subsidiary runners took off from these diagonally and fed a gallery or circular horizontal gate, which in turn fed the in-gate fitted to the top of each bucket.

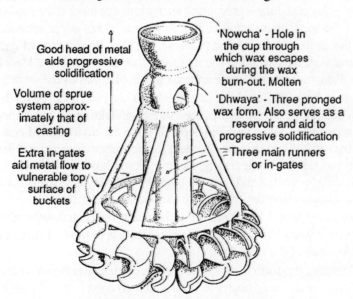

Good head of metal aids progressive solidification

Volume of sprue system approximately that of casting

Extra in-gates aid metal flow to vulnerable top surface of buckets

'Nowcha' - Hole in the cup through which wax escapes during the wax burn-out. Molten

'Dhwaya' - Three pronged wax form. Also serves as a reservoir and aid to progressive solidification

Three main runners or in-gates

Figure 72. The Newar method of spruing and gating a small Pelton mould

A weakness we found during our first experiments with Pelton wheels, cast using the Roman method (a weakness incidentally which had nothing to do with the method), was a failure of molten metal always to fill the top edges of the buckets.

The Newar casters used no degreasing fluid (alcohol or soda) and yet the first slurry coat (consisting of equal parts of clay and cow dung) had no problem wetting the surface. This is because the first coat of slurry was allowed to stand and ferment for several weeks. It therefore etched the wax surface, and thus needed no degreaser.

To prepare the slurry coat the dung was sieved, and all undigested matter removed, then mixed with clay and a little water. This mixture was then sieved again through a finer mesh into a bowl. These casters use two different kinds of clay, apparent from the different colours visible in the clay store.

The clay used in the first coat is critical. It must dry with reasonable speed and yet not so fast as to develop cracks in the surface. For this reason the coated waxes are dried in the shade, not in direct sunlight. The clay used in the first coat is a special, rather rare clay called 'mashincha'. Its special quality lay in a combination of fineness, plasticity and hardness when dried. A potter in Baktapur later told me that mashincha is a grey clay with a yellow tinge found near natural deposits of potters' black clay called 'kalimati'. Both these clays were found near the brick fields of Lalitpur (now renamed Patan).

Each wax was dipped in the slurry, the bubbles blown off or tickled out with a chicken feather, then the slurry allowed partially to dry in the shade where a warm breeze circulated. A second coat was applied that evening. Fortunately the weather was warm and the set of Pelton wheel waxes with their investment dried quickly, despite the rain clouds which seemed to grow more massive and threatening each day.

The third, fourth and fifth coats resemble porridge, or dhal (or in Africa the maize porridge known as *posho, nsema* or *ugali*) in consistency. The first slurry coat is put on one side and a fresh slurry of clay and dung mixed to cream consistency. Rice husk

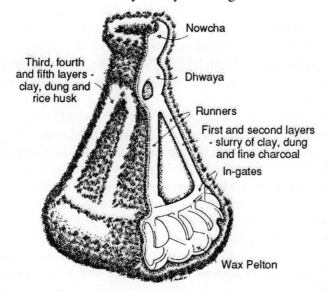

Figure 73. Newar mould, cut away to show fine inner coats and coarse outer coats of slurry

81

is added to this until the right paste-like quality is achieved. The addition of rice husk not only allows the investment to breathe, but, when fired, adds amorphous silica to increase the refractory qualities.

These subsequent coats took longer to dry than the first and second. Even with a warm, drying wind the process took a week. A second batch of Pelton moulds took much longer to dry because of the wet weather and rising humidity, a period of between fourteen and twenty days. This, as I have already said, is the method's one major drawback, but you can provide an artificially dried atmosphere – a cheap electric fan circulates warm air admirably.

Once dry, the moulds were warmed over a charcoal brazier until warm enough to melt the wax, then the 'nowcha' (hole inside of the cup) was pierced and the wax poured out. About 50% of the wax is recovered by using this method. Some of the wax remains in the investment in any process, and this must be removed. To do this the moulds were placed in a simple wood-fired kiln for about five hours.

While kiln and moulds were still very hot the crucibles of metal were lifted from the furnace. The molten metal was poured while the moulds were as hot as could be handled, using (in this case) sacks which smouldered and sometimes caught fire.

A steady supply of metal is a problem for the Newar casters. Copper is mined in Nepal, as are silver and gold; tin appeared to be in short supply. The statues that they cast are made of either copper or brass. I did not see any bronze castings, undoubtedly because of supply problems. However, gun-metal was to be found in this instance in a Patan scrapyard in the form of scrap parts from oil tankers imported from Singapore.

When the moulds were broken open some hours later the castings proved to be accurate, with a minimum of faults such as feathers, potatoes, or blow holes.

Like any foundry, east or west, the Shakya family observed that they never had casting faults (everyone does have faults, of course, though nobody talks about them). I discovered later that the Shakyas repaired only very small faults. If a major fault occurred they simply melted the casting immediately and recast the faulty piece.

There was no sign that flow welding was used as it is by the Bamoum casters, but all the Newar foundries I visited made occasional use of oxy-acetylene welding.

West African casters, from Ghana through Nigeria to Cameroon, use a melting and filling method to cope with copper oxidization which I have not seen anywhere else, and as far as I know is unique.

A hemispherical crucible is made to suit the size of a particular wax pattern, then the correct amount of scrap bronze is assessed by eye and placed in the crucible. After the wax is melted out, the crucible is fitted onto the cup end of the mould and then sealed. This prevents both air and impurities reaching the molten copper. (The Akan casters use this method for brass castings, but it is particularly well-suited to copper.)

The combined mould and crucible is placed in the furnace with the crucible at the bottom. The metal is melted and, at the same time, all traces of wax gas are burnt out of the mould. The white, sweet smelling fumes of zinc are unmistakable. Once these appear over the furnace the mould and crucible combination is removed from the furnace and inverted. The molten metal flows into the mould without being exposed to oxidization or hydrogen pickup.

This method is not practical for large castings. It is only used to cast objects below the size of a human head, so it is used particularly by jewellers and silversmiths. Illustrations in some European text books show the casters of Benin forming life-size heads by this method. The Bamoum casters laugh at this suggestion and point out that the problem of turning both mould and crucible when they are hot and fragile would make large castings impossible, which is why the Bamoum use it only for small objects. The Newar do not use it at all.

Many of the Newar moulds used in Nepal were large. Figures or couples well over life-size were common. The Shakya family solved the problem of size in a practical and ingenious way. The wax workers dismembered the hollow wax model, and then cast it in several pieces, not forgetting the Roman joints on each section which would eventually locate one part into another. Finally the statue, or couple, was fettled, metal finished and polished and assembled.

This method has many advantages. The most obvious is the ease of handling several medium-size moulds instead of one huge one. The second is the open ended nature of each wax pattern, avoiding the notorious problem of the enclosed core. And the third is more commercial than technical. Packing a giant sized sculpture piece is a major headache. It is far easier to transport a couple of large and amorous deities in sections and fit them together on arrival, so long as you know which bits fit where.

The clay slurry method combines immense sophistication and faithful reproduction of detail with simplicity and, no less important, with cheapness of materials and equipment. No one but a fool would import expensive material for his business if the material is lying near to, or within easy reach of, the foundry.

Inca silver

The final example describes a method which is not a lost-wax, though is closely related to it. It is neither die casting nor sand casting, and therefore difficult to position in a list of techniques.

Clay pressing, found in the Andes, is possibly the only pre-Columbian metalworking technique to survive the ruthless destruction of the Conquistadors. It is still used as a common technique by many self-employed silversmiths, or small jewellery companies in Peru, Colombia and Ecuador. A hand-made model, or master, complete with its sprue system, is pressed between two slabs of clay which resemble large biscuits.

The clay is a mixture of a fine pale clay of the kaolin type, with very fine, sieved silica sand. The biscuits are pale grey, almost white.

The master is lightly oiled between each pressing, and a series of four or five pairs of slabs made in this way. Each slab, or pair of biscuits, has an in-gate (or runner) and two air vents (or risers). The in-gates are connected to a single large cup, made of the same clay mixture. The risers vent outside the cup. Finally the edges are sealed with soft clay and the assembly of small moulds baked in a crude oven. At the same time the silver is melted in a small furnace, fired by charcoal, with a hand-powered blower to raise the temperature.

The silversmith removes the mould assembly from the oven while it is still very hot, using tongs. He holds it horizontally while the molten silver is poured into the cup. The

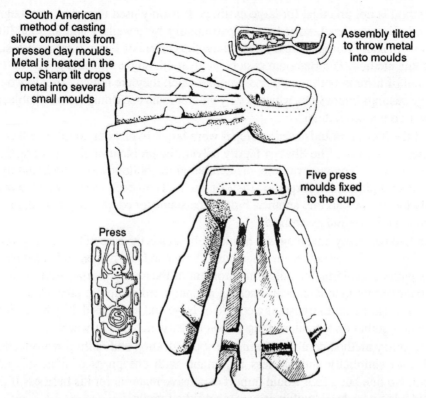

South American method of casting silver ornaments from pressed clay moulds. Metal is heated in the cup. Sharp tilt drops metal into several small moulds

Assembly tilted to throw metal into moulds

Five press moulds fixed to the cup

Press

Figure 74. Clay pressing: a hand-made model complete with sprue system is pressed between two slabs of clay to make a mould

assembly is then turned to a vertical position with a vigorous movement which projects the molten silver into the group of moulds.

Once filled with metal the clay assembly is plunged into water. The clay cracks away leaving the silver jewellery clean, still attached to its sprue system.

Young boys and girls (apprentices) then cut each silver ornament from its sprue and clean up any positive faults, or 'stub ends', remaining from the in-gate or risers. If there are any negative faults (air bubbles or cold shuts for example) the silver is remelted.

During my visit I saw very few faults. Though the technique is simple, the results were remarkable for their accuracy and complexity.

7. The ceramic shell process

The ceramic shell process developed out of the Indian and West African clay and dung slurry method of casting described in the previous chapter. It is much closer to this thin-walled, porous method than it is to either the Italian block or the Shaw process. Rolls Royce in the UK pioneered the ceramic shell method during World War II to make precision aircraft parts, particularly the blades for gas turbine engines whose interior surfaces were so complicated that they could not be machined. Most casters and engineers believed at that time that the system would only work in large and lavishly equipped foundries with precision machinery and measuring instruments.

The system was not generally available to small foundries until the late 1960s and early 1970s. On experimentation with the new method I quickly discovered two major advantages. First, ease of investment. Unlike the Italian method which demanded manual ability and craft apprenticeship training, provided that there is a supervisor somewhere nearby to make sure that the quality and condition of the materials are maintained exactly, the ceramic shell method is well-suited to the small foundry. The second major advantage is the de-waxing process. Ceramic shell avoids the lengthy, patient and tiring period of kiln firing which is crucial to the Italian method. Ceramic shell has one or two major disadvantages also; we will come to these later. At first sight it seems like the answer to all the caster's problems. There were many legends, myths and theories about this new and, by repute, magical process. Closer acquaintance and familiarity prove that it is by no means perfect, especially where climatic conditions are less than consistent.

Handbooks on the ceramic shell process are highly technical and specific. They specify the viscosity of the slurry and its exact pH. Temperature, humidity, slurry mixers and fluidizing beds are all tightly controlled. The list goes on and on. The textbooks are, of course, concerned with high technology. The machinery and test equipment that they specify is expensive. Medium or appropriate technology is outside their field. Where these books fail, in what is otherwise excellent information, is in their insistence that ceramic shell works only if you follow their method to the letter. Their method invariably involves large capital expenditure on precision machinery. Practice and experiment by various iconoclasts in America, Australia and Europe (in the back yard, rather than the laboratory) proved that this is very far from the truth (see Sheffield case study, page 74).

In fact, ceramic shell needs less equipment than the block method, because you can manage without a kiln. A kiln is useful but not essential. What you must have, and here the handbooks are correct for alternative as well as high-tech casting, is good quality material. To make the slurry you need colloidal silica, which is a manufactured product, and you need three sizes of refractory.

Different refractories are used in different parts of the world. These include silicas (electrofused silica and unfused silica), alumino-silicates (molochite, remasil, chamotte, mullite), fused alumina and zircon. All of these refractories have to be milled precisely. You need one other manufactured product to build your own furnace and de-waxing chamber, and that is ceramic fibre blanket. Provided that you can get hold of these three: colloidal silica, molochite and ceramic fibre blanket, and you have the use of a small welding machine, you should have no problem building a small-scale foundry. The problem lies in obtaining these materials. In some areas they may either be too expensive or unobtainable.

Aficionados of the ceramic shell method tend to be dogmatic about their own particular method, asserting that it is the only modern way of investment casting. All the others, they insist, are obsolete. There is no doubt that ceramic shell is an excellent method; for certain industries it is superior – aerospace we have already mentioned. It is also used to manufacture gun parts and some precision optical and camera pieces as well as certain pieces of medical equipment. But ceramic shell is not the only way, and for certain purposes it is inferior to the Italian block method. Every method has advantages and disadvantages.

Ceramic shell is not practical in parts of the world where the temperature fluctuates wildly – in the Andes, for example, or in Nepal. This presents no problem if you have a room with a controlled temperature. If you do not then you are faced with a major problem: the slurry will not set to its green strength below 20° C, and the colloidal silica is ruined if it drops below freezing point.

No less important, variations in temperature cause the wax to expand and contract. The shell is not flexible, nor is it strong in its green state. The movement of the wax cracks the shell, which will open up and leak when it is filled with molten metal. This causes feathering at the cracks and inaccuracy in the thickness of the casting. For these reasons ceramic shell would be a difficult process to control for a small foundry which could not afford a room with temperature control and central heating, for example, someone setting up in business in Cuzco or Kathmandu.

Equipment

First check that there is someone in your area who can supply you with material and at a reasonable price. If this is the case, then the equipment you need is simple, easily made and cheap. You will not find this point made in any of the standard textbooks, but it is the biggest single advantage of the process for a caster setting up on a small budget. If you plan to make small-scale, precise castings, the equipment is not heavy, which is another advantage.

I have a complete portable foundry which I built for ceramic shell demonstration and teaching purposes. Using bottled gas as a fuel this packs into a small van and trailer.

To build this you will need two 200 litre (40 gallon) drums, some scrap mild steel, angle or flat stock, and a few lengths of round steel bar. The insulating material is ceramic fibre blanket. You will need a standard sized roll of 20mm (1in) thick fibre. You will also need silica sand, or green sand and about 20 refractory fire bricks. Ordinary house bricks are also useful. A grating supported by four lengths of steel water pipe, or angle, about 1.75m (5ft) long, makes up the de-waxing stand, with a tray or large pan at the bottom to catch the wax (this can be reused for the back-up coat).

Obviously you need a crucible to melt the metal in, and you need a heat source, gas, oil or paraffin. One burner will do, two is a luxury. If you already possess a conventional furnace, you are fortunate. All you need is a burner of some kind, gas, oil, or paraffin fired, to de-wax and to keep the moulds hot after de-waxing.

For details of construction of this equipment, see Chapter 11.

The ceramic shell process in outline

Ceramic shell bears little or no resemblance to the Italian block investment method. In principle it is the same as the clay and dung slurry method used in India and Africa for centuries (and probably in South America in pre-Colombian times).

The shell is built up in layers starting with a very fine-grained dip-coat which is then dusted with a fine powder (molochite or zircon). Once the first coat is set hard, the wax is dipped a second time. Again, this is of fine material and it picks up any bubbles or fine points missed by the first coat. The third, and successive, coats are dusted with a coarser-grained stucco. This coarser aggregate builds up the strength of the shell.

Handling the wax during this dipping and stuccoing process is a problem, but practice and experience overcome most of the handling difficulties. Here again the makers specify special slurry mixers rotating constantly; fluidizing beds, or 'rain' machines for the stucco; drying cabinets and autoclaves for de-waxing.

Certainly, anyone watching the automated investment process at the Rolls-Royce aero-engines factory in the UK must be filled with admiration for the ingenuity and precision of the equipment. But the process works well without machinery, where the dipping and stuccoing is done by hand.

The two key factors in successful casting in ceramic shell are:

o   Flash de-waxing (melting out the wax very fast)

o   Pouring the metal into hot moulds.

The pouring temperature of both metal and mould depends on the thickness of the casting. Generally speaking the shells should be red hot, or certainly pink hot (700–800°C).

The process in detail

Designing machine parts for the ceramic shell process

Castings are improved by following a few simple rules:

1.   If possible avoid major changes in thickness. Make contours as smooth as possible, use fillet radii to soften sharp internal edges.

2.   Flat surfaces and right angles are difficult to cast. Blended contours make better castings.

3.   Place runners (in-gates) on surfaces that are not critical and can be easily machined.

4. The same rule also applies to core nails, if these are used.

5. Flatness is difficult to achieve with any form of lost-wax casting, adding ribs will minimize distortion or twisting. They will also help the flow of the metal.

Wax

Most of the comments on wax in the earlier chapter still apply, but with this difference. The qualities required for wax using the ceramic shell method are of more critical importance than with the block method, and the caster must be more particular about the mixture that he uses. In the latter the slurry is painted, flicked or poured on. The wax pattern is not handled during the investment part of the block method. In ceramic shell, on the other hand, the wax has to be handled and turned during the investment. Alternatively, as in the aircraft industry, the wax can be suspended by a stainless steel frame attached to the sprue.

It is important to remember that the ceramic slurry has no green strength. It becomes strong only when it is fired, when a chemical change takes place, like the chemical change in any other fired ceramic object. Until this happens, the strength of the unit, both the casting and the sprue, lies in the wax. In the block method, the strength, or brittleness of the sprue is not important, because no pressure is put on the sprue.

In the ceramic shell process the cup and sprue have two functions. Their prime purpose is to flow metal in and let air and gases out, just like any other casting process. Secondly, and uniquely, the cup and spruc arc handled as the wax is stuccoed. For this reason the wax, from which the sprue is made, has to be both tough and flexible. Flexibility, or its opposite, brittleness, varies according to the ambient temperature. Therefore you have to adapt your wax mixture according to a winter temperature or a summer temperature in the foundry. (See *Qualities of different waxes* in Chapter 6.)

There is nothing more discouraging, or infuriating, than to see bits of wax break off as the weight of the slurry increases.

As a simple test, cast some runners (about 20mm in diameter). Let them cool to room temperature, then bend one of them. If it bends very slightly, yet with good resistance, it is ready to use. If it snaps, it is too brittle and you must add something to soften it, and possibly something to add more toughness. If it is sloppy and bends easily, or will not keep its shape, then you must make it harder.

I use the same basic mixture of paraffin wax and resin (see previous chapter). To this I add a soft microcrystalline, or beeswax, to soften it, and to add toughness I put in a small quantity of styrene wax, bought from a specialist wax supplier. In Peru we had no styrene wax so we used shredded polyethylene plastic bags. If you do this you must be careful to use the right kind of plastic.

You can blend an excellent wax using different grades of microcrystalline wax, or you can pay an expert to do it for you. This is what happens in the aircraft industry where the specifications of the wax must be exact and it must show minimum contraction. It is not a cheap service. It may be worth considering, however, because one of many problems we encountered making the waxes for Pelton wheels was the varied contraction of the waxes we used. The contraction of the wax fluctuated between one batch and another. The paraffin wax was reliable, so, to my surprise, was the beeswax, but no two batches of the microcrystalline were the same.

Moulding the wax pattern

This is exactly the same as for the block process (see Chapter 6).

The sprue system

This differs from the block process. It has one advantage in that you do not need risers. Because the shell is so thin (compared to the bulk of a block investment), the air and gas will escape through the gaps between the grains of molochite. However, in certain castings you may need vents in some places, not so much to let the air escape when the metal is poured in, but to allow the wax to flow rapidly out of the shell.

The less trouble the wax has escaping during flash de-waxing the better. Some foundries also nick the shell in strategic places to help the wax out, covering these small saw nicks with slurry during the reinforcement and final coat. Another minor difference is the size of the cup and main runner, or head of the sprue.

Italian sculptor-casters from Cellini to Giambologna made a comprehensive and delicate runner system with an elegant cup. You can see this attention to detail in designs that have survived from the foundries of the Renaissance, and in foundry scrap which has survived by accident; the tradition continues in some Italian foundries and in Germany to this day

Perhaps because the ceramic shell method started in the aircraft industry, and during a war, the sprue system tends to look more functional, or even brutal, to one trained in the Italian tradition. There is no logical reason, however, to suppose that a system which looks better will perform more efficiently compared with one which looks crude and oversized. Certainly most shell casters believe that the volume of cup and runners should be equal to that of the wax pattern. There is no doubt that this system is an aid to correct progressive solidification.

Degreasing

This also is of more critical importance than in the block process. If the wax is not degreased completely, the first dip coat tends to slide off, or the wax rejects the slurry.

There are several ways of degreasing: soda, soap, detergent, or a mixture. Liquid detergent works better than solid as the latter tends to settle out and sink. The purer the detergent the better the result. Any additives, like colour or scent, tend to have negative side effects. In practice the cheaper detergents are usually better. The most effective degreaser we found was alcohol with a very small proportion of detergent suspended in it. Isopropanol is excellent, but any methylated spirit or commercial alcohol works well.

First test and check your wax and sprue for any weak points. Pull very gently on the runners to make sure that they are securely welded on. Pour the alcohol into a bowl, adding 0.05% liquid detergent (or about one squirt from the detergent bottle to one litre of alcohol). Dip the wax into the alcohol, or pour the alcohol over it, making sure that the degreaser reaches every part including internal corners.

Leave it to dry, either standing the wax on its cup, or suspending it with a stainless steel hook. The alcohol evaporates, leaving a microscopic layer of detergent. Remember that the alcohol will chill the wax as it evaporates making the pattern contract. You must allow sufficient time for the wax to return to the normal ambient temperature. If you do not and you coat the wax in slurry too early, it may cause hairline cracks as the wax warms and expands. At this point it is as well to check that the wax stands up, or is suspended securely, so that it cannot fall over and be damaged. Remember that the shell adds weight to the wax which may make it unstable as the layers build up. Avoid major differences in temperature between the room where the wax is dried and the investing room.

The first dip coat

Successive coats of slurry and stucco are held together by colloidal silica. This is a factory-made chemical liquid, much stronger than sodium silicate (waterglass). Colloidal silica comes in various forms. It can be alcohol-based or water-based. Some types use an acid catalyst to set the mixture. In others the shell is placed in a fume cupboard, containing ammonia to make it gel. So long as you follow the suppliers instructions, the procedure is similar. I have concentrated on water-based colloidal silica because although the water-based type takes longer to dry, it is much simpler to use and, as far as fumes are concerned, far less unpleasant. Both the alcohol-based liquid, and the ammonia catalyst, can be very unpleasant to use in a small confined workshop. On the other hand, many casters favour these systems because they are so much faster.

The final casting is as good (or bad) as the first coat. In our first experiments when trying to find a low-cost way of using the ceramic shell method, we encountered several major problems. The first was the slurry sloughing off the wax. There were two reasons for this. The first, already mentioned, was inefficient degreasing. The second, we discovered, was mixing the slurry too thin. When we added more powder to the colloidal silica the first coat stayed in place.

Experience proved that a very small quantity of liquid detergent added to the slurry helped it to 'wet' the surface of the wax and stay there. Later, when the whole process was completed, we discovered another problem, the primary coat was so hard that parts of it stuck to the surface of the metal. (See Appendix F for ways of removing clinging fragments of investment). With much trial and error we found that we could weaken the first coat without affecting the quality of the casting. The colloidal silica could be thinned down by as much as 50% with distilled water (filtered rainwater will do). *Note*: This only applies to the first and second coat. For all the subsequent coats you must use the colloidal silica at full strength.

When adding the fine molochite, or zircon flour, the opposite is true. The first coat must be thick and creamy, otherwise the wax will not be covered sufficiently. At first attempt the tendency is to make the slurry too thin.

To repeat, the first coat is crucial to the whole operation. Time spent experimenting to get the right consistency is not wasted. Make the slurry as thick as you can, though obviously not so thick that you cannot pour it over the wax or dip the wax into the slurry.

As soon as you have dipped the wax, coat it with the fine stucco layer. You must do this immediately before the slurry starts to dry. Instructions in early manuals advised the caster to let the first layer dry without stucco. Experience proved that stuccoeing with fine powder makes a tougher bond with the next layer. For obvious reasons, a smooth surface is more likely to crack away from the second layer. There is one other problem, slurry tends to build up in crevices and hollows; the ideal to aim for is an even coating. If there is too much slurry and powder in a hollow it may not dry properly. Here too, the first coat is the tricky one. You must make sure that every part is dry before the next coat goes on.

Leave the first coat to dry for several hours (depending on the ambient temperature the shells will take anything from three to six hours). If you can leave it to dry overnight so much the better (see also suggested timetable, page 186). The shell needs a moving current of warm air (but not hot air). This air current must reach, or be directed into, the inner hollows and cavities. The temperature must not drop below 15°C (60°F) or the silica solution will not gel. A perfect situation would be a gentle temperate wind blowing through the foundry door and across the shells, but such breezes do not come easily, except by divine order. So it behoves ordinary mortals to invest in a cheap electric fan. Make sure that the breeze blows into any hollow parts of the casting.

You may find that some of the hollows are too deep for the air to reach. The air must circulate to draw off the humidity, so it will pay you to take tubes or air ducts from a second fan, or an old hairdryer if one is available, taking an air tube to each hollow. (An old glove with tubes taped to the open finger ends works well.) Try to keep the temperature as stable as possible and the humidity low. If the temperature drops at night you may have to build a drying cupboard (see Chapter 11). Do not put the shells in hot air. If you use a hairdryer, keep it set on cool.

A final note on temperature. A technician and I made our first experiments in the ceramic shell method in the heated atmosphere of an art school. Though we later modified several aspects of the process, the first results were good. The issue of temperature did not occur to me, nor did the handbook used refer to it. The next major experiment, which I carried out for a client, took place in a farm shed in mid-winter. The shells possessed no green strength, nor did they gain strength when heated: every single one collapsed and disintegrated during the de-waxing operation. This was not only embarrassing, but caused me to lose a good client. The handbook, written in sunny California, USA, did not consider frozen cowsheds. The moral of this experience is: temperature and humidity are vitally important factors in the setting of ceramic shells.

The second coat

The second coat uses the same slurry and stucco as the first but in different proportions. The liquid is the same (50% colloidal silica, 50% distilled water), but this time you must mix in less molochite flour. The first coat had to be thick to coat the wax. The second coat needs to be thinner in consistency, to wet the first stucco. If the second coat is too thick it will tend to 'ball up' or roll off the stucco. A correct mixture will flow well and cover any air holes or tiny blemishes in the first coat. While you are handling the wax, some parts of the sprue system will lose their surface coating. This cannot be avoided. When the shell is coated and you have placed it in its drying place, then take a small quantity of the slurry and touch up the blemishes.

The third coat

The major change comes with the third coat. This time use the colloidal silica neat, straight from the plastic drum. Mix it with the finest grade of molochite, as before. The second change is the stucco, which for this coat and all subsequent coats, is the coarsest grade. Because the stucco is coarser, the coat takes less time to dry. In mild weather (30 to 40°C) the third and subsequent coats should each take about 1–2 hours to dry.

The fourth coat

This is a repeat of the third.

The fifth coat

There are two alternatives for this coat:
1. You can form the fifth coat exactly as the fourth, by dipping and stuccoeing.
2. You can de-wax the shell and then put on the fifth coat. This is called the back-up coat. If it is a large or very irregular casting you will need a sixth coat. In this case, de-wax after the fifth.

The back-up coat (fifth coat)

The choice for this coat depends on the size and shape of the casting. Some castings that have sharp edges or protruding pieces must be reinforced. Large sections or large shells also need reinforcing. The best reinforcement is fine glass fibre dipped in slurry. It must be borne in mind that glass fibre is weakened by extreme heat if it is applied to the shell before de-waxing. In the case of a very large casting, or where you consider that the shell needs strengthening, use stainless steel wire bound to the shell by glass fibre dipped in slurry.

Note: Do not use iron wire or galvanized wire because both rust and zinc oxide will affect the strength of the slurry. In the USA, casters use stainless steel chicken wire to strengthen large moulds. I have never seen this useful material anywhere else in the world.

Because the wax is removed before the back-up coat, there is no danger of expanding and cracking the shell. For this reason the back-up coat can be dried rapidly, using a gas flame.

Final note: After de-waxing, be very careful not to drop any investment or glass fibre into the cup of the shell. The shell is not strong before firing, and the wax inside it is vulnerable to expansion and contraction caused by changes of temperature. Once the shell is de-waxed and fired, a chemical change takes place and the shell becomes stable and strong. The fired shell can be stored for years, though quite obviously you must take precautions against dust or small objects falling into it. Like any other ceramic material, it will break if dropped.

Mixing and re-mixing the slurry

If the slurry is not mixed frequently, or kept moving by some means, the powder (molochite or zircon) will settle and separate out from the colloidal silica, forming a mass at the bottom, rather like cement. It has been stated in at least one handbook that it cannot be re-mixed. That is nonsense – it can be re-mixed, but if the container is very large, the mass of hardened slurry may take so long to chop and stir back into usable condition that the foundry manager may decide that it is cheaper to throw it away, and mix up a second batch. Dough mixers, colloids and hand mixing are all satisfactory ways of returning the slurry to a usable condition.

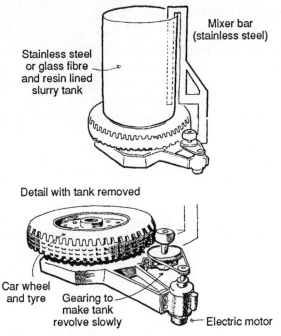

Stainless steel
or glass fibre
and resin lined
slurry tank

Mixer bar
(stainless steel)

Detail with tank removed

Car wheel
and tyre   Gearing to
make tank
revolve slowly   ← Electric motor

Figure 75. Improvised slurry mixer

The most common cause of this annoying and wasteful state of affairs is a power failure, such as a power-cut, or fuse blowing in the middle of the night. The author has experienced this personally. The power went off briefly, when nobody was supervising the slurry mixer. By the time the electricity came on again the slurry had settled. Unable to turn properly in the thickening mixture, the paddle burned the motor out.

There are in fact, various electronic safeguards to avoid this happening. A mixer is not hard to make: using a car wheel; a pair of pulley wheels; an electric motor; a paddle made up of flat stainless steel, and last, but not least, a drum or circular container. Placed on the car wheel, the drum rotates, while the paddle or scraper remains stationary (see Figure 75). The drum can be of the type used for food processing purposes. A dairy or similar establishment may well have one which will suit your purposes, being no longer suitable for the mixing of food. Failing that, use a 40 gallon drum. If this is an ordinary oil drum you must first line it if there is no plastic lining (some chemical drums are lined) or the steel will contaminate the colloidal silica. You can line it yourself using polyester resin and glass fibre.

93

The handbooks often say that you must have a slurry mixer, and there is no doubt that this is true if you are making a lot of shells, virtually a production line operation. If, like me, you use it occasionally, for certain specialized jobs, or for teaching purposes, then there is no point in wasting capital and space by owning a slurry mixer. There is a small-scale alternative. Various colloids on the market (some of them developed for thixotropic paints) will help to suspend powders in liquids. The best known is 'Seaspen' made in the USA, but any chemical company manufacturing colloids should be able to supply one.

If you only use the process very occasionally, the other alternative is to mix the slurry each morning during the process. This is hard work but the results are no less satisfactory than the most expensive mixer that money can buy.

Store the slurry in a plastic container with an airproof lid. So long as the liquid is kept above freezing (which alters the state of colloidal silica irretrievably) you can store the slurry as long as you like. To re-mix the stored material, carefully pour the liquid into another plastic container. Next dig out the solid, taking care not to puncture the plastic container, and put the lumps of molochite on a stainless steel tray or a galvanized sheet. Use a spade to chop up the hardened molochite. When the lumps are as small as you can make them, replace them in the plastic bucket and pour in a little of the liquid, stirring with a stainless steel rod or hardwood pole. With a lot of stirring the mixture will return to its original consistency. If you leave it overnight, use the same procedure. It will not be so laborious as the first mixing.

The fluidizing bed and the rain machine

There are two ways of covering the wax with stucco while it is still wet. The most luxurious is a fluidizing bed. This is a drum with an air pump underneath it which blasts air upwards through a fine sieve. The current of air makes the solid grains of stucco behave like a liquid. You can dip the slurry-covered wax into the machine, covering it with stucco in exactly the same way as if you had dipped it into the liquid.

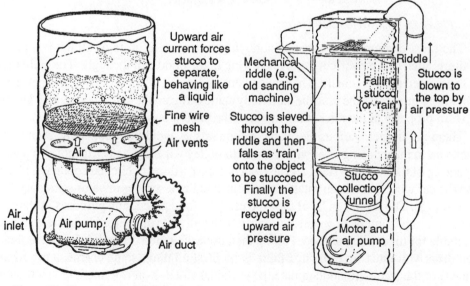

Figure 76. Home-made fluidizing bed   *Figure 77.* Mechanized stucco rain cabinet

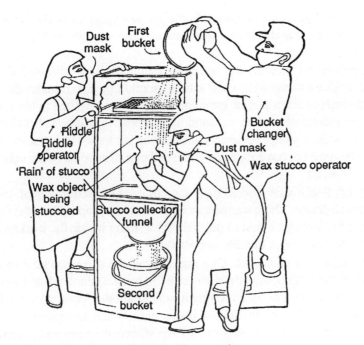

Figure 78. Simple stucco rain cabinet in operation

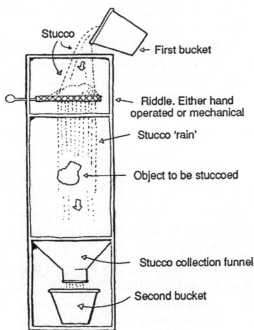

Figure 79. Cross-section of simple stucco rain cabinet

There is no doubt that one of these machines is a pleasure to use. A fluidizing bed is not hard to make, and the home-made ones I have seen work as well as any other type. If, however, you are contemplating making large castings, then you will either need a very large fluidizing bed, or to find some other way of doing it. The second way is to build a cabinet with a chute at the bottom to funnel the stucco into a bucket. Above the cabinet, a mechanically shaken sieve 'rains' stucco down on the wax that you are turning underneath it.

The particular example I describe has one electric motor which drives the shaker at the top and also works a pump with some kind of suction pipe to transfer the stucco from the bottom chute to the top. One ingenious caster I have visited made a similar machine using the mechanism of an old sanding machine to agitate the riddle at the top. Instead of a vacuum pump, he simply rotated the buckets. However, if you are short of space, you may not have room for either a large drum or a bulky cabinet. In that case, stucco by hand.

One small foundry that I have worked in, in the UK, was housed in a small building that had been a coach-house. There was no space for machinery, apart from the furnace. The kiln was outside, through a hole in the wall. Everything inside the workshop was portable, to keep the foundry as flexible as possible.

Investing was a matter of teamwork. One man rotated the waxes on steel rods, one wax at a time, while his mate poured the slurry over an inclined chute of stainless steel. Then the next pair took the wax, one rotating it while the other poured stucco from a large bowl. The stucco fell into a similar bowl underneath. When the top one was empty, he changed over the bowls. A fifth person took the stuccoed waxes and placed them on a shelf covered in clear plastic to make a simple fume cupboard. Under this cover sat several saucers of ammonia. For speed setting this particular foundry used the ammonia setting variant of the process.

A peculiarity of this foundry was backing the completed shells with ludo, reinforced with chicken wire. A purist would be shocked by such an odd hybrid of processes, but this particular foundry achieved some very fine castings. In my own foundry we use all three methods: the Shaw process, the Italian block method, and ceramic shell, without any mechanical aids. We dip and stucco by hand. *Whichever method is used, the wearing of an efficient dust mask is strongly advised. Any form of silica is dangerous as all cause silicosis.*

De-waxing

There are several types of de-waxing furnace (see illustrations in Chapter 11): toploading, top-hat, counterbalanced or, simplest of all, a lift-off type. I have called it a furnace to emphasize that it is not a conventional kiln.

For example, the de-waxing kiln, for the block method, builds up heat slowly, while with the de-waxing furnace you need the opposite effect. The ceramic shell has quite amazing resistance to thermal shock. On the other hand in its green state, it can easily be cracked by any expansion of the wax. To prevent this damage, the shell is plunged suddenly into an intense heat. The outer skin of wax melts instantly. This 'skimming' relieves pressure on the shell as the thicker, inner mass of wax expands. Finally, this melts and drops through the cup to a tray placed below to retrieve and recycle the wax.

Some foundries do not bother to use a separate de-waxing furnace, but plunge the shells into their metal-melting furnace. In using the metal-melting furnace in this way, they argue, they save on equipment and save space. I am all for saving space and equipment but this seems to me a wasteful and messy practice. It is then impossible to recycle the wax which is very expensive, and, secondly, the wax burns, making smoke and fumes in the foundry.

Assuming that you do not use the metal-melting furnace, you will need a simple de-waxing furnace. This should be placed on a frame well above the ground: if the wax is flaming as it comes out of the cup (as it often is) it will cool and the flames go out before the wax hits the collection tray. An old tin bath, or large baking tray are ideal to catch the wax.

Do not make the mistake that I made when I first tried it, and put water in the tray. As wax behaves very like oil, water only increases the fire. The simplest de-waxing burner that causes least bother and is simplest to operate, is a large torch using bottled gas. This again is simple to make. The next best is a kerosene burner working on the primus principle. An oversized plumber's lamp is ideal. Keep the shell in the flame and inside the de-waxing furnace for a few minutes, until the flames and smoke have ceased. Most of the shell should be white or a pinkish colour. Traces of black or grey indicate carbon, meaning that some wax gas is still inside the mould. Do not worry at this stage, the holding kiln will remove this wax at a later stage.

A de-waxing furnace, as I have said, is very simple to make. Being light in weight, you can haul it up into the foundry roof or hang it on the wall when you are not using it.

If the shell needs reinforcing, it is advisable to do this after de-waxing, when you put on the fifth coat (or sixth coat, if the mould is large or angular). Once the wax has gone, and the shell is fired, it is a good idea to spend some time checking all the shells, and reinforcing the larger ones and those small ones that show signs of cracking or having weak points. The cup will probably need some attention: resting the shell on the cup inevitably causes some abrasion and weakness at the lip. Dip the glass fibre in some spare slurry and model it onto the surface of the shell. Be very careful at this point that nothing falls into the cup. One way to prevent this is to wrap some cotton wool with thin plastic and place it in the cup.

Flash de-waxing

Pre-heat the flash de-waxing container until the ceramic fibre glows pink. Remove the container and place the shell on the grid. Replace the container immediately. This process needs two people, one to lift the container and one to place the shell. At first it is a good idea to turn down the burner during this operation, but a little practice should make this unnecessary. You can see when the shell has stopped flaming by looking under the grid. As soon as the shell is ready, lift the container, remove the first shell, using ceramic fibre pads, and place the next. Leave the shells to cool in a safe dry place.

Kiln firing

It has already been stated that you do not need a kiln for the ceramic shell method: that is, you do not *need* a kiln in the conventional sense. If you have one, then it is an advantage. What is necessary, however, is a heat-retaining container. A kiln does the job. If you do not have one then you can build a heat-holding kiln without difficulty from a ceramic fibre blanket and the other half of the 40-gallon drum that you used for

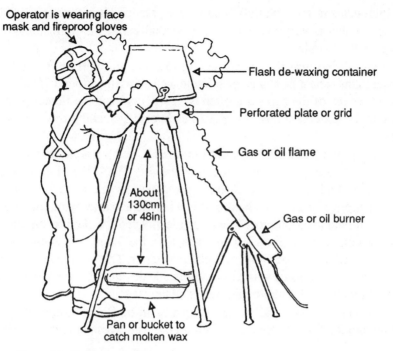

Operator is wearing face mask and fireproof gloves

Flash de-waxing container

Perforated plate or grid

Gas or oil flame

About 130cm or 48in

Gas or oil burner

Pan or bucket to catch molten wax

Figure 80. Flash de-waxing

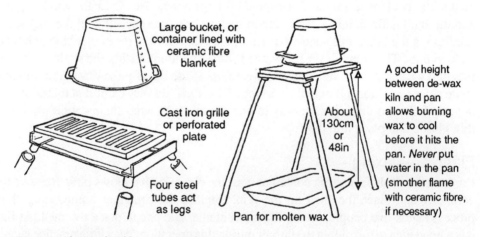

Large bucket, or container lined with ceramic fibre blanket

Cast iron grille or perforated plate

Four steel tubes act as legs

About 130cm or 48in

Pan for molten wax

A good height between de-wax kiln and pan allows burning wax to cool before it hits the pan. *Never* put water in the pan (smother flame with ceramic fibre, if necessary)

Figure 81. Improvised burn-out equipment

the furnace. Normally the moulds are reheated up to pink heat in this holding kiln. This removes the last traces of carbon and wax gas and preheats the moulds to receive the metal. Using ceramic fibre pads to protect your heat-resistant gloves, remove the moulds at the last moment and place them ready to fill with metal. The advantage of using a holding kiln is that you can take out just the number of moulds that you need to fill, leaving the remainder hot and protected.

One of the problems encountered with ceramic shell is the speed with which the shell cools. I noticed a very interesting trick at the Rolls Royce factory. The shells are de-waxed in the autoclave, then fired in a kiln. Removed from the kiln, they are placed

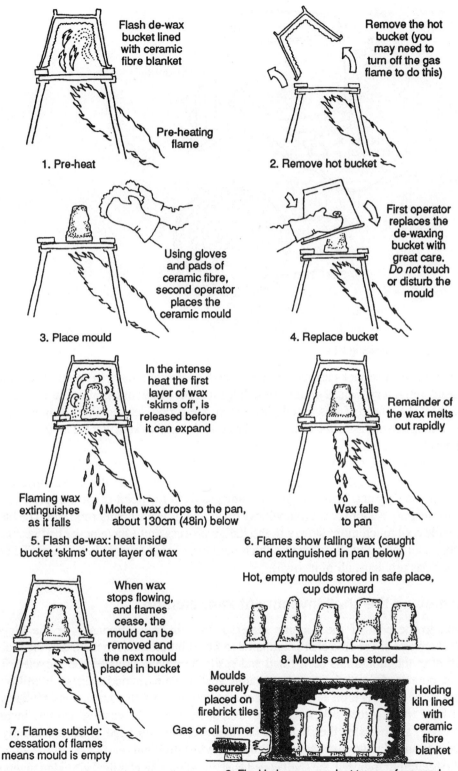

1. Pre-heat

Flash de-wax bucket lined with ceramic fibre blanket

Pre-heating flame

2. Remove hot bucket

Remove the hot bucket (you may need to turn off the gas flame to do this)

3. Place mould

Using gloves and pads of ceramic fibre, second operator places the ceramic mould

4. Replace bucket

First operator replaces the de-waxing bucket with great care. *Do not* touch or disturb the mould

5. Flash de-wax: heat inside bucket 'skims' outer layer of wax

In the intense heat the first layer of wax 'skims off', is released before it can expand

Flaming wax extinguishes as it falls

Molten wax drops to the pan, about 130cm (48in) below

6. Flames show falling wax (caught and extinguished in pan below)

Remainder of the wax melts out rapidly

Wax falls to pan

7. Flames subside: cessation of flames means mould is empty

When wax stops flowing, and flames cease, the mould can be removed and the next mould placed in bucket

8. Moulds can be stored

Hot, empty moulds stored in safe place, cup downward

9. Final bake removes last traces of wax and gas, and pre-heats moulds for filling

Moulds securely placed on firebrick tiles

Gas or oil burner

Holding kiln lined with ceramic fibre blanket

Figure 82. De-waxing procedure

99

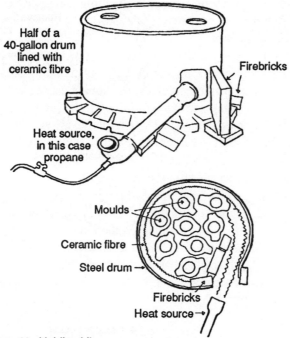

Figure 83. Holding kiln

in a trough of firebricks and held in place; bedded down, in fact, in hot mullite. This is a black refractory, whose grains are so large that they look like granite chippings. Gas jets heat the whole of this trough, heating up the firebricks, the chips of mullite, and last but not least, the shells. Using this clever device makes sure that the metal is poured into red hot moulds.

One investment foundry I have visited in Sheffield, UK, had so refined this process that they could vary the flame jets to cool the bottom of the shell after it was filled while keeping the cup hot. This has great advantages from the point of view of progressive solidification. A more conventional way of doing this is the exothermic cup. The block moulds cool much more slowly in the Italian process and I have never had problems with metal failing to flow because the mould has cooled (except in the case of silver, which has problems all of its own).

Removing the shell investment after casting

Next to the cost of the ceramic material, this, in my experience, is the biggest disadvantage of ceramic shell, compared to block investment. In the latter, the ludo is soft after the mould has been filled and easily removed, crushed and recycled. The most notable characteristic of the ceramic shell is its extreme hardness. It will blunt your metalworking tools unless you remove all of it. Nor will your customer thank you for hard white pieces adhering to crevices or details in the casting. Do not despair, however, all traces of the shell can be removed, but you need to think carefully in advance and plan your workshop to cope with this problem.

In the aircraft industry, the shell is first shaken off on a mechanical vibrating machine. I watched one at Rolls Royce and was surprised how much came off at once, mainly because the casting was made up of smooth surfaces. Something with a surface texture or deep grooves is more difficult. The next step was an air-tool called a needle gun, and the third is sand-blasting the surface.

Engineers in industry select the right grit with great care, or else use beads, to avoid damaging the surface. The final stage is to immerse the castings in boiling caustic soda (see Appendix F). If you turn pale at the thought of a vat of boiling caustic soda in your workshop, you are not alone. So it may surprise you to learn that in a large aircraft factory it is considered safer than the alternative. The alternative is hydrofluoric acid: also an exceptionally dangerous liquid, but easier to use in a small workshop. *Used with the proper precautions* this method is both safe and effective. But please be warned: *you must follow the safety directions to the letter*.

Hydrofluoric acid attacks silica, so it removes the silica in the ceramic shell most efficiently. It also attacks the calcium in your body. When I have to use it I wear a gas mask, thick rubber gloves and boots, and a chemical protection suit which covers the whole body. Before I take off this protective clothing I wash off any signs off spillage with plenty of water. Fortunately, lime makes the acid completely harmless, provided that you are able to take precautions, the danger is negligible. *If, however, you cannot protect yourself and others in the workshop properly, on no account should you use hydrofluoric acid.*

Final safety note: all acids must be kept in a locked cupboard or strong room, with labels to identify them.

8. Die casting

This is the most expensive method of producing a short run of castings. On the other hand there is no doubt that it is one of the cheapest and simplest ways of mass-producing a continuous run of simple articles.

The complexity and expense of the top end of the industry should not blind us to the possibilities of this method on a much simpler, low budget scale. Blacksmiths in Zaire, Zimbabwe, Zambia, Sri Lanka, Malawi and Nepal, and in many other countries, have made simple but effective and long-lasting dies out of mild steel using local blacksmithing techniques, sometimes with the aid of an arc welder, and possibly some simple grinding tools.

Examples of the technique

Below are three examples of the technique observed by the author.

Example 'A', Nepal

The Nepali die was made up of three steel blocks with the negative surfaces cut or ground into them. These blocks slid into a steel box, rather like a breech block on a cannon.

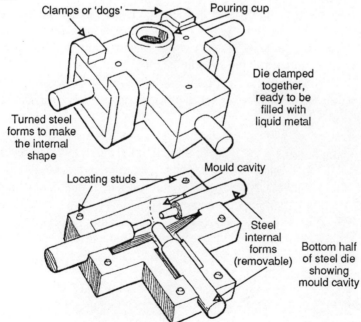

Figure 84. Simple steel die for sprinkler head

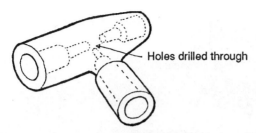

Figure 85. Finished casting of sprinkler head in zinc-based alloy, Nepal

A foundry labourer held this preheated assembly over a patch of sand while the caster poured aluminium from a ladle into the opening at the top. They had several of these simple dies. As the first one of the battery of dies cooled, another labourer opened it, removed the casting and replaced the die pieces in the steel box ready to be refilled. The owner of the foundry showed me one of the castings, a piece for an agricultural irrigation water sprinkler head. The casting was bright and clean. Apart from cutting off the button of extra metal at the top, and two thin strips that had filled the vents either side, little had to be done to finish it.

Example 'B', West Africa

An even simpler die was made by a blacksmith in Nigeria. This was one of a range of dies of all sizes for the mass-production of spoons. The die was made up of two halves that locked together, hammered out of steel sheet with the negative of the handle cut or ground out of the solid metal. Put together, the two sides left a spoon shaped cavity in the centre and a small cup, or button, at the top.

The heated die was filled with molten aluminium which cooled quite rapidly. The labourer had no difficulty in separating the two halves and removing the spoon.

Though larger domestic ware that I saw in Cameroon was cast by the green sand method, small calabashes or spoons were cast in simple dies. These, the market trader told me, were not quite as smooth and modern as the Nigerian imports, but they were much cheaper and did the job of putting food in the mouth just as well.

Though the initial expense is high, the caster might well find it rewarding to work out the cost of making these dies with a local blacksmith, possibly with the aim of working on a profit-sharing basis.

The problem in East Africa was not a technical one but rather caused by the vagaries of market forces. Though the caster had the skill to make the dies (he was a blacksmith and mechanic first and a metal caster as an afterthought), Lilongwe market was full of pressed stainless steel spoons, made in China and selling at prices well below their true value. The blacksmith discovered, however, that frying pans, imported from Tanzania, were over-priced. When I last saw him he was using an old European pan as a pattern and casting excellent copies. These sold well at a fraction of the price of the Tanzanian articles. They were, of course, too big to die cast, so he adapted his technique to make them using the green sand method.

Example 'C', Peru

A two-piece aluminium die was used to cast small aluminium propellers for fishing boats.

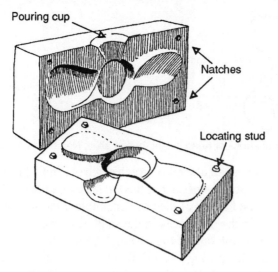

Figure 86. Die for casting aluminium propellers for *peque-peque* fishing boats,

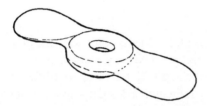

Figure 87. Finished casting of propeller

Finding and correcting faults in the castings

Example: the use of metal dies for casting buckets for Pelton turbine wheels
I was given two small brass Pelton wheel buckets which had been made in Sri Lanka. These Pelton buckets were accompanied by photographs of the die-casting process.

The two-piece bronze dies were held together manually. There were no clamps or iron dogs; the craftsman simply held a steel gas pipe in each hand, the end of which fitted over a pin on the back of the mould. He held the two firmly together while a second craftsman poured in the molten metal.

The advantages of this process are:

o   Speed of manufacture

o   The low cost, relative to other methods

The disadvantages are:

o   Loss of accuracy

o   Problem of joining small parts together.

Other significant observations were that the crucibles were very small, obviously locally made. A crucible of metal had to be melted for every one or two dies. A larger

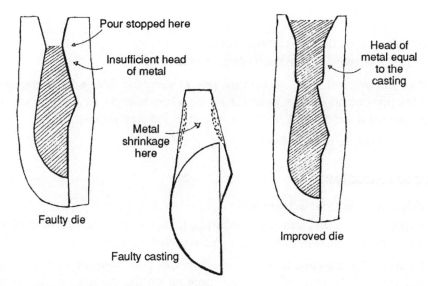

Pour stopped here

Insufficient head
of metal

Metal
shrinkage
here

Head of
metal equal
to the
casting

Faulty die

Faulty casting

Improved die

Figure 88. Die for Pelton buckets, Sri Lanka

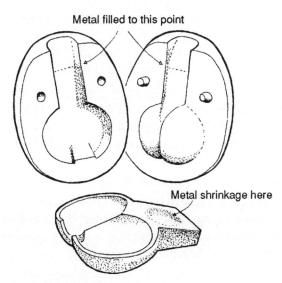

Metal filled to this point

Metal shrinkage here

Figure 89. Two-piece metal Pelton die, showing insufficient head of molten metal
and consequent shrinkage

crucible is always more economical on fuel and has a less debilitating effect on the
alloy. Small crucibles, obviously enough, are cheaper in the short run but more
expensive over a long period.

Last but not least, when using a small crucible there is a tendency to skimp on the
amount of metal poured into the die, instead of filling the cup of the die with a generous
head of metal, thus ensuring a reservoir of metal which aids progressive solidification.

Furthermore, I wondered how the heel of the bucket was joined to the boss. It is
unusual to assemble so small a Pelton. Pelton runners up to 175mm PCD are usually
cast in one piece by the lost-wax process.

105

Faults

The faults obvious on the two castings were:

1. 'Sinks' (contractions) on the heels of the buckets.

2. Poor surfaces inside the buckets and pitting along the sharp edge of the splitter ridge (the central sharp edge on the Pelton wheel bucket). Needless to say these are the areas which most need to be accurate and well-defined.

3. The buckets are crudely finished.

Possible remedies

The problem appears to be in two parts:

1. A *sink* (or shrinkage, also called 'drawing'). This occurs when the head of metal is too small to allow for logical progressive solidification.

   To avoid this, increase the head – in other words, increase the size of the sprue and cup. The volume of the metal backing up the casting should be equal (approximately) to the volume of metal in the finished casting.

   To achieve this you will need to re-design and re-cast the die. A second solution would be to allow the casting to solidify first, retaining heat in the cup and sprue as long as possible. Wrap insulating material round the cup (ceramic fibre wool, if obtainable). As a last resort, use an exothermic cup (I think it unlikely that this will be necessary).

2. *Pitting*. Given the type of casting, and the use of a die, there is little that can be done about the pitted surface, though painting the die with a fine refractory wash and baking it might help. (The UK foundry-chemical firm FOSECO have a branch in Bombay where they manufacture a refractory called FIRIT, which I suspect is mainly kaolin or some other fine china clay.)

   Along the splitter ridge, design in a little extra metal (known as sacrificial metal). To achieve a complete and accurate ridge the extra can be ground away later using a die grinder or flexidrive grinder. These are, however, expensive tools. A small amount of extra metal could be removed using a file.

9. Melting and pouring metal

In simple terms the object of melting the metal is to heat it to the temperature at which it flows most easily into all parts of the mould, and not to heat it beyond that point, or keep the metal in a molten state longer than necessary (known as 'stewing' the metal).

Molten metal will pick up gases from the air (see Chapter 10): these must be either excluded by using a cover flux, or removed using de-gassing chemicals. De-gassing means what it says, expelling or neutralizing harmful gases. For example, phosphorus is used to remove oxygen in copper alloys. Aluminium alloys have a marked tendency to pick up hydrogen. This is removed using a de-gasser. Very often a sodium modifier is used to modify and refine the grain structure.

For bronzes and brasses the simplest chemical treatment used in cannon and sculpture foundries for hundreds of years was charcoal, which was thrown on top of the molten metal. The charcoal consumes the oxygen as it burns, and so prevents it reaching the metal. The second chemical treatment used was borax, to flux the metal just before it was poured.

A primitive form of cover flux was broken bottle glass thrown onto the melt. In its molten state glass excludes both oxygen and hydrogen and also coagulates the dross and impurities on the surface of the metal. This is a good precaution in theory, and an Egyptian foundry I visited in the 1960s still used the method because they used home-made crucibles with a very short life. In practice it damages the crucible, which is not a good idea if you are using an expensive silicon carbide crucible with a comparatively long life.

Chemical treatment of aluminium is complicated (see Chapter 10 on alloying).

Summary

1. Warm up the crucible slowly: this prolongs its life.

2. When the crucible is red hot, place a pre-heated ingot or large piece of scrap in it, using tongs. Crucibles are not physically strong, so never drop lumps of metal into one. Use a cover flux (see page 118) if you have one; charcoal can be used as a satisfactory alternative.

3. Feed in more pre-heated metal as the previous feed melts.

4. Furnaces vary in efficiency, so melting time varies. Experience and the notes in your foundry log should give you a good idea of how long the metal will take to melt. Thus you can plan the movement of your foundry crew. (It goes without saying that the second and subsequent melts will be quicker than the first because of the furnace warm-up time.)

Figure 90. An Italian foundry in the 1960s: the boss takes charge of pouring; his assistant wears goggles – the exception rather than the rule as bronze casters disliked protective clothing, saying that it made the foundry workers clumsy, but protective clothing is now compulsory throughout the EU.

5.   Once the metal has melted, check the temperature frequently. Use a pyrometer if you are fortunate enough to have one; if not, there are various well-tried methods of testing temperature. Aluminium can be checked visually by its colour. It should be silver with the slightest tint of pink around the edge of the melt, *never* red hot. The traditional way of testing the temperature of bronzes and brasses was, and is, a clean pre-heated steel rod. If the metal clings to it then the melt is too cold. If it leaves the rod clean then it has reached the correct temperature.

Once the metal has reached its molten state, your foundry crew should be ready and waiting. Pre-heat all the foundry irons to prevent thermal shock to the crucible. Allow no distractions at this stage. This is an extremely important principle. Any delay or interruption of the process may cause either overheating or 'stewing' of the metal (see above). The result will be poor-quality alloy.

6.   Using the lift tongs, raise the crucible out of the furnace and place it in the pouring shank.

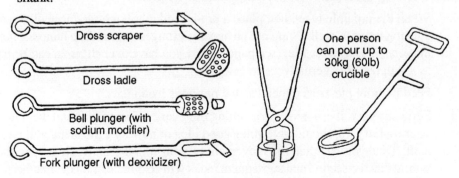

Dross scraper

Dross ladle

Bell plunger (with sodium modifier)

Fork plunger (with deoxidizer)

One person can pour up to 30kg (60lb) crucible

Figure 91. Melting and pouring irons

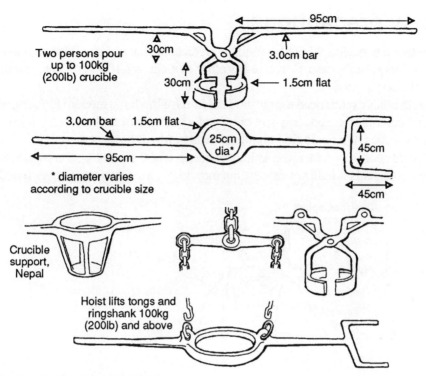

Figure 92. Crucible lifting irons

7. Remove the dross by skimming the surface of the metal with a rake. Plunge in the deoxidizing tube (or use borax) for copper alloys. Carry out the de-gassing and modifying procedure if using aluminium. (This varies according to the type of foundry chemicals you use. FOSECO, for example, will supply you with directions for use of their chemicals.)

8. Check the temperature again using a pyrometer, if you have one; if not, be guided by colour for aluminium. For bronze and brasses, test with a clean skimmer or rake. If the metal slides off the skimmer, the metal is ready. If it rejects the rake fast (slides off rapidly) then it is too hot. Pouring bronze too hot will cause too much contraction. In a lost-wax mould it will also cause 'black scale'. If poured too cool, the metal will not flow into all the extremities of the mould.

9. A very small crucible can be lifted and poured by one person. A very large one must be lifted with a hoist. The most usual procedure is a 'lift and pour' movement by two casters, while the third rakes the dross off the surface off the melt and then uses the rake to hold back any remaining fragments of dross. Finally, the third caster holds back the crucible with the rake should it show any signs of slipping forward.

10. After the moulds are filled, the third caster scrapes off any dross left in the crucible, and then the two pourers replace it in the furnace.

11. Relight the furnace. Start to charge the crucible immediately. Repeat the melting procedure.

Safety precautions

Generally the behaviour of molten metal is predictable, but you should not assume that this will always be the case. Fire, like any other element, is full of surprises: you should expect the unexpected.

The author has experienced a large modern furnace in a large modern foundry, which appeared controllable, suddenly spit out about a half-kilo of molten metal. It missed a visitor by inches. We could find no logical reason why it happened.

One could quote other, far more serious accidents where several workers were injured or killed. Accidents should not happen, but they do, even in the most efficient foundries.

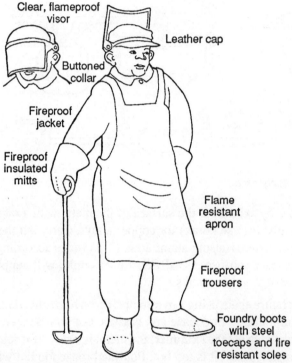

Figure 93. Foundry protective clothing

To prevent accidents:

1. Always pre-heat the ingots of scrap metal and be particularly careful to examine scrap for combustible materials. For example: gun-metal often contains valves and joints from oil tankers. These are not always clean despite the scrap merchant's assurances that he is indeed selling you 'clean scrap'.

2. Pre-heat foundry irons.

3. Wear full protective clothing if you have it, but AT LEAST wear a minimum which protects eyes, hands and feet. If you place any value on your genitals protect them too.

10. Metallurgy and the low budget foundry

Many foundry handbooks leave out any reference to metallurgy, or to metallography. Metallurgy, in its widest sense, covers all the sciences and arts concerned with extracting metal from its ore, mixing metals to form alloys, working metals and the study of their physical and chemical properties. Today it is usually a shorthand term referring to the last-mentioned. The metallurgy laboratory in a large, modern foundry is a specialized, extremely complicated and expensively equipped area, staffed by highly-trained scientists. Metallography is concerned with the examination of the microscopic structure of metals and alloys.

The metal caster, setting up his own foundry, needs only a superficial knowledge of metallurgy, but there is no doubt that a basic knowledge of how metals behave when melted, and their structure as they solidify, will help him or her both to design better pattern and sprue systems and identify problems when faced with a poor quality or defective casting.

The solidification of molten metal in the mould is far from a simple change, especially in alloys. For example the grain structure of the casting varies according to the rate of cooling, and this is affected partly by relative thicknesses; metals pick up gases when in liquid form; certain chemicals reduce the negative effects of gases, or help the metal to flow; some alloys lose some of their constituent metals when heated, this in turn affects the qualities of that alloy. In an area where there is probably no ready supply of proprietary foundry chemicals, and a shortage of basic raw materials, the caster needs some background information.

Sometimes valuable help can be found in old books. Between the late nineteenth century, and the middle of the twentieth, a vast number of technical help and self-improvement books were printed in Europe and America. These often give basic formulae, using materials commonly found in agricultural areas. This is something you never find in books written within the last few years.

The structure of metals

The microscope is the most useful tool the metallurgist has in his laboratory. Through it the skilled observer can detect the structure, history, and any weaknesses of a piece of metal or alloy.

Metals are opaque, so the microscope is designed to examine the surface using reflected light. One face on the metal test piece is filed flat, ground and finally polished to mirror surface. Any faults, cracks, gas holes or inclusions can now be seen under the microscope. Next it is etched in a suitable chemical solution and re-examined.

Microscopic examination shows that the metal is made up of numbers of tiny grains. The etching fluid attacks the grain boundaries more easily than the grain centres, and so a network of minute channels can be picked out. Looking at these boundaries the metallurgist can study the grain structure.

Used in reference to metal the word 'grain' does not mean quite the same as the word in common use. A grain of sand or sugar is not the same as a grain of metal. These other grains are brittle and easily crushed, whereas most metal grains are ductile. Secondly, grains of sand or sugar do not hold together unless used with a binder (see Chapter 5), whereas in a block of metal great force is needed to separate the grains. On one or two metals the grain structure can be seen by eye; zinc in galvanized steel sheet, for example, or worn and polished brass, but the majority can only be examined under a microscope.

The grain size of the metal depends on the casting temperature, the impurities in the metal, and the mechanical working and heat treatment it has undergone.

Heat treatment

New grain structures can be created in alloys by heating. This is known as recrystallization. To achieve this the casting has to be heated to the right temperature for the correct length of time, and the cooling period also has to be over the right period of time (see below).

Dendrites

Under laboratory conditions it is possible to produce a metal which has no crystalline structure. On the practical level, however, all metals used in engineering are crystalline. Pure metals have several valuable qualities, particularly conductivity, both thermal and electrical. Pure metals pass from the liquid to the solid state rapidly, setting

Figure 94. Formation of dendrites as alloy 'freezes'

112

predictably in layers. Alloys react differently, they have a state when they are neither liquid nor solid, described as a 'mushy' state. The slower rate of solidifying relative to pure metals makes them easier to pour, and to flow more readily in the mould. Bronze, for example, is a much easier metal for the caster to use than pure copper.

When a molten alloy begins to freeze, minute crystals begin to form at various points in the liquid, these grow branches in various directions.

These branches are called 'dendrites' and have been compared to pine trees in shape, or to the formation of frost patterns on a window pane in winter. These patterns, often very beautiful, can only be seen under the microscope after the metal has been polished and etched. Each branch of a dendrite is restricted when it meets another; the spaces between continue to fill until the entire mass of metal is solid.

A factor of particular importance to the design of castings is 'grain impingement'. Grain boundaries form by the impingement of other growing grains. The effects of the grain boundaries depend on the change of orientation at the boundary, and on the special properties of the boundaries themselves. Under certain circumstances these can form paths for crack propagation. In castings the bad effect of grain impingement is noticeable at sharp corners, in rectangular sections and at perpendicular surface junctions. Most of these defects can be remedied by intelligent design of the casting (which of course means the design of the pattern).

Development of grain structure

The crystalline structure of a metal breaks down at its melting point. There are no grain boundaries and the metal has no useful mechanical strength. The solid crystal structure re-forms on cooling. On solidifying, energy is given out in the form of the latent heat of fusion, so the rate at which solidification proceeds depends on how quickly heat can be removed. When the cooling of the liquid metal is slow, a few of the large clusters of atoms in the liquid develop interfaces and become the nuclei for the solid grains that are to form. During solidification at a slow cooling rate, the first nuclei increase in size as more and more atoms transfer from the liquid state to the growing solid. Eventually all the liquid has transformed and large grains have developed. The grain boundaries represent the meeting points of growth outwards from the various nuclei initially formed. When cooling is rapid, many more clusters develop and each grows rapidly until it meets its neighbour. More grains are formed and the grain size in the solid metal is finer.

The final grain size depends, to a large extent, on the rate of cooling. When the cooling rate cannot be controlled, the desirable fine grain size can be promoted by introducing foreign nuclei into the metal to cause crystal growth to begin in more numerous places. This is called 'inoculation' or 'grain refinement'. Grain size has a direct effect on the mechanical properties.

If no foreign nuclei are introduced, most cast metals are *dendritic* in structure. If the alloy is polished and etched, the course of the formation of these dendrites can be seen under the microscope. As described, the composition of the first part of the alloy to freeze differs from the middle and final freeze areas. The result is a 'core structure' (see Figures 95 and 96).

These differences can be altered to some extent by heat treatment, which gives a more uniform structure.

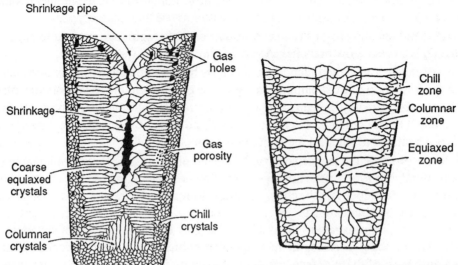

Figure 95. Section of ingot macro-structure

Figure 96. Grain structure of ingot showing chill, columnar and equiaxed zones

Eutectics

Alloys melt at a lower temperature than their parent metals. A common example is solder made of lead and tin. Lead melts at 327°C, tin at 232°C. A solder composed of 80% tin and 20% lead starts to solidify at 203°C, changes to a porridge like state and then like paste and finally becomes solid at 183°C.

The alloy of a particular range which has the lowest freezing point is called a 'eutectic'. This is of particular importance in solders and brazing rods, where the joining metal must have a lower melting point than the metals to be joined (quite different from welding, where the metal fusing metal of the same type is added using a filler rod).

Selection of scrap metals for casting

Appearance and qualities of common scrap metals

The foundry industry conventionally divides metals into ferrous and non-ferrous, but this note on the selection of scrap refers to iron and steel briefly as well as to the aluminium and copper-based alloys.

Scrap merchants deal in any metal they can obtain. Small foundries depend largely or totally on scrap, so the caster needs to know one metal from another in order to pay only for the metal required. For example, stainless steel can bear a superficial resemblance to some aluminium alloys used in aircraft construction. A simple test of relative weights, or a test for hardness using a file, will reveal the difference.

Separating alloys of the same base metal is more difficult. The best guide is a knowledge of the type of product cast in a particular alloy. Steel is easy to spot because it rusts, as does cast iron. The hardness and machinability of cast iron can be tested by its colour when fractured with a hammer. Grey cast iron is more ductile and machinable, while the harder, more brittle cast irons have a paler appearance and are called white irons.

Scrap cast iron varies in quality and hardness. The oldest and simplest method of selection is to match like with like. For example, to cast an iron base or support, look for a similar structure in the scrap heap. To cast a flywheel, look for scrap wheels.

Next to iron, the most common casting metal is aluminium. It is also the most commonly confused. The two alloys which are confused with – and put into the melt with – aluminium are magnesium-aluminium alloy and the zinc-based die-casting metals. The latter have a dull, yellow-grey appearance, whereas aluminium turns white as it oxidizes. Another clue is the sharp detail and clarity of lettering which is the mark of a die casting.

Magnesium is more difficult to pick out because its appearance and weight are close to those of aluminium. Only knowledge of the parts that are cast in magnesium will help you. Compared to aluminium, magnesium is expensive and used only for luxury items such as racing cars and aircraft, and certain lightweight tools such as chainsaw cases. Magnesium alloys appear most commonly in scrap in the form of Volkswagen engine blocks and gearboxes. Magnesium can be separated from the aluminium content of the alloy, but this technique is beyond the scope of a small foundry.

The next common mistake in scrap identification lies within the range of bronze alloys. Bronzes and brasses are copper-based alloys. Phosphor bronze is often thrown into the same bin as gun-metal, the bin labelled 'bronze'. Phosphor bronze is used for non-magnetic electrical parts and for bearings. It is harder than gun-metal with a higher melting point. The gun-metals (including leaded gun-metals) are softer, with excellent resistance to corrosion. They are used for marine taps and levers, particularly on oil tankers. This alloy is also used for propellers, but only on small boats and other water craft. A file test detects the different hardness, while shiny pinkish-orange marks distinguish gun-metal from the cold yellow of the brasses.

Summary guide to common scrap metals

Cast steel's hardness depends on the percentage of carbon. It is used for high-grade cutting tools, die steels, railway wheels, and good quality agricultural and mining tools.

Cast iron has good fluidity and mould filling during the casting process with low shrinkage on cooling. Hardness and brittleness are influenced by silicon and manganese. 'White' iron is hard and brittle, and is used for cutting and mining tools. 'Grey' iron is used for supports or bases for heavy machines, pressure pipes, vehicle engine blocks, gear and flywheels, and all kinds of agricultural machinery.

Aluminium is used in its pure form only in the laboratory. It is a light metal with excellent conductivity both for electricity and heat. It can be alloyed to produce a variety of useful qualities including strength, hardness, and resistance to corrosion. All aluminium alloys are easily melted and cast, although the speed with which it oxidizes makes it difficult to weld.

Copper is a soft metal of beautiful appearance which is resistant to corrosion and a good conductor of heat and electricity. It is most commonly used for electrical wiring and hot water pipes. The bronzes and brasses include:

LG2 (a common bronze gun-metal used for marine taps) which consists of 85% copper, 5% tin, 5% zinc, and 5% lead.

The cold-drawn brass used for cartridge cases contains at least 64% copper and less than 36% zinc.

Brasses are cold yellow in colour, ductile, machineable, easily cast, drawn or cold-worked. There are many different alloys with a variety of uses. The type of brass depends on the ratio of copper to zinc.

Phosphor bronze is a warm, pinkish-orange colour. Tough, resilient, hard, non-magnetic, it is used for springs and electrical contacts and for all kinds of bushes and bearings.

Gun-metals, originally used for cannons and statues, are now used for marine or decorative purposes, pump bodies, high-pressure steam plants, hydro-electric turbines, and sculpture.

Aluminium bronze is notorious for difficult casting and welding because it picks up hydrogen from the atmosphere, but it is strong, corrosion-resistant, and comparatively lightweight, and is used for marine and aircraft parts.

The use of tin bronze and arsenical copper is as old as metal casting. Neither is much used now, except in the laboratory.

Tin is a soft, expensive metal which is used in great quantities to produce tinplate (tin-coated sheet steel) and also used for electronic and electrical equipment. Not least is its importance as an additive to form alloys such as bearing metals, pewter, bronze.

Zinc is also used to form alloys, particularly brass and zinc-aluminium die-casting metals. Zinc is much used as an anti-corrosion coating for steel (galvanizing and sherardizing). Zinc die-casting alloys form carburettors, vehicle pumps, builders' hardware, and electrical housings.

Lead is soft and heavy with corrosion resistance and a low melting point. In the past it was often used as a roof covering or for guttering; now it is used for battery plates, water pipes, sound-proofing, anti-radiation protection, and the sheaths on power cables. It is also used in paints and a wide variety of chemicals.

Nickel is an expensive, attractive metal used for corrosion resistance, plating, and in high quality alloys with copper or steel. It is used in stainless steel alloys.

Magnesium can be alloyed with aluminium and zinc to form components and structures of great strength and light weight. It can be turned, drilled or cut easily, and is used for aircraft, racing cars, tool casings and sports equipment. Most common scrap is Volkswagen engine blocks and gearboxes. Because it reacts violently with oxygen, magnesium is difficult and dangerous to cast. Casting is usually done by specialist foundries.

Titanium is a heavy, expensive metal with an extraordinary resistance to corrosion, which is why it is used as both a container and a conductor of corrosive chemicals and for surgical implants. Titanium alloys combine lightness with great strength.

Battlefield scrap

Many of the poorest countries became so through invasion or civil war. War zones can be a lucrative source of metal, particularly copper and brass. Most of the replica Benin bronze statues exported by Nigeria after the Biafran War were cast from cartridge cases.

This type of salvage demands caution and specialist knowledge; many French farmers lost their lives trying to remove the copper driving bands and fuses from unexploded shells.

Alloying

Alloying was practised in ordinary foundries for thousands of years. There is no mystery; it is simply that it has been largely forgotten in the West.

In developing countries the situation varies from country to country. Even in a country like Peru, which has abundant supplies of copper, zinc and tin, we encountered a major problem of supply. Peru is such a vast country that supplies to the Amazon area were uncertain at the best of times. My visit to Pucalpa was far from the best of times. Pucalpa is the industrial centre for the region. Iquitos, though larger, and an international trading centre, has little industry.

The foundries that cast propellers for the river boats, small or large, are all in or around Pucalpa. The only available metal came off these same boats, and so it was used and reused over and over again. With the cargo boats, some of which have very large bronze propellers, the usual procedure was to remove the damaged propeller, take a mould from it, repairing the damaged form, or even replacing it in the mould. This was done either by modelling the sand mould in negative, or else replacing the damaged piece with a carved wooden insert. The bronze propeller was then melted down, with whatever scrap brass that could be begged, borrowed or stolen added to it, and poured into the mould. With increased guerilla activity, and a security clampdown by the army, even the most meagre sources of supply dried up.

Herein lay the problem: reusing scrap bronze. The problem was simple enough, and even the theory not too complicated, but solving the problem under these circumstances was a very different matter, far removed from the text book.

The heart of the problem is degradation. The metal becomes degraded because each melt loses zinc (which volatilizes) and loses a smaller quantity of tin. The best solution is to mix in 50% new metal, or more. This solution is not always available to the caster, as my brief description of Pucalpa illustrates. Failing a ready supply of the constituent metals, there are various measures that one can take to minimize further losses.

Bronze and brass

1. Heat the metal as quickly as possible but do not overheat it.

2. Minimize the loss of zinc by using a cover flux.

If possible, replace losses by adding zinc and tin. Add some new metal to the scrap. In either case, use the correct alloying procedure (see note on page 118).

Aluminium

Aluminium degrades and picks up harmful gases (particularly hydrogen) at high temperatures. Do not overheat the alloy, or leave it in the furnace. Pour as soon as it reaches the right temperature. If you do not have a pyrometer, judge it by colour: silver where the light falls on the surface, pink in the shade.

For alloys containing silica (such as LM6) use a sodium modifier and a de-gasser. Both of these are hard to obtain away from large, industrial areas. Metal casters in Papua New Guinea reported good results when they used the ash from burnt torch batteries as a substitute for a sodium modifier.

Modifying aluminium LM6

Dr Aladar Pacz discovered in 1920 that certain aluminium alloys were improved by adding a small quantity of sodium-potassium fluoride. Today sodium modifier is sold under the brand name 'Navac' by FOSECO. The sodium is contained in a small aluminium can. When plunged into the melt it modifies the grain structure. This makes the molten metal flow better and, equally important, improves the machining qualities and the surface of the aluminium.

Alloying bronze

Melt the least fusible metal first. This means the one with the highest melting point (which is, of course, copper). There is very little doubt that proprietary foundry fluxes and coveralls are the most convenient, but in many countries these are either expensive or unobtainable, so one has to fall back on ancient recipes.

Home-made fluxes

- Tree resin (used in Nepal)
- Salamoniac (ammonium chloride)
- Borax and powdered bottle glass (used in Peru).

Keep 'poling' or stirring the alloy. Do not use an iron rod because iron will contaminate the bronze; use a wooden pole (picking up another as the first one burns away) or a copper rod.

Late nineteenth or early twentieth century technical books yield much useful information. The hints on alloying listed below come from the old craftsman Guettier, as reported by J.F. Buchanan in 1911 and are particularly appropriate where chemicals are hard to obtain.

Method

1. Thoroughly clean the melting crucible.
2. Fire the furnace and bring the crucible to red heat.
3. Start the melt with a small quantity of good quality scrap bronze.
4. Melt the metals in order, starting with the metal with the highest melting point, in this case, copper. Introduce the copper, pre-heated.

5. Place a layer of charcoal on top of the molten metal to reduce the absorption of gases.

6. When the copper is molten, remove the crucible from the furnace and let it stand until the copper is about to congeal. Take a piece of borax the size of your thumb and drop it into the melt. Then immerse the pre-heated zinc into the copper.

7. 'Pole' the alloy. Cover the melt with a mixture of powdered charcoal and bottle glass.

8. Adding the tin is easier because it does not evaporate as easily as zinc.

9. The melt must be 'poled' continuously to mix the metals.

10. Pour the bronze into ingot moulds.

Note:

○ Zinc has to be introduced in this way because of the disparity in melting points. Copper melts at 1083°C; zinc melts at 419°C and boils at 913°C. If the two metals were put together cold and then heated, the zinc would vaporize and burn off as zinc oxide.

○ *Zinc and tin must be pre-heated (but not overheated) near the furnace before they are put into the molten copper.* One of the most common causes of accidents in foundries, large or small, is failure to pre-heat the metal. A steam explosion in a crucible is messy and often extremely dangerous.

Aluminium bronze

J.F. Buchanan also says that aluminium bronze can be alloyed in the same way. He writes that 90% copper and 10% aluminium is a good mixture; more than 10% aluminium makes the alloy brittle. 100 parts copper to 10 parts aluminium makes a more malleable alloy.

Metal melting

Both manganese bronze and aluminium bronze present problems for the founder (see below). For this reason Naval brass or a standard bronze, such as LG2, are preferable for a foundry that does not have sophisticated temperature controls or foundry chemicals.

Manganese bronze

The molten alloy tends to form a tenacious oxide skin. The alloy is very sensitive to variations in metal pouring temperature. Feeding is a problem and the metal needs extra large risers to avoid shrinkage cavities forming.

Aluminium bronze

Aluminium bronze is a notoriously difficult alloy. Precision castings for marine or aircraft engineering, are usually made by specialist foundries. A senior metallurgist

Table 2. Bronzes and brasses in common use

	Copper	Tin	Zinc	Lead	Nickel	Aluminium	Iron
			Percentage composition				
Naval brass	60	1.5	37	1.5	—	—	—
Leaded gun-metal	85	5	5	5	—	—	—
Admiralty gun-metal	85	10	2	1.5	1.5	—	—
Aluminium bronze	81	—	—	—	4.5	9.5	5

Manganese bronze: *Copper* 55–63%; *Tin* 1.5%; *Manganese* 3% (max); *Lead* 0.5%; *Nickel* 1% (max); *Aluminium* 2.5% (max); *Iron* 0.5–2%; *Zinc* balance

told me that it is possible, in theory, to alloy this metal. Then he laughed and said that they had trouble making it using the most modern, computerized control equipment.

The main problem with aluminium bronze is the ease with which it picks up hydrogen. It also absorbs sulphur dioxide, from the fuel gases of the furnace. To make matters worse, the alloy forms a heavy layer of dross through oxidization. To minimize all these problems, use a cover flux and melt and pour the metal as quickly as possible. Aluminium bronze is described as 'self-annealing'. This means that the grain structure of the alloy grows and becomes coarse if the casting is allowed to cool naturally. Slow cooling makes the casting brittle and reduces its mechanical properties. Castings must therefore be removed from the mould as quickly as possible.

Brasses

The alloy is relatively simple and straightforward. However, the high percentage of zinc (see Table 2) and its propensity to volatilize, prevents oxidization of the copper and also hydrogen pick-up. Unfortunately, the melting point of brass is well above the boiling point of zinc (913°C). If the brass remains too long in its molten state you will lose zinc both by oxidization and volatilization. Once again, and this cannot be stressed too often, melt the metal as quickly as possible and do not allow it to overheat or 'stew'. In practical terms this means that the moulds should always be ready for the metal, never the other way about.

Last, but by no means least, the vapour from the overheated zinc, inhaled by the caster or furnaceman, will make him or her feel very ill. Unlike lead, zinc vapour is not fatal, but anyone who has suffered from 'brass founders ague' will tell you that it is extremely unpleasant. At best the symptoms resemble a bad attack of flu, sweating violently one minute, shivering with cold the next. At worst, there is pain in every joint, in every bone and in the chest. Apparently women suffer from metal fumes more severely than men, supposedly because of the relatively small size of many women. The effect of the fumes is related to the proportion of water in the body, very similar to the effects of alcohol.

De-gassing and fluxing bronzes

In the early twentieth century, nitrogen was successfully used to remove hydrogen gas from copper alloys. Hydrogen causes severe sub-surface porosity (see below). This worked well as a technique, but from a practical foundry point of view, it had certain major disadvantages. To force sufficient nitrogen gas to the bottom of the melt, founders had to use high pressure cylinders, which were difficult to handle, especially in the crowded space of a small foundry. Metal lances could not be used for obvious reasons, and ceramic lances were brittle and broke easily.

A second gas problem is called 'steam reaction'. This is not steam as we recognize it, coming from a damp mould, but in a chemical sense. Molten metal has a solubility for hydrogen. This gas is ejected from solution as the alloy cools and freezes. Cuprous oxide is also soluble. This is formed by a reaction between copper and the atmosphere, or water vapour. During cooling, hydrogen can react with cuprous oxide to produce copper and water vapour (in other words, steam). This steam can remain trapped beneath the surface of the metal as a form of porosity. Many a bronze caster has picked up a casting which appears to have an immaculate surface, only to find the pin holes underneath as soon as he starts to file and polish it.

The oxidization–deoxidization process

The process most commonly used today creates an oxidizing atmosphere, which precludes other gases, and then removes the oxygen itself.

Regulate the flame in the furnace to create an oxidizing atmosphere. A cover flux also helps to prevent hydrogen entering the molten metal. When the bronze has reached the right temperature remove the crucible from the furnace and plunge in a deoxidizing tube.

If you cannot obtain the foundry chemicals, use powdered charcoal on the surface of the melt, and borax, as a flux, just before pouring (see Alloying bronze, page 118).

Dry silica sand acts as a slag coagulant. A mixture of borax and powdered bottle glass is used as a covering flux in many countries. I have seen powdered tree resin used in Nepal. This is used on the melt itself, and also thrown into the cup of the mould as the molten metal is flowing into the cup. The resin acts both as a flux and as a heat source to keep a high temperature in the cup – a simple and cheap version of the exothermic sleeve.

Summary

In practice, the two most common causes of porosity and gas holes in castings are:

1. Pouring the metal too hot
2. Too much moisture in the mould.

In investment casting, or lost wax, the natural instinct to pour the metal hot, in order to flow into the thin sections of the mould, needs to be balanced against the danger of a reaction between the metal and the mould surface.

This can take one of two forms, either gas pick-up, causing pin holes and porosity, or scabbing. This is where the overheated metal breaks down the surface of the mould, causing an uneven scabby surface on the casting.

Metal flow and solidification

Designing the sprue system

The sprue system is an arrangement of conduits which allows the metal to flow into the mould with the minimum of hindrance or turbulence, and smaller vents which allow air and gases to escape from the mould. A well-designed sprue system facilitates progressive solidification of the metal.

Terms vary in different types of casting (e.g. sand casting or lost-wax casting). Generally speaking, the conduits taking the metal in are called runners or feeders, while those allowing the air to escape are called risers or vents.

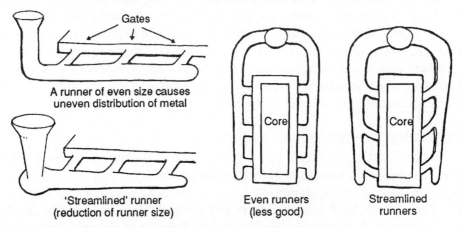

A runner of even size causes
uneven distribution of metal

'Streamlined' runner
(reduction of runner size)

Even runners
(less good)

Streamlined
runners

Figure 97. Conduits taking the metal, known as runners or feeders

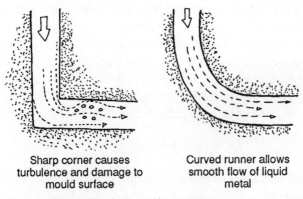

Sharp corner causes
turbulence and damage to
mould surface

Curved runner allows
smooth flow of liquid
metal

Figure 98. Metal flow in the gating system

The following notes are a general guide to the subject (see Figures 97 and 98):

1. The runner, at the point where it feeds the casting, should be approximately the same thickness as the casting wall.

2. Just as you try to avoid sudden changes of size in the casting, so avoid sudden changes of size in the sprue.

122

3. Avoid sudden changes of direction. If the sprue must make a right-angle bend then make a fillet and round the joint.

4. Consider carefully how metal will flow and solidify. Plan the flow so that most of the shrinkage takes place in the header, main runner and cup.

5. If a major change of thickness cannot be avoided, then you must make sure that the thicker parts are 'fed' by a reservoir of metal on the sprue system or by an extra large runner.

6. Avoid hot spots, consider the use of chills and denseners (see page 125).

7. It is a great advantage to have some method of keeping the metal in the cup hot as the casting cools. To aid progressive solidification some foundries use exothermic sleeves. Casters understood this aspect of their craft in early civilizations and used materials such as resin to increase the heat at the cup. Silversmiths, who suffer severe problems with cooling because of the efficiency of silver as a conductor of heat, play a flame onto the cup and actually pour the metal through the flame.

8. The main channel from the cup, through which the metal flows to the subsidiary runners, is called the gate. The most simple form of gate is a straight tube from which the runners take off at right angles. There are many other, much more complicated forms such as the 'horn gate' and the circular gate. Some forms of gate double their function by having reservoirs built in to feed the thicker parts of the casting with extra metal.

9. Headers and blind risers are tubes into which the metal flows in the opposite direction to the flow in the runners. In other words, the molten metal is flowing away from the casting. These have two functions: first, to push any air or dross or inclusions away from the casting, and secondly to feed the casting with yet another reservoir of molten metal and thus make contraction less likely on the casting itself.

These points show clearly how sophisticated is the craft of the pattern maker, who needs to understand very clearly the different characteristics and idiosyncrasies of different metals. Aluminium, for example, though it has a much lower melting point than bronze, needs a thicker runner system, to prevent distortion caused by contraction, and a main gate and cup very much larger than the type you would design for bronze.

Metal solidification

As metal changes from liquid to solid state it passes through three changes in volume at pouring temperature, liquidus temperature, and solidus temperature.

1. Liquid shrinkage occurs between pouring temperature and liquidus temperature.

2. Solidification shrinkage happens between liquidus and solidus temperatures.

3. Solid shrinkage (which is also called contraction) occurs between solidus and room temperature (this is the point at which the legs break on the bronze horse).

Making allowance for shrinkage

Any change of section should happen gradually. An abrupt change causes shrinks and hot tears and will set up stresses in the casting which may cause trouble later. Use fillets to round the corners, but do not make them too large or you may cause hot spots.

Where a major shrinkage cannot be avoided you should plan the sprue system to use 'progressive solidification'. Contraction should be designed to take place in the feeder head rather than in the casting itself. Oversized risers, known as headers, have the same effect.

Stresses and faults in the finished casting can usually be cured by intelligent pattern design or by modifying the sprue or gating system.

'Progressive solidification' means exactly what it says: the gradual, planned freezing of the metal. The intelligent designer plans both the pattern and the sprue system so that the molten metal cools gradually, with the last to cool being the metal in the cup and headers. The situation to avoid is one where several thin sections cool first while large sections are still liquid. If these larger sections have no reservoir of metal to draw from, in contraction they will draw on the thin sections, then at their weakest stage of

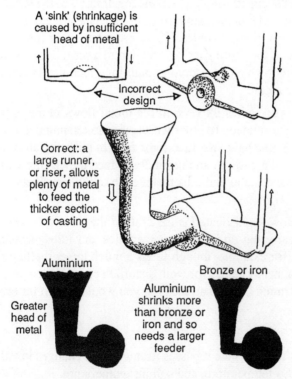

A 'sink' (shrinkage) is caused by insufficient head of metal

Incorrect design

Correct: a large runner, or riser, allows plenty of metal to feed the thicker section of casting

Aluminium

Greater head of metal

Bronze or iron

Aluminium shrinks more than bronze or iron and so needs a larger feeder

Figure 99. Sinks or 'draws' caused by an insufficient head of metal

solidification, and tear them. Because the ideal is rarely possible, in casting, as in life, the designer has to compensate for the thick-thin problem by providing reservoirs, headers or blind risers for the thicker sections to draw from. The most efficient heat-retaining form is the sphere, the next is the cylinder. The former is the normal solution in lost-wax casting. A spherical reservoir, or riser, is less easy to form in green

124

sand moulding, cylindrical risers are very easy to form and, therefore, more commonly used. There is an alternative to providing an extra supply of molten metal, and that is to make the thick section cool rapidly. To do this the designer turns to chills and denseners.

Chills and denseners

A chill is a material or component of high thermal conductivity used to accelerate the cooling of the metal in the mould. Chills can be made of copper or cast iron, the latter is more usual. The chill is set into the face of the mould, against the pattern surface. The surface of the chill is painted with spirit-based shellac to prevent oxidization.

A densener is inserted into the mould or core face, or protrudes into the mould cavity, to promote localized solidification. Denseners are surrounded by molten metal during pouring. Made of the same metal as the product, they are fused into the casting sections and are not recoverable.

Exothermic material

Exothermic materials aid directional solidification by generating heat. The most common location is in the cup or header, but exothermic material can be built into the mould at any point where the setting time of the metal needs to be retarded. When it comes into contact with the molten metal, a chemical reaction takes place which produces heat. The metal in the riser or cup becomes superheated and remains molten for a longer time, forming an insulating layer as the metal inside the mould solidifies. There are many exothermic cups and risers on the market and they contain various ingredients including powdered magnesium. A common form of exothermic is to mix some oxide of the metal to be cast with powdered aluminium. Starch is used as a binder and the mixture painted, or moulded, onto the surface of the cup or riser. If the mixture is used inside the mould, then it is mixed with facing sand and formed like a core. It should be baked very gently, or dried in the sun. It is then placed where the extra heat is needed to aid directional solidification.

11. Kilns and furnaces

Time used in research before building a furnace and wax burn-out kiln will prove time well spent. The author's own are both double-insulated and fuelled with natural gas. They are also simple and easy to maintain. The kiln uses four simple gas jets. The furnace, rather more complicated, uses an American system which works rather like a carburettor. It has only one manual control. The supply of gas is governed by an air valve called a proportionator. Using a zero governor to create a balanced pressure, a second governor, controlled by the air valve, makes sure that the mixture of gas and air is always constant. Apart from this sophisticated control equipment, and a well-engineered burner and flame retention head, the furnace is simple, and I built it myself, from digging out the furnace pit in an old stable to constructing the chimney. The furnace is tough and reliable, and I am well-pleased with it.

Despite this, I am tempted at times to be wise after the event. If I knew then, nearly ten years ago, what I know now, I would have built it from cheaper materials. A simpler design would have saved a lot of money.

I have in mind two products in particular which were developed for the large-scale aerospace industry in the 1960s and 70s. It is a delightful irony that the most lavishly funded, most wasteful and most advanced industry should potentially benefit one of the oldest and most basic.

I am referring to the ceramic shell method of casting, described in Chapter 7, and ceramic fibre insulation. This comes as ceramic fibre blanket and also in sheet form. Used as the heat shield on the first spacecraft, this amazing discovery has simplified and cut the cost of both furnaces and kilns. If available, ceramic fibre is appropriate for the small foundry, the business starting on a low budget in a developing country, or in an industrialized country, the artisan or teacher who finds himself unemployed, as I did, and decides to set up his own business.

Ceramic fibre has little mechanical strength, so the furnace built from it will not last like a brick or refractory cement furnace will.

The same is true of a kiln, but the great advantages are lower cost and ease of construction. The craftsman can begin a business without being indebted to the bank for the rest of his life. Once the business is running, then he can plough back the profit and re-equip with more permanent, more expensive machinery. Secondly, it will be discovered that businesses do not develop in the way one foresees when first planning them. We all imagine an ideal organization and plan it as realistically as we can. Yet, experience teaches that the business in reality is not as we pictured it, for good or ill.

The first furnace I built was made of brick and concrete, in the conventional way, because that was the only way I knew at the time. Its construction was laborious and expensive. On the credit side this furnace is simple to operate, fuel-efficient and robust.

It still serves me well, ten years after I built it. Subsequently I built furnaces out of anything I could find on the farm dump nearby, from galvanized feed bins to 40-gallon oil drums. In each case I used ceramic fibre blanket as an insulator, glued with sodium silicate. Painting the surface of the fibre with left-over slurry from the ceramic shell process strengthens it, but it is never as hard-wearing as brick.

In East Africa I learnt that one can make a furnace out of almost anything, from a termite mound to a tin drum lined with river mud and cow dung. These furnaces were fuelled with waste motor oil and were all placed above ground. I pointed out to a blacksmith on one occasion that he would save heat, and therefore fuel, if he sank the furnace below ground, with the lid a few inches above the foundry floor. This has a second, no less important advantage, safety. Lifting the crucible from floor level is less arduous, and very much less dangerous, than lifting it chest high. This is especially true if the furnace attendants have no protective clothing.

The furnace drum

Different types of burners mean slight variations in the quarl, but apart from that there is little variation. The flame always enters tangentially: this is the most efficient way of heating and does less damage to the crucible. Within reason, the more insulation you can put round the furnace drum, the more fuel-efficient it will be. Obviously this depends also on the efficiency of the burner.

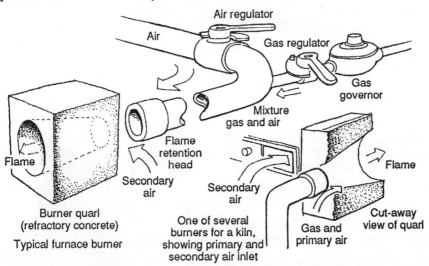

Figure 100. Simple layout for gas and forced air, showing quarl, retention head, regulators and gas pressure governor

The simplest possible design is a pit furnace, using a facing layer of clay, and clay sand and dung as an insulator. An excellent natural insulator is kyonite or fired rice husk ash. Another, if you are lucky enough to find a deposit, is diatomite (also known as *kieselguhr*).

A 40-gallon drum lined with refractory cement is also a practical furnace. As a substitute it can be lined with a mixture of silica sand, rice husk ash, plumbago and fireclay.

127

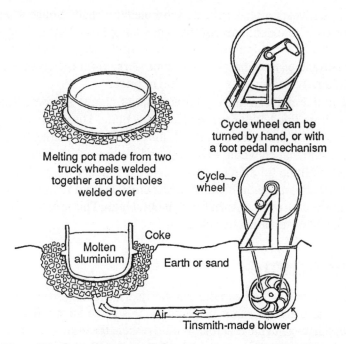

Melting pot made from two
truck wheels welded
together and bolt holes
welded over

Cycle wheel can be
turned by hand, or with
a foot pedal mechanism

Cycle
wheel

Coke

Molten
aluminium

Earth or sand

Air

Tinsmith-made blower

Figure 101. Coke and air blast aluminium furnace, Douala, Cameroon

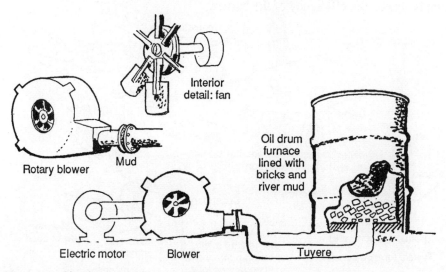

Interior
detail: fan

Oil drum
furnace
lined with
bricks and
river mud

Rotary blower   Mud

Electric motor   Blower   Tuyere

Figure 102. Simple charcoal furnace, Pucalpa, Peru

The life of a brick furnace will depend on the quality of the bricks. Hard, high temperature fire bricks will last a long time, while ordinary house bricks last a very short time, although you can prolong their life by facing them with one of the simple refractory mixtures described above. A mixture of clay, dung and white sand (silica sand) will protect the surface of the bricks, though you may have to renew it every two, or three melts.

A 40-gallon drum lined with a ceramic fibre blanket is another variation. For a furnace of larger diameter, three drums can be cut lengthwise, opened out and welded together.

Two further variations are an open-hearth furnace for recovering aluminium and (see separate section) a cupola furnace for melting iron.

Types of furnace burners

1. Using kerosene (see Figure 103). This is a type of burner which was very common a few years ago. The burner itself is a modified weed burner, working on the Primus stove principle (the 'Sheen' burner). The kerosene and air mixture is compressed in the pressure vessel from an ex-army cooker. One of these burners will melt a small amount of metal (30kg). Using two burners, opposed tangentially, you can melt much larger amounts of metal (up to 90kg)

2. Kerosene and water as shown in Figure 104 (Danish method, Kathmandu)

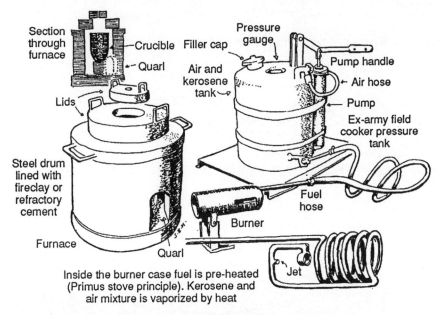

Inside the burner case fuel is pre-heated (Primus stove principle). Kerosene and air mixture is vaporized by heat

Figure 103. Kerosene furnace, Chelsea School of Art, London

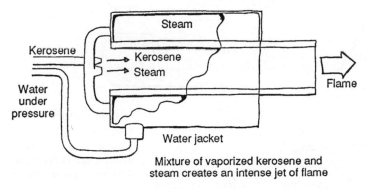

Mixture of vaporized kerosene and steam creates an intense jet of flame

Figure 104. Kerosene and water furnace burner

3. Used engine oil. There are two types:

   ○ drip feed (Figure 105)

   ○ jet (using an air fan – Figures 106 and 107)

4. Bottled gas (Figure 108)

5. Coke (Figure 109)

6. Charcoal (Figure 110).

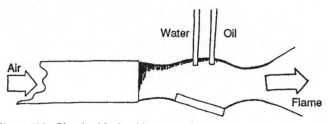

Figure 105. Simple drip-feed burner using waste motor oil

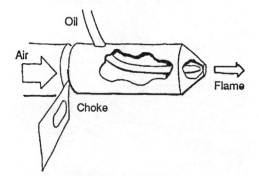

Figure 106. Air jet burner using waste motor oil

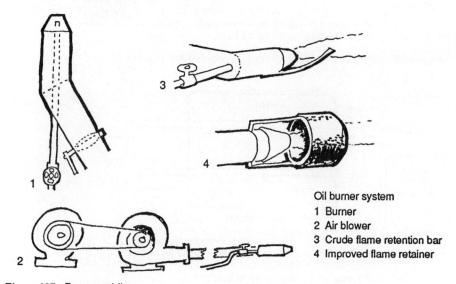

Oil burner system
1 Burner
2 Air blower
3 Crude flame retention bar
4 Improved flame retainer

Figure 107. Burn-out kiln

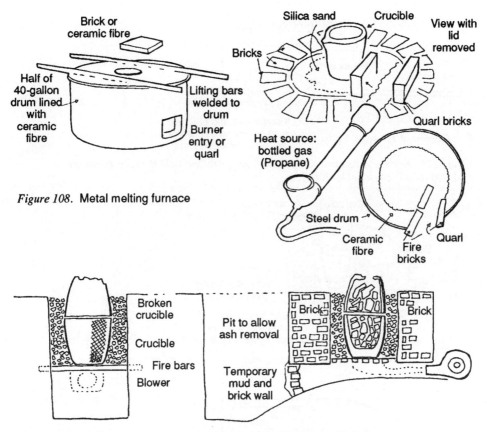

Brick or ceramic fibre

Silica sand   Crucible   View with lid removed

Bricks

Half of 40-gallon drum lined with ceramic fibre

Lifting bars welded to drum

Burner entry or quarl

Heat source: bottled gas (Propane)

Quarl bricks

Figure 108. Metal melting furnace

Steel drum
Ceramic fibre   Fire bricks   Quarl

Broken crucible

Pit to allow ash removal

Brick   Brick

Crucible

Fire bars

Temporary mud and brick wall

Blower

Figure 109. Simple coke furnace with electric motor air blower, Nepal

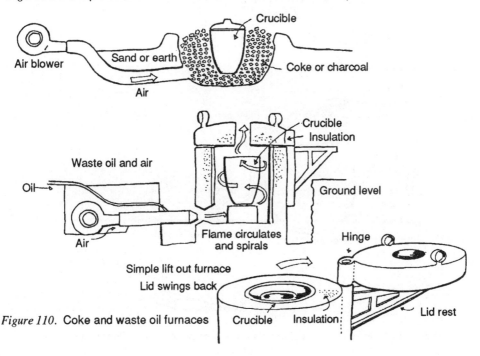

Crucible

Air blower   Sand or earth

Coke or charcoal

Air

Waste oil and air

Crucible
Insulation

Oil

Ground level

Air

Flame circulates and spirals

Hinge

Simple lift out furnace
Lid swings back

Lid rest

Figure 110. Coke and waste oil furnaces   Crucible   Insulation

131

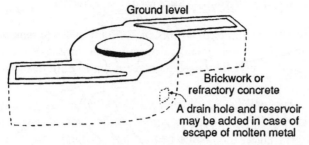

Figure 111. Kerosene furnace for melting 100kg bronze: hole is first marked out and dug to suitable level for furnace

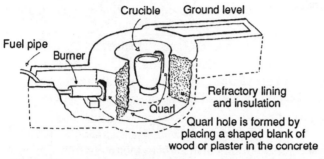

Figure 112. In this furnace the fuel was kerosene and air under pressure, but burners vary

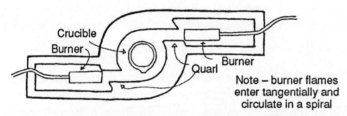

Figure 113. Plan view of kerosene furnace

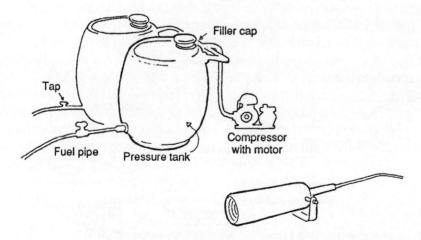

Figure 114. Fuel tanks and agricultural weed burner working on a Primus principle

132

Building a simple two-burner pit furnace

This type is based on the one built by the Arnatt brothers for their lost-wax foundry in Berkshire, UK. They used an 80kg crucible, and cast many large pieces of sculpture using this furnace. To burn out the wax they used a coke-fired kiln built of old house bricks.

First consider what type of furnace, what size of crucible and what type of fuel you are going to use. This sounds elementary, but it is surprising how many casters build a brick furnace and only worry about the source of heat later (which usually means expensive and time-wasting alterations to the brickwork). A sensible way of working is to lay out all the pieces for the furnace on the foundry floor before starting. This is partly to make sure that you have everything you need, and secondly to check the size of the furnace pit.

Dig an oval-shaped pit to a depth of about 36in (900mm) and then concrete the bottom of it. Make sure that the concrete is level. Allow time for the concrete to cure. The simplest way of making the base of the furnace is to draw out a pattern on cheap paper (old newspaper will do). This pattern should show the internal shape of the furnace, including the quarls and pits for the burners. You will need to adjust these pits to fit the burners that are going to be used. For example, an oil burner with an integral air blower will take up more space below ground than a gas burner with a piped supply of air and a large fan which is sited above ground.

Cut out the pattern and lay it on the concrete. Unless you are employing a skilled bricklayer, make a rough drawing of the way the layers of brick are going to overlap each other. You may decide that you need a safety plug in order to drain off the molten metal should the crucible split in the furnace. We all hope this will never happen, but sometimes it does. In this case, you will need an extra pit to catch the molten metal. If you need to adjust the burners in place, you can combine this pit with the access pits for the burners. To protect the burners from molten metal, the quarls are placed above the furnace floor and the crucible raised on a pot stand (which could be a simple fire brick).

The design of the quarl depends on the design of the burner, so it is hard to give any hard and fast rule. The burner and quarl must be so placed that it is the refractory material of the quarl that receives the heat of the furnace and not the burner. Burner and quarl may be so simple in design that the quarl is merely a few fire bricks placed at the entrance to the furnace. Or it may be designed with precision and moulded out of refractory cement. The burner is placed close enough so that the maximum heat enters the furnace, but not so close that the tip, or nozzle, of the burner melts. All furnace burners (though not all kiln burners) mix air and fuel to form an intense flame. This air is the primary air supply. Most furnaces need a secondary air supply to reach and maintain full heat in the furnace chamber. This is the air sucked in around the quarl. The flame (or flames) should never be directed against the crucible, but always enter the furnace barrel tangentially in order that the flame and heat take a spiral path around the crucible.

The quarl may be one or two bricks higher than the furnace bed. When the first two courses of bricks are laid, cement the two quarls in place. Before the cement sets, check

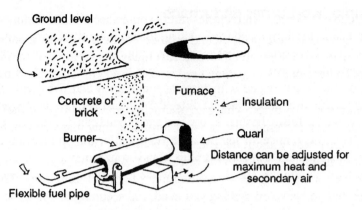

Figure 115. Cut-away view through the earth to show burner and quarl alignment

that the burners can be bolted or fixed easily onto the quarls. Now build up the furnace walls and the walls of the two pits. If you are lucky enough to have high-temperature facing bricks for the furnace, there is no need to waste these on the furnace pits. Little heat leaks into these, so ordinary house bricks will do perfectly well. Cover the furnace pits with a grating or steel plate. These protective covers must be removable, in order to adjust, clean and service the burners; but they must be sufficiently secure so that they do not tip or slide when you are walking around the furnace. The collapse of a pit cover while you are lifting the crucible could cause a very serious accident, possibly fatal.

Earth will make a satisfactory insulator, but a back-up layer of refractory concrete is better. If you are fortunate enough to find a supply of ceramic fibre board or wool, place a layer of this around the bricks and then back it up with concrete. Rice husk ash makes an excellent insulator. Once again, there is no need to insulate the furnace pits. There is one exception to this, and that is the brickwork above the quarls, an area which takes the direct heat of the furnace.

The furnace must have a cover. Some furnaces have chimneys, others make do with a hole in the cover controlled by a smaller cover. The simplest way to form the cover is to make a hoop out of (size ¼in × 3in) steel and weld handles onto it. The hoop is then filled with refractory concrete (see below). This will make a crude but effective lift-off cover. With a little extra effort, however, you can make a swinging cover, which is much more convenient.

Place the hoop on a flat piece of plywood or metal which is covered with thin plastic sheet or greased newspaper. Place a cylindrical piece of wood or large tin to form the centre hole and then shovel in the refractory concrete. Tamp it down well to drive out any air pockets. While the cement is setting, cover it with a damp cloth or sacking. In a hot climate, damp the cloth by sprinkling water on it twice or three times a day until the concrete is thoroughly cured. Do the same to make the smaller secondary cover for the centre hole. If you cannot obtain refractory concrete then make the lid out of steel with a rim welded onto it, and line it with any refractory you can find. you will have to replace the steel frequently, when it burns out under the intense heat of the furnace.

Allow sufficient time for all the materials to dry before you fire the furnace for the first time. Bricks, mortar and concrete should be given plenty of time to dry. You will need patience. Rushing the job at this stage may well weaken the furnace and waste much time and valuable materials. Refractories rarely come cheap. Some casters light a small wood fire inside the furnace, once it is dry, to complete the curing process. Many smiths and casters have some kind of ceremony, religious or secular, to celebrate the commissioning of the furnace.

A furnace should always be treated with respect, maintained and fired with close attention. Time spent thinking about, and tending, the furnace is never time wasted. Like the sea, or the wind, the fire in the furnace can be a good friend or a dangerous enemy.

Take the first firing slowly, raise the temperature very gently, and do not take it too high. If the foundry makes castings in both aluminium and bronze, or brass, it is sensible to make your first melt aluminium and do not allow the temperature to rise once the aluminium is molten.

Care of the furnace

A certain amount of metal, oxide and flux falls to the base of the furnace. This forms a hard, glassy layer which is much harder than the bricks themselves. To prevent this layer from rising up to the level of the burner quarls it should be chipped out periodically. A power chisel saves time, but the dross can be chipped out with a large, long handled, coal chisel. Be careful not to go through the layer with too much force and damage the brick floor of the furnace.

Burners using gas as fuel rarely need attention, but oil is a dirty fuel and the burner jets should be checked and cleaned out frequently. The electric motors on the air fans should be protected against damp and dust. (For care of crucibles, see pages 145-6.)

Check the quarls for obstructions and the furnace walls for spurling of the brickwork. If the furnace is unused for several months, or under very damp conditions, the furnace should be fired slowly to allow steam to escape, before the temperature is raised to red heat.

Kilns

These can use all the types of fuel listed in the section on furnaces (above). A kiln can also be fired using wood as fuel. In the engineering industry the term 'furnace' is used for both the melting process and various other forms of heating, such as heat treatment or annealing. In the investment casting industry it is more usual to use the term 'kiln' to describe the brick box, or oven, in which the wax is removed from the refractory mould by heating.

There is not much difference in principle between a bakers oven, a potters kiln, a wax burn-out kiln and a heat treatment furnace. The difference is mainly one of temperature. This governs the refractory strength necessary, and therefore the cost of the firebricks.

There is another difference, and that is the sophistication of kilns used for firing out pots or other ceramic ware. This only concerns us in this book in a negative sense. The wax burn-out kiln should never exceed 900°C, In construction it is nearer to the bakers oven than the potters kiln. For this reason you can ignore much of the advice in the many books on building pottery kilns (excellent though some of this advice is). There is no reason why you should not use a kiln for both purposes, or even share the cost of building a kiln with a potter. But if the kiln is for lost wax alone, then almost any refractory brick will do, because the normal burn-out temperature is between 650 and 750°C. It is perfectly feasible to build a kiln out of ordinary house bricks, taken from derelict buildings. These will not last as long as proper fire bricks, but they do the job well enough and can be replaced as soon as they start serious spurling.

The simplest burn-out kiln I have seen is in Patan, the industrial suburb of Kathmandu, in Nepal Dhalout Udyog, the foundry owned by the Newar family of Mr Shakya. This was built from house bricks, with a raised platform in the centre to hold the moulds, with a gulley down the middle of the platform to catch the wax. The kiln was fired from both ends using wood as the fuel. The roof was removed to retrieve the moulds and replaced for the next firing. This roof was made in slabs which were simply constructed with scrap steel frames welded together, the centres being filled with cement, which was mixed with some refractory, probably silica sand and rice husk ash. Once the fire was burning well and the temperature rising inside the kiln, then more of these concrete and iron slabs were placed over the openings at each end. The Shakya family used clay and dung slurry moulds and their kiln took about four hours to fire out the wax. The kiln watcher knew when the moulds were fired when the smoke ceased escaping from the cup. (Moulds were, of course, inverted, as is the usual practice.)

Kilns – variety of designs

Newar, Nepal Already described above, though the traditional Newar kiln is different, and is in fact a type of combined kiln and furnace as found in West Africa. (See Appendix B, Bamoum casting.)

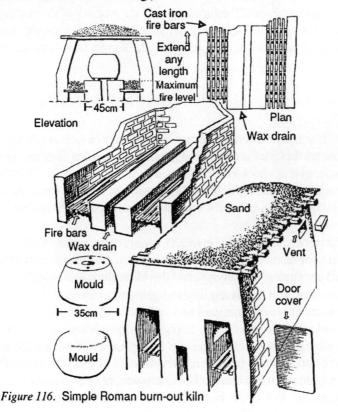

Figure 116. Simple Roman burn-out kiln

136

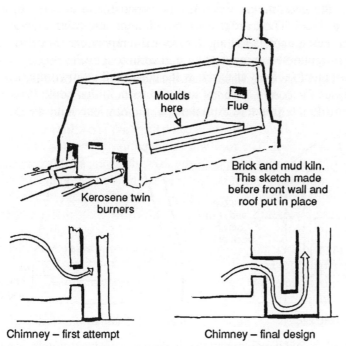

Moulds here

Flue

Kerosene twin burners

Brick and mud kiln. This sketch made before front wall and roof put in place

Chimney – first attempt

Chimney – final design

Figure 117. Burn-out kiln for lost-wax casting, Cuzco, Peru

Roman Albert Angeloni, the master craftsman in charge of the foundry at the Royal College of Art (RCA) came over to London from Italy at the age of ten, by which time he was trained to look after a Roman-style kiln. In middle age he designed and built a Roman kiln in the middle of South Kensington where it remained until the RCA sculpture school moved in 1992. Generations of foundry students learnt to fire this kiln with coke throughout the night. Small moulds took 15 hours and large ones as much as 36 hours. If you were the only student making castings, as I was in my year, this was hard work.

The kiln was built of low temperature firebricks above, and house bricks below the fire level. As in the Newar kiln (described above) the moulds were inverted and placed on a raised brick plinth with a wax escape channel down the middle. There were trenches on either side of the plinth, with raised fire bars to support the coke. The two lines of fire were started with wood. Slowly coke was introduced until an even level of red-hot coke was maintained. There was no chimney: draught was controlled by using loose bricks at the top rear end. By removing or replacing these bricks the student could increase or choke down the draught, and thus increase or reduce the heat. The brick walls were roofed over using warped old fire bars as support, followed by a layer of scrap corrugated iron. Dry sand was shovelled on top of the corrugated iron. A good thick layer of silica sand made excellent insulation. Once he or she had learned to stoke the kiln, the foundry student could keep a good even heat, by stoking every hour.

Roman arch My own kiln, and those built by most of the lost-wax casters that I know in England, uses straight brick walls reinforced with angle iron braces and tie rods, while the roof uses a conventional Roman arch held in place by wedge-shaped bricks. Bag walls inside protect the moulds from direct flame (which causes serious, and

137

damaging, spurling of the investment). Coke is now expensive in the UK, so most casters use oil or gas as a fuel. There are many types of automatic control devices on the market which will regulate the flame and control the temperature inside the kiln. Some of these can be programmed to regulate the entire burnout cycle. Because of the huge cost of such equipment (at least as much as the cost of all other components of the kiln, sometimes twice the cost) I have not included them in this book. It is much cheaper to regulate the kiln jets yourself, even though you may lose some sleep.

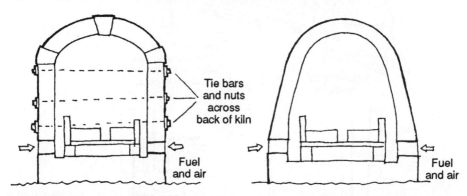

Figure 118. Roman arch kiln   *Figure 119.* Catenary arch kiln

Catenary arch This is a recent development in kiln design, and an extremely practical solution to construction of brick without steel supports (see illustration). To hold the bricks in place while you complete the arch, you must build a wooden support, just as you would for a roman arch. The side of the kiln can be built up with normal bricks, but the top part of the curve will have to be made of shaped bricks. The main advantage of the catenary type of kiln is its shape, which encourages a good flow of heat around the moulds (though this is less important at low temperature than it would be for pottery firing). Furthermore, its shape makes angle iron or other steel reinforcing unnecessary.

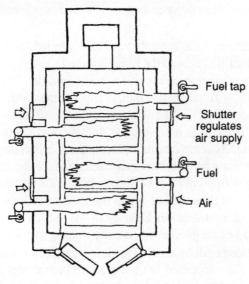

Figure 120. Floor plan and burner arrangement for gas or oil fired Roman or catenary arch kiln

138

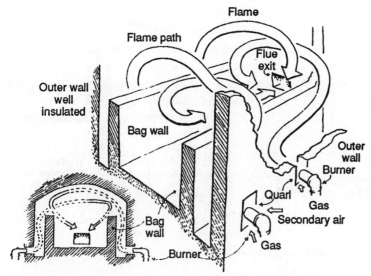

Figure 121. Movement of flame over bag wall down to flue

The top-hat kiln The 'top hat' is another recent type of kiln, and one that would not be possible were it not for developments in refractories stimulated by the aerospace industry. Building it depends on being able to obtain a supply of ceramic fibre blanket, normal brickwork is too heavy for the counterweight mechanism. A discarded 40-gallon oil drum is ideal for the casing of a small kiln. Line this with two or three inches (50–75mm) of ceramic fibre blanket and cut a disc of the same material for the top. There are two ways of fixing the soft blanket in place. One is to glue it with sodium silicate (also known as waterglass), the other is to make small button-like washers out of stainless steel sheet. These hold the blanket in place, fixed with stainless steel wire which is passed through the blanket and the steel drum. The top hat sits on a base of firebricks with the flame entering tangentially. You must create a flame passage, using a short bag wall, or baffle, to protect the moulds. A steel scaffold supports the chain or

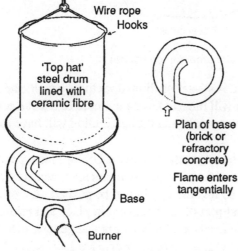

Figure 122. Home-made 'top-hat' de-waxing kiln using ceramic fibre

139

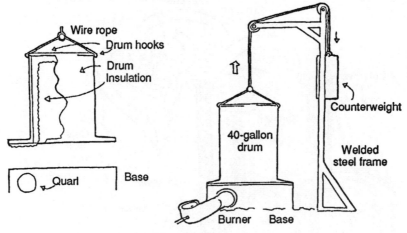

Figure 123. Top-hat de-waxing kiln: elevation

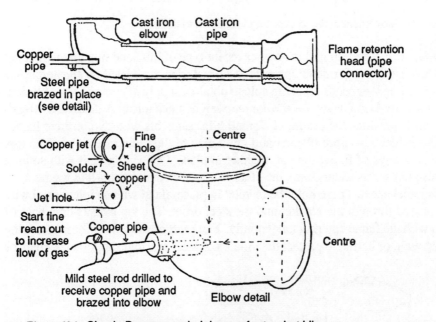

Figure 124. Simple Propane and air burner for top-hat kiln

cable of the counterbalance weight. A 40-gallon drum does the job well, and costs very little. For a larger top-hat kiln you will have to have a cylinder of sheet steel rolled up to your design. Naturally the counterweight and the scaffolding will have to be scaled up in proportion.

Trolley kiln (more usually known as a shuttle kiln in the USA). This type of kiln uses a flat bed of refractory brick on a steel frame which is mounted on wheels. The flanged wheels run on track or angle iron so that the trolley can be pushed into, or out of, the kiln. Usually the door is an integral part of the bed, held in place and reinforced with a steel framework. The trolley kiln needs a lot of welding and general metal work, so it is expensive to build, but it has several advantages over more usual kilns. The Roman

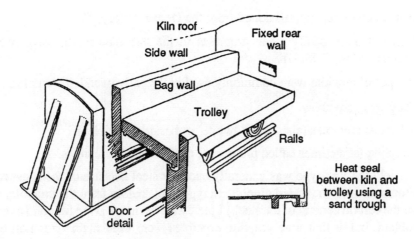

Figure 125. Detail of trolley or shuttle kiln

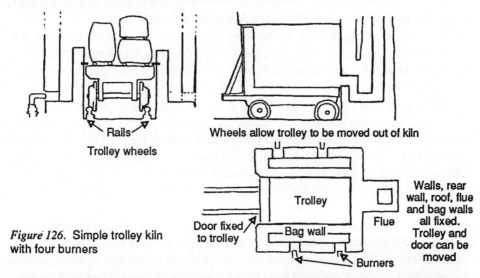

Figure 126. Simple trolley kiln with four burners

type of refractory moulds are heavy when wet and brittle when fired, so the trolley kiln has the major advantage of stability. Moulds can be placed on the trolley easily without having to crawl into the kiln with the risk of damage to your back. When fired and still very hot, the moulds can be scrimmed up on the trolley (see Roman lost-wax casting, Chapter 6). Once safely jacketed in scrim and plaster, the moulds can be turned right way up and placed in sand ready for metal filling. This saves the even greater discomfort of working inside a hot kiln. The construction of the outer box and the bag walls is the same as with any other kiln. A trolley kiln can be either Roman or catenary arch.

Crucibles

Crucibles imported from Europe or the USA are expensive. Even if the small foundry can afford the price, they are difficult, sometimes impossible, to obtain.

Intermediate Technology initiated research into crucibles which could be made locally, concentrating in two areas:

- A local crucible, commissioned from the Dedza Pottery, Malawi
- Research into locally made crucibles in the late nineteenth, early twentieth century in Sheffield, UK.

Three types of crucible were commonly used in the early twentieth century:

1. Clay–grog crucibles
2. Siliceous crucibles (also called 'white' or hessian crucibles)
3. Graphite (sometimes called plumbago, or black lead) crucibles.

In Sheffield the first type was generally used for steel because of the sensitivity of the carbon content. (The added graphite in type 3, picked up from the crucible, would increase the carbon content of the steel.) Later, various means were found to overcome this problem, but at that time graphite crucibles were used mainly for non-ferrous casting. Hessian crucibles were used, almost exclusively, for laboratory testing.

Clay crucibles go back to the earliest metalworkers and are still made, and used, in West African and Indian foundries (see Appendices A and B).

In Sheffield, crucible making by 'potmen' was a specialized skill and trade. Fortunately, some of these craftsmen lived until the last decade, and some left accounts of their work. These give the formulae, the types of clay, and the proportion of refractory material, as well as precise directions on fundamental stages of crucible making, especially in the mixing of the components, and the drying and baking stages.

During the European Industrial Revolution, Germany was the leading exporter of fine crucibles, of the siliceous or 'hessian' type, used for laboratory, chemical, or metallurgical test work. Graphite, or plumbago, crucibles were a later discovery. Joseph Dixon of New Jersey, USA, advertised his new, patent 'blacklead' crucibles in London papers in 1827. In 1851 Dixon exhibited his crucibles at the London Great Exhibition. In the mid-nineteenth century, Morgans, the ceramic importers of Battersea, London, started to make their own crucibles using graphite imported from Sri Lanka (Ceylon as it was then). In 1857, Morgans 'Patent Plumbago Crucible Co' was exhibited at the Crystal Palace, London. Crucible makers in the USA had the advantage of local sources of graphite, with abundant supplies over the border in Ontario and Quebec, Canada.

Morgans searched the world for their own sources of graphite, and it is useful to learn where they found it.

Apart from Sri Lanka, the original source, the Battersea company also mined graphite in Travancore in southern India, Kenya and Madagascar. There are deposits in the former Czechoslovakia, Mexico, the Caucasus and Siberia.

In 1988 we found graphite on the surface in Malawi (see Appendix C). In Sheffield, powdered coke was used as a substitute for graphite. Many potmen preferred coke to graphite. Coal, on the other hand, is too gassy and burns too easily to be of any use.

Graphite, like diamond, is a mineral form of elemental carbon. Manufactured graphite is related to silicon carbide (which is also used in modern crucibles). The most important advantage of graphite is the speed with which heat passes through the crucible to the metal. Metal in a graphite crucible reaches melting point much quicker than a clay–grog crucible. This saves both time and fuel.

There are also other advantages to graphite, which:

o   Increases the crucible's resistance to thermal shock
o   Reduces the tendency of the metal to oxidize
o   Remains useable much longer than the clay type
o   Can be used repeatedly until the wall becomes too thin for safety.

Composition

Clay and graphite are the chief constituents. Grog and free silica are added to keep shrinkage within convenient limits.

Sheffield potmen used various clays but found none better than plastic fireclay, or a mixture of fireclays. It is essential that the clay is plastic enough to retain a large amount of graphite (graphite is a much lighter material than clay; though the weight may be about equal, the volume appears disproportionate).

Desirable qualities in clays include high binding power (also called 'fat' clay). The binding clay must not have too high a shrinkage, so the limits of its plasticity are narrow.

It need not be highly refractory. It should sinter (vitrify at the surface) at a low temperature but retain its shape at a much higher temperature (in other words, have a long range of vitrification). The clay must also produce a material of great mechanical strength (both tensile and crushing).

Sheffield potmen realized quickly that no single clay has all these qualities, so they used a mixture of several clays. Two types of clay were used: 'white' (or china clay) and fireclay. The first came from some distance, the second was from local clay beds. The local (Derby) clay is rich in alumina and highly plastic (for a fireclay). Local clays were cheap (avoiding the cost of transport) and their qualities were discovered by trial and error.

Crucibles: approximate formulae

1. *Clay–grog crucibles*

    1 part clay, 2 parts grog (replace 0.25% of grog with old crucible material, ground to powder). Use a coarse grog, reject the fine particles.

2. *Siliceous crucibles*

    Equal weight of silica and clay (using a very plastic binding clay).

3. *Graphite (plumbago) crucible*

    Formulae range from equal parts clay and graphite (by weight) to 1 part clay to 4 parts graphite. Brassfounders preferred 50% graphite.

Two formulae for crucibles for copper alloys			*A German formula*	
Graphite	8	12	Fireclay	36
Fireclay	67	50	Coarse grog	23
China clay	—	13	Powdered coke	23
Grog	25	25	Graphite	18

Mixing: treading, panning and pugging

Records kept by the potmen in 1943 show that the clay and grog were mixed by spade and then 'trodden' for three or four hours. Early photographs show that this means what it says. The potmen turned the mixture with spades, then trod the clay with bare feet until their experienced feet and toes told them that the clay was ready. The alternatives were panning, using a centrifugal mill, or more commonly a pugmill (screw mill).

A.B. Searle made many tests on different mixes in 1917. He reported that the powered pugmill mixed and prepared the clay quicker than treading, and he could find no evidence that the crucibles made this way were inferior. He reports, however, that the potmen insisted that treading produced a superior crucible.

Either method had the same purpose, to expel air pockets or lumps of extraneous matter, and mix the clay to an even consistency.

Manufacture

Once he judged that the clay was ready, the potman cut the clay into pieces which he judged to be the right size for the crucible mould. He weighed them and rolled each into a ball. The iron mould defines the shape of the crucible exterior and a steel form suspended above it makes the inner shape. A hole in the base of the mould receives a spike. This registers the position of the inner steel form ensuring that the wall of the crucible is an even thickness (it hardly needs saying that a crucible of uneven wall thickness will create all sorts of problems and hazards during the melt process). Both mould and steel inner piece were greased to prevent the clay sticking, and the ball of clay was then put into the iron mould.

Pressed down into the mould, the steel inner form forced the ball of clay against the wall of the outer mould and squeezed the clay upward into the required shape as the spike located the register hole at the base of the inner form. Clearly this action required much force. A small crucible works would use manpower, hammering the steel into place with a heavy sledge hammer. In a larger factory, a simple but robust machine would force the form into place in the mould by lever or screw action.

The surplus clay would then be scraped off evenly at the top, the steel centre removed and the crucible ejected. The pouring lip would then be pinched or modelled into shape by hand.

There were several alternative methods for manufacturing smaller crucibles. The most common methods were to either throw on a wheel or produce mechanically on a simple machine known in the English potteries as a 'jolley and jigger'. The jolley, an iron or plaster mould, rotated, while a steel profile, or jigger, was brought down into place to press the clay against the jolley (an action rather similar to spinning metal).

Drying and dry storage

Whatever means is selected to make the crucibles, one rule applies to the drying process. Crucibles *must* dry slowly and uniformly, free from draughts or direct sunlight, otherwise they will crack. Store them in a warm dry place. Above all avoid frost. At this stage crucibles are particularly susceptible to frost.

144

Thorough and even drying necessitates prolonged storage, as much as three months. Crucibles should always be stored mouth downwards, both during manufacture and between uses. This minimizes stress on the crucible and also prevents the accidental inclusion of debris.

The next stage was known as 'warming through' in a very low temperature kiln or oven. Once again, this should be very gradual.

The final stage, the firing process, was known as 'burning'. For grog crucibles the kiln was fired up to 1230°C to 1250°C; for plumbago crucibles 710°C to 900°C. The latter were packed in muffles or saggers, with coke dust or sand, to prevent undue combustion of the graphite.

Once again (and one cannot emphasize this too strongly) the rise in temperature was slow and gradual. To reach 110°C takes 48 hours, and another 48 hours or more to reach the final temperature. Cooling should also be slow.

Lining

Crucibles were usually lined, or glazed. This was particularly true in the case of crucibles for the iron and steel industries, in order to prevent the intrusion of graphite into the melt.

Glaze 1 Felspar and whiting in water

Glaze 2 A solution of 70% water, 20% waterglass, 10% salt or soda.

Care of crucibles

Avoiding unnecessary wear or damage to crucibles prolongs their life and prevents accidents. Whether imported, or made locally, crucibles are a major part of the running cost of any foundry. It is worth taking extra trouble to extend their working life.

The most likely sources of premature wear are either poor storage conditions, or badly made or ill-fitting lifting irons.

1. Store crucibles in a warm dry place, off the ground on shelves or wooden pallets, or on dry straw. They should be placed mouth downward. Crucibles should never be stacked on top of each other, or on their sides.

2. Discard or rebuild mis-shapen tongs or ring shanks. Make sure that the irons fit the crucible centrally and snugly. Crucibles come in many shapes and sizes, which means using more than one set of irons. If possible, standardize crucible sizes and check the fitting of the irons frequently. Extreme heat warps the irons, so they need to be checked often. A smaller size of crucible can be used in a larger ring shank by using 'dogs' (steel spacers) of the correct size. Check that the dogs are a good fit.

3. 'Packing' or 'wedging' a cold crucible with ingots or scrap is a bad practice and may damage the crucible. The metal expands more than the refractory and may force it or crack the walls. Pre-heating the crucible and then placing one ingot, or a small quantity of scrap, is the correct practice, feeding in more as the first charge starts to melt.

4. The use of fluxes or covers is common practice with brasses and bronzes, many would say it is essential. During the rapid absorption of oxygen, borax and other fluxes corrode the crucible at the top of the melt. Unfortunately there is no way of avoiding this, but wear can be minimized by varying the height of the melt, thus spreading the area of corrosion.

Conclusion

Resistance to thermal shock is in the nature of any refractory, but resistance is a matter of degree. Major temperature changes cannot be avoided, but the speed at which this change takes place can, and must, be controlled.

Sensitivity to the nature of refractories and care of all tools, instruments and equipment involved in the heating and melting processes will save you money, time and much frustration.

Furnaces, kilns and crucibles vary widely, but one generalization that can be made with confidence is their aversion to damp. Unless the furnace has been in use the previous day, and is still hot, you must build up heat slowly. A warming period of 20–30 minutes is sufficient when the furnace is in regular use. If the foundry has been closed for repairs or a holiday period, or when commissioning a new furnace, you *must* warm the brickwork first and then build up the heat very gently and slowly. If you do not take this precaution then the brickwork will crack and spurl.

Crucibles should always be kept dry and warmed before use.

Damp is the enemy of all refractories. To give one extreme example: a damp crucible that is heated too fast for the steam to escape naturally will explode like an artillery shell. Anyone who has experienced this will tell you that it is a lesson not likely to be forgotten.

12. Faults, fettling and finishing

Common faults in castings

Sand casting

Blow holes; gas holes; porosity; pin holes

Blow holes are round or elongated cavities, usually smooth-walled. They are found on, or close under, the surface of the casting.

Gas holes are either caused by insufficient venting of the core, or the core prints are not large enough to allow the gas to escape.

Pin holes and porosity are caused by the absorption of gas in the molten metal. The reason for this is incorrect fluxing or de-gassing procedure.

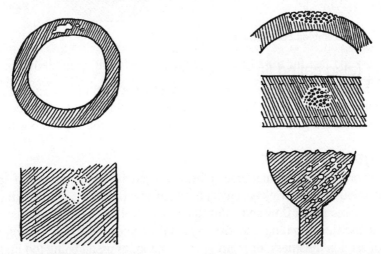

Figure 127. Large holes called 'blow holes', caused by steam or gas in the metal

Figure 128. Pinholes, called 'sponginess' or 'honeycombing', caused by moisture (steam), aspiration or gas in the metal

Inclusions: oxide, dross, sand, drop

Oxide and dross inclusions are caused by the entrapment of surface oxide, or other foreign matter, during pouring of the molten metal.

Sand inclusion and drop result from careless ramming or withdrawing of the pattern, leaving loose sand in the mould cavity. This will be included in the casting. Drop is when the upper surface of the mould cracks and pieces of sand fall into the mould cavity. This is caused either by sand of too low a green strength, or by soft ramming.

Scabs

Scabs are rough, irregular projections on the surface of the casting containing embedded sand or refractory. There are two types: expansion and erosion scabs.

Expansion scab A small area of the sand surface lifts, allowing metal to flow beneath it. This usually occurs at the top surface of the mould where the sand becomes pre-heated by radiation of heat from the molten metal. This causes the thin outer layer of sand to dry up and expand, leaving an air gap between the dried surface and the green interior.

Erosion scab This type is caused by uneven running of the metal, or bad design of the gating system. Molten metal scours (or erodes) sand at points that are not streamlined, or at badly designed parts of the mould or core which impede the metal flow. This erosion point leaves an unwanted 'positive' on the casting, while the displaced sand may find its way to the top of the mould, resembling a dirt inclusion.

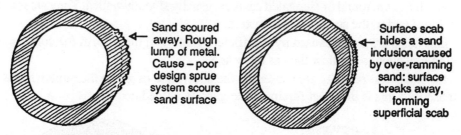

Sand scoured away. Rough lump of metal. Cause – poor design sprue system scours sand surface

Surface scab hides a sand inclusion caused by over-ramming sand: surface breaks away, forming superficial scab

Figure 129. Examples of scabbing

Flashing (also called fin or feather)

This is the formation of an unwanted run of metal at the parting line, caused by leakage of molten metal into the space between two halves of the mould. This may be caused by poor mould making, or by insufficient weight holding the cope in position.

Shrinkage or contraction

Contraction cracks are irregular cracks formed when the metal pulls itself apart while the mould is cooling. A shrinkage cavity is a void or depression caused by uncontrolled solidification (see Metal flow and solidification, page 122). The causes may be wrong location or inefficient gating and riser system; or poor design of casting or abrupt changes of section thickness; or pouring temperature of metal being too high.

Shift; swell

Shift is the result of a mismatch of the sections of the casting, usually at the parting line. The most likely cause is carelessness. Misalignment of flasks, incorrect mounting of pattern plates, or worn locating pins are the first things to look for. Core shift is caused by undersized (or oversized) core prints, or chaplets (locating pins) of the wrong size.

Swell is the term describing an unwanted positive, usually caused by weak, or inconsistent ramming of the sand, or by the cope lifting because there is not enough weight holding it down. Occasionally a swell is caused by metal flowing into the mould too fast, so building up too much pressure.

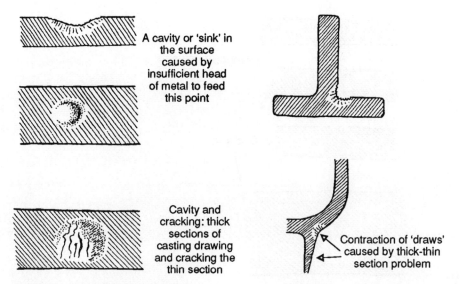

Figure 130. Shrinkage and cracking caused by poor design or technique

Figure 131. Contraction necessitates the redesign of runner and feeding system

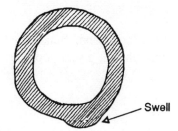

Figure 132. Swell of metal is caused by weak or haphazard ramming

Warp

Warped castings are rare in small foundries. This is more often encountered in large, or flat, castings where insufficient camber allowance has been estimated. On a smaller scale, other causes are: (a) flasks too small, which causes rapid cooling at the edges or ends of the casting; (b) weak flasks, allowing movement of the sand; (c) too narrow a gating system, which will not allow metal to reach the mould cavity fast enough; (d) excessive strength in cores.

Cold shut or missrun

A cold shut looks, at first sight, like a crack, but its smooth rounded edges betray its true nature. It is produced when two streams of metal, flowing in different directions, meet without fusing together. This is rare in bronze or brass, but very common in aluminium, a metal which oxidizes rapidly. A layer of oxide, pushed ahead of the melt, prevents the two flows of metal fusing.

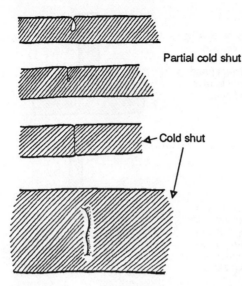

Partial cold shut

←Cold shut

Figure 133. Metal poured too cold or a badly designed runner system can cause a 'cold shut' or missrun; aluminium is particularly prone to this

Rough surface; metal penetration

The most common cause is poor quality facing (surface) sand. Sand which has high permeability, large grain size and poor green strength will give a poor surface to the casting. The other cause is soft ramming.

Lost wax

Note: Faults in lost-wax casting can often be traced to the wax rather than the casting process. For example, pin holes, or an uneven surface on the metal casting may not be due to faults in the investment or gas in the metal, but quite simply a badly made wax with air bubbles near the surface. Thorough quality control of waxes, therefore, is essential.

Assuming a perfect wax, the following are four common casting faults.

Gas holes (porosity)

These are caused by:

○ Insufficient heat-soaking time during the burn-out process
Moulds must stay in the heat long enough to remove all trace of wax gas from the core. This is particularly important when there is an enclosed core. Allow sufficient time in the heat. Fit a core vent.

○ Gas in the metal
This will only occur if the correct fluxing and de-gassing procedure is neglected.

Flashing (also called feathers)

These are either a sign of poor quality investment, or (more likely) over-baking the moulds. Either too high a temperature or too long an immersion in the heat. Flashing can also be caused if the mould is exposed to flame if, for example, the bag wall is broken or fissured, so that the flame plays onto the mould surface.

Scabs

These are most likely to be caused by pouring the metal too hot. This causes a metal-to-mould surface reaction, breaking down the surface of the mould. Too thin a first coat, or failure of the first to bond onto the second coat could also be responsible. This is the reason for a middle layer of 'one, one and one' (see block investment, page 68). A combination of first and outer coat which do not bond efficiently, and too high a firing temperature can cause a metal 'cocoon' around the casting. This usually looks worse than it is, and can be chiselled away with care.

Potatoes

(From the Italian casters' 'patati'.) These are round, smooth, organic looking positives attached to the surface of the castings. These are caused, invariably, by air bubbles in the investment slurry. Sometimes the potato is formed in a crevice in the casting, when it is a real nuisance. The most important advice is not to panic. A potato is never as bad as it seems. The air bubble is usually formed in the second coat of the investment (only gross carelessness will have been responsible for an air bubble on the first coat where it is so easy to spot and remedy). The potato is attached to the casting by one point or a thin feather, rarely more than that. Using a chisel or hammer to whack the potato free is a mistake, because it will break off a shred of metal from the casting, which will have to be repaired later. The correct procedure is to use a grinder, fine saw, or fine chisel, to reduce the solidity of the potato until only a thin layer is attached to the casting. Finally this too can be chiselled away (see also Metal flow and solidification, page 122, and Fettling and finishing, below).

Fettling and finishing

The finest most precise casting can be ruined by clumsy and imprecise metal finishing. Surplus metal must be removed logically and with patience.

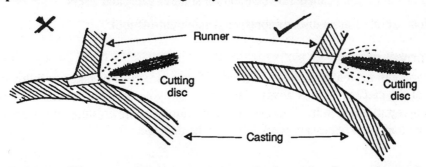

Figure 134. When removing the runner, never take the cutting disc too close to the casting: digging in with the disc can ruin the surface

The point of greatest risk is the first cut-off of sprues and feathers. This is often handed to the youngest and clumsiest apprentice. By the time the casting reaches the most skilled worker, the damage is done. Therefore, the first cut-off should be done by a skilled, experienced artisan. This simple lesson cannot be over-emphasized.

Some of the cleaning methods used for ferrous castings are not suitable for non-ferrous, firstly because the metal is more easily damaged, and secondly because, generally speaking, the castings are smaller and of thinner section.

Shaking out

Shaking out takes place as quickly as possible for economic reasons. You must, however, consider the nature of the metal and the effect that rapid, or gradual, cooling will have upon the casting.

Fettling stages (sand casting)

1. Knocking out of dry sand cores
2. Removal of gates and risers
3. Removal of fins and unwanted projections
4. Fine finishing
5. Cleaning castings
6. Repairs to castings

1. Knocking out

Both pneumatic and hydraulic tools are used in larger foundries. The smaller foundry will find a long steel bar and hammer the cheapest and most versatile method.

2. Removal of gates and risers

Knocking off, or breaking with a hammer, is a common method of removal with grey iron castings, but this is not suitable for copper or aluminium alloys. For these you will need:

o Metal cutting saw; either a power saw or hacksaw

o Sprue cutter (also called a bolt cutter) for smaller gates and risers

o Most useful of all, a disc, or abrasive grinder, cut-off tool.

3. Removal of fins

For this you will need a saw, chisel or grinder. Great care must be taken to follow the contour of the casting. This is always important, but you must be especially careful when using a portable grinder. Hasty or impatient cutting off or finishing with a grinder can cause hours of unnecessary work to repair the damage.

4. Fine finishing

Metal finishing tools in common use include:

- o Pneumatic or electric angle grinders. These are smaller than the large cut-off grinder.

- o Pneumatic or electric die grinder. This can be fitted with rotary files or abrasive points of various sizes.

- o Electric flexible shaft grinder. Less versatile than the die grinder, but safer and less likely to cause accidental damage to the casting.

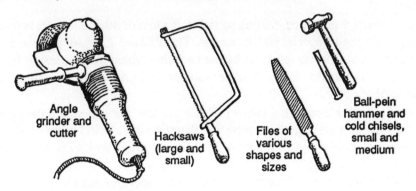

Angle grinder and cutter

Hacksaws (large and small)

Files of various shapes and sizes

Ball-pein hammer and cold chisels, small and medium

Figure 135. Metal finishing tools

- o A variety of small metal cutting chisels. For fine finishing work you will need cutting edges of different sizes and shapes.

- o Hacksaw, normal size. For fine work a small hacksaw (sometimes called a butcher's saw) is a useful tool.

- o Files. For bronze you will need a variety of small but coarse-toothed files. Do not use these for steel until they will not cut bronze cleanly, then they will be suitable for work on mild steel.

Note on filing aluminium: aluminium work-hardens and sticks to the file. If allowed to remain, these hardened pieces of swarf will scar and damage the surface of the casting. The way to avoid this is to lubricate the file using tallow mixed with turpentine or to use talc. The talc must be applied often, but it is less messy than the tallow. Use a wire brush on the file to remove the aluminium swarf.

5. Cleaning castings

Preliminary cleaning

With the exception of aluminium, magnesium and zinc-based metals, most castings come out of the mould with sand, scale or investment sticking to the surface.

In small foundries, shaking off the sand, knocking out the sand core, or knocking off the investment material is usually a manual rather than a mechanical process. In larger foundries, vibrating tables and pneumatic hammers are commonly used. Whatever the method, care must be taken to keep down, or contain, dust. *Foundry workers must use efficient masks or, preferably, air pressurized helmets.*

153

Surface cleaning

TUMBLING

The castings are put into a large steel container which is supported on trunnions (see Glossary). Small pieces of white iron are put into this barrel with the castings. The barrel is rotated and the castings and iron fragments tumble against each other. This peening process removes any flashes or sharp edges and also cleans and polishes the castings. Tumbling is generally used for iron or steel castings of medium size, not for delicate non-ferrous castings.

SANDBLASTING

A stream of compressed air containing particles of sand, or other abrasive, is directed at the casting through a special nozzle, or gun. The abrasive is drawn into the mixing chamber of the gun from its reservoir by the vacuum created by the passage of air at high velocity. The abrasive is usually either sand or steel grit, though sometimes glass beads are used.

Small castings are cleaned in a cabinet with a window through which the operator can see the flow of sand onto the casting and therefore control it. Larger castings are cleaned in an enclosed room with a perforated floor through which the sand drops to be re-used.

Because of the danger of silicosis or eye injury the operator must wear heavy-duty rubber gloves, protective clothing, and mask or face protection. The most efficient lung protection is an air-pressurized helmet.

HYDROBLAST

This is a less hazardous method using a cabinet, or in the open, and one particularly well-suited to a small-scale foundry doing precise castings.

A water pump forces a stream of water at high velocity past a side tube which conveys fine sand. The sand is sucked into the mixer. Sand and water are directed at the casting. This method is more suitable for non-ferrous than ferrous castings, because the latter are corroded by the water. There are various means of separating the water and the sand. Perhaps the simplest is to stand the casting in a pit or lined basin with a shallow dam to allow the water to trickle out while retaining the sand to collect later, dry, sieve and use again.

The second advantage of hydroblast is that the water prevents the abrasive dust from floating about, where it can do damage to both workers and machinery.

SHOT BLASTING

This is more usual in large foundries and for large castings. Steel shot is hurled against the casting using a centrifugal impeller wheel. Some units use a rotating table others tumble the casting as the steel shot hits the surface with great force.

PICKLING

Pickling is used for bronze or brass castings, not for aluminium, magnesium or zinc-based metals.

Either nitric or sulphuric acid makes a satisfactory pickle. Assuming that the acid is 95% to 98% concentrate, a dilute mixture of 1 part of acid to 8 parts water cleans the surface of the casting well. *Always add acid to water. Never the other way round.* Add the acid slowly; do not allow it to splash or froth. *All fumes from concentrated acid are toxic and highly corrosive.*

(Aluminium can be etched with hydrochloric acid provided that the metal is suspended face down in the acid and agitated occasionally, to allow the precipitate to fall from the etched surface.)

Keep the pickle in a plastic or ceramic container. Do not allow pickle used for copper alloys to become contaminated with iron.

6. Repairs to castings

Aluminium castings can be gas welded, or tungsten inert gas (TIG) welded using alternating current (AC). Either system demands a welder with a high degree of skill; the myth found in some handbooks aimed at the small foundry that any garage car-repairer can weld aluminium is nonsense. For aircraft production during World War II, women proved to be the best aluminium welders because male instructors discovered (to their own chagrin) that women were much more responsive to the slight visible change in the surface of the aluminium as it melted.

Bronze and brasses can be welded with oxy-acetylene, direct current (DC) arc, or TIG welders. For an experienced welder, TIG is the easiest and most satisfactory method, but the equipment is extremely expensive and requires a supply of the appropriate gas. DC arc is not difficult to master. Oxy-acetylene is the cheapest and also the most difficult method.

The rules for welding any form of casting are the same: a clean surface, pre-heating before welding, and slow cooling after the weld is completed. For large castings, or those of dissimilar thickness, it may be necessary to build a brick muffle (see Glossary), fill it with coke and place the casting inside it. Gentle build-up to an even heat, and slow cooling will prevent cracking around the weld.

Castings are vulnerable to thermal shock. They must be pre-heated gently and evenly, and cooled slowly. No traces of scale, dirt or investment refractory must remain on the surface to be welded.

Thorough knock-out, pickling and hydroblasting usually do the job. Time spent in cleaning saves much time and frustration during the repair welding stage.

Flow welding

This method was much used in ancient times. It is rarely, if ever, used where the founder has access to welding equipment. I have only seen it done twice, once by an Italian master craftsman using the Roman method, and once in Foumban, Cameroon, using the clay slurry method. In each case it worked well (see Appendix B).

Traditional Nepalese bells (background) and Pelton turbine wheels drying in the sun after first, second and final coats of investment using the Newar method

Appendices

A. Newar casting in Patan, Nepal

Patan is now a part of greater Kathmandu, but it used to be the independent city of Lalitpur, divided from Kathmandu by the river. Most of the traditional industries are found in Patan, except for ceramics which is centred on Baktapur, another of the ancient and powerful city states of the Kathmandu valley. The Newar are the original inhabitants of the valley and famous for their skill. As far back as the seventh century, the rulers of Tibet sent for craftsmen from Kathmandu to teach them the art of lost-wax casting. In the thirteenth century the Emperor of China, Kublai Khan, placed a Newar craftsman in charge of the Imperial metal restoration workshops.

In Patan two different foundry traditions have been established in the same industrial area, in some cases side by side, and the ITDG team worked within two foundries, each following one of these separate traditions. National Structures Engineering, owned by the Mittal family, is an Indian sand foundry whose technique originated in the railway foundries of the British Raj, and Nepal Dhalout Udyog, the small foundry belonging to the Shakya family, follows the Newar tradition. Technical differences appeared small compared to the social or class barriers.

The Mittals' engineering business and foundry used conventional Western technology, of a type common in Europe thirty years ago. The Shakya family foundry used an ancient technology which was well-suited to the conditions in the Kathmandu valley. Observations on Newar casting are all based on what I saw, not what I was told. I am sceptical about what artisans tell strangers. They are in a competitive business, using skills passed down through the family, or through hard-earned apprenticeship. They may tell you some of what they know, but they will always leave out some process, or material, vital to the whole. Any formulae or recipes should be used with caution.

The Newar casting method

The wax

The wax is hand-modelled. There is no mass-production or use of flexible moulds, but some details, such as faces, hands or ornamental details are press-moulded into hard wax negatives. Traditional waxes in Nepal are made from tree resin (often called rosin), beeswax and ghee, which is a type of melted butter (see Summary at the end of this appendix for recipes and proportions).

The design

The Newar technique allows form to follow function. Whenever possible the wax component takes the form of a hollow cylinder. The line where one piece is jointed to another becomes part of the design. Unlike European sculptors who often work against the nature of the process, the Newar avoids thin, complicated, horizontal shapes.

Though the decoration on the surface is complex, the basic form is simple. This makes the whole process of casting straightforward and reliable. Though each piece is unique, in the sense that it is hand made, each is made to a formula which minimizes risk.

The sprue system

Small section runners take the metal to all the extremities. No risers are necessary because the air and the gases escape through the porous surface. The Newar technique uses small cups and tends to be skimpy about the volume of the metal in the sprue. A peculiarity of the Newar method is the 'dhwaya'. The dhwaya is a three-pronged wax runner which is attached to every wax between the runner system and the cup. The purpose of this is both practical and religious. The religious significance is complex and difficult for an outsider to understand, but possibly symbolizes some kind of trinity of gods. From a practical view, the dhwaya increases the head between the cup and the model, and also, being thick in section, helps progressive solidification.

The investment

The first and second coats are invested by dipping into a refractory slurry. Subsequent coats are thicker, resembling porridge. Each coat is dried before the next coat is applied.

The Newar do not use alcohol, soda, or any other degreasing liquid. Speaking through an interpreter, and with some difficulty, the aunt of the Shakya family told me that the slurry first coat is left to ferment for a long time before it is used, and the mixture etches onto the wax. Whatever the reason, it works. There is no problem of the first coat wetting the wax; it sticks first time. The wax is dipped into a large bowl of slurry, air bubbles are blown off, or removed gently with feathers. It is dipped again and then left to dry. The proportions of each coat stay the same, but accounts of the materials used vary – sometimes yellow clay, sometimes black clay, I suspect that the darkness of the slurry was caused by charcoal.

The first coat is a slurry of clay and dung: 60% clay to 40% dung (cow or goat) sieved fine and then wetted down to a creamy mixture.

The second coat is of the same material and similar technique to the first, but thinner. More dung is added to the second coat (to a proportion of about 50/50).

Drying

Investing and drying were carried out on the flat roof of the workshop. The first coat was left to dry in the sun for a very short time. It was then moved into the shade where there was a breeze, and left to dry out slowly (a minimum of 24 hours). Each coat is dried before the next is applied. The total drying time may be three or four days in dry

158

weather, up to two weeks or more in the monsoon (this was the one major disadvantage in the Newar method).

The third coat shows a change of technique. A stiff paste like porridge is kneaded thoroughly and pushed onto the wax with the fingers. This paste is made up of equal quantities of clay, dung and rice husk.

The fourth coat is the same. The total thickness is between 15 and 20mm.

De-waxing

The cup on a Newar mould looks odd to the eyes of anyone trained in the Italian tradition. For one thing it is small by those standards, and secondly, the inside of the wax cup is coated with investment in exactly the same way as the rest of the wax. A small hole is left in the middle of the cup, and this is plugged with clay. This hole is called the 'nowcha'. When the mould is dry and ready, it is held and turned over a 'makal' (a thick clay fire pot containing burning charcoal). The mould is turned regularly to heat the clay evenly. When the whole is above the melting point of wax, the nowcha plugs are removed from either end of the mould, and the liquid wax poured out into a metal bowl. Some of the wax permeates the clay and is lost. Mr Shakya claimed that he recovered 75% of the wax, though later he agreed that it was nearer 50%.

The core

In this method there is no core in the sense that the Italians use the term, nor in the way West African casters use it. The Newar method uses the same mixture, and system of coats, inside and outside. Core nails, when they are needed, are much smaller than one might expect because of the sensible shape of the wax. This same open-ended form is used in West Africa, except that there the core is pre-formed out of clay, and with the Newar technique it is not, but is invested both outside and inside at the same time. Finally, the inside is stuffed with the clay and husk 'porridge'mixture.

Baking the moulds

I visited several Newar foundries and saw a variety of kilns and furnaces, using fuels which ranged through coke, wood, kerosene, and waste oil. National Structures Engineering also made biogas generators so, in theory, one could run a kiln on methane produced from animal dung. Bottled gas could be bought in camping shops in Tamel, but it was expensive. Among this bewildering variety of heat sources, I did not see one of the traditional type that they described. I hasten to add that this does not mean that such a furnace does not exist.

I spent a lot of time with the Shakya family and they used a system very similar to that used in European foundries. That is to say, a separate burn-out kiln and metal-melting furnace. The kiln burnt wood and the furnace coke which, at that time, had to be smuggled across the closed border with India.

Tending the kiln was the responsibility of the aforementioned aunt, who also invested the moulds. The kiln was her area. It was a simple, practical way of heating the moulds, very similar to a Roman kiln. Because it burnt wood, the kiln had openings at each end to load the two fire troughs. The ends, like the roof, were blocked with slabs of cement mixed with silica sand cast in an iron frame. The moulds rested on a central platform of brick, similar to a Roman kiln. This had the same type of trough in the centre, so that the kiln supervisor could watch the flames at each cup.

Unlike the Italian moulds' 15–20 hours, the Newar moulds are baked for 3–4 hours, until cherry red heat is reached. A team of aunts then maintained the temperature, watching the mould cups closely to see the flames or, on one occasion, smoke which one of the youngest members of the clan ignited with a burning kerosene-soaked rag on an iron bar.

When it was clear that no trace of wax gas remained, the kiln was closed up, and all the joints sealed with clay except for two small holes at the bottom to allow a little air to enter. While this was happening, the furnace team cleaned out the brick furnace and loaded it with coke. The electric fan blower was brought out from the metal store.

Large silicon carbide crucibles are beyond the purse of small companies or family businesses like the Shakyas'. National Structures Engineering used large graphite crucibles, inferior to silicon carbide, but still very expensive because they were imported from India. All the Newar foundries that I saw used batteries of small crucibles which melted, at a rough guess, 25kg of brass each and lasted for three, four or at most five melts. The family kept a plentiful supply of fresh ones. They did not themselves make them, though Mr Shakya had been apprenticed to a potter as a child.

Once the kiln was closed, there was a pause while the family did other jobs, always keeping an eye out for the progress of the furnace. At last, when the metal was nearly ready, the kiln was dismantled. The moulds were left in the embers until the last possible moment, and only taken into the courtyard when the metal was ready to be poured. The moulds were so hot that some of the sacks used to carry them caught fire.

Metal preparation

The weak point in the Newar casting system lies in the metal. This is not only because good quality scrap is very hard to find, and properly alloyed and certified ingots almost unobtainable, but because the Newar practitioners that I saw took a very *laissez faire* attitude towards the preparation and pouring of the metal. Despite the poor quality of the scrap, fluxes, de-gassers or deoxidizers seem to be unknown. Neither borax nor the old furnaceman's trick of powdered glass were used, nor any charcoal to remove oxygen. Possibly the burning coke made this unnecessary by creating a reducing atmosphere.

The second thing which perturbed me was the nowcha, which I have described earlier. This seals the cup to prevent any inclusions during the kiln firing – a sensible precaution – except that the worker entrusted with the job of unsealing the cup was so clumsy that pieces of nowcha clay fell into the dhwaya, or main triple runner (that, in an Italian foundry, rated instant dismissal).

My admiration for the Shakya family and the Newar system of casting is clear from my earlier remarks, but this carelessness at the climax of the process explains why some engineers, and Mr Mittal in particular, believed that 'the Shakyas are not in the world of the turbines'.

The discipline and team work of the Shakyas, on the other hand, was superb. Pouring small crucibles into big moulds is no easy task because the flow of metal must not be interrupted. As the molten metal delivered by one pair comes to the end, the next pair start pouring from the opposite side. The mould for the base section of one large figure took three crucibles to fill it. 75kg is not a problem for a foundry using large crucibles, but no easy task when you have to maintain the flow from three small ones. The aunt stood beside each mould in turn, a stick in one hand and a copper bowl of powdered resin in the other. She threw a small quantity of resin into the crucible and then pushed back the dross with the stick. As her two nephews poured the metal, she threw a larger quantity of *sal-dup* (tree resin) into the mouth of the mould where it gave off a great flare of yellow flame. I had never seen resin powder used in this way before, but it is a sensible trick: firstly because it heats the cup in the same way as the more sophisticated (and much more expensive) exothermic sleeve, and secondly, resin is an excellent and well-tried flux. It also probably acts as a deoxidizer.

Three moulds had cracks, one of these more than a mere weep of metal. In each case, Mr Shakya, seeing what was going on, seized a handful of mud and husk which stood ready, and plastered it onto the smoking mould with his hands. This porous poultice dried instantly and barred the leak of any more molten metal.

The furnace contained 14 or 15 crucibles, but on one occasion they used a second smaller furnace containing 5 or 6. On this larger pour they melted and poured something like 20 crucibles in an afternoon. Even then there were some moulds left over. This did not trouble the Shakyas. The moulds were of course baked and void of wax, a condition known as 'sdya' in Newari. The aunt plugged the nowcha holes with great care, and stored the moulds on their sides in a dry store room, where women made the wax components.

Metal finishing

The metal workers appeared to be itinerant, yet they were also family. The metal working section was large: five or six men and their immediate families, also two Shakya sons and a cousin, who joined in after a big metal pour.

First, the ludo was removed and stored in an outhouse where it was re-ground. Then the remnants of the clay were washed and scrubbed off and the brass or copper castings dried in the sun. The men sat in a row chiselling, matting or filing the castings. The fine finishers used chisels, files and various abrasives. The women and children finished the polishing and burnishing.

The foundry was too far off the beaten track to attract tourists. Mr Shakya sold to the larger, more tourist-orientated Udyogs, or to dealers in Tamel or Baktapur. All the foundries I saw followed much the same pattern, locating the metal finishers at the front of the workshop. This was the obvious side of the industry. Tucked away behind the scenes in a dirty shed at the back were both oxy-acetylene and arc welders for welding up repairs or faults in the castings. They also had large and small angle grinders, though they did not appear to use these very much.

161

Summary – materials and quantities

Wax

As a rough guide, equal quantities of sal-dup or rosin, beeswax and liquid butter (*choorighee*) were used. Exact proportions depend on the ambient temperature. In cold weather more fat should be added, in hot weather add more rosin. (In practice the IT team did not use ghee but added Vaseline and soft microcrystalline wax.)

Investment

For the first and second coats, cow or goat dung and clay of the kaolin type are used. This is dried and sieved or rubbed through a fine mesh to remove undigested impurities. It is then mixed with water to form a fine creamy slurry. The Shakyas left this slurry to settle and mix for several weeks before using it. I suspect that either fine powdered charcoal or rice husk ash (kyonite) was added.

Third and subsequent coats

Clay and rice husk are used in equal quantities. The proportion of clay is increased on the final outer coat to give it a smooth surface. Each coat is allowed to dry. It is damped superficially before the next coat is applied.

These materials are available locally; they are cheap and efficient. Dung, being full of chopped fibres, is not only an excellent binder, but also porous. Rice husk further assists porosity. When it is fired it turns to ash (kyonite). This is amorphous silica, a stable refractory. The mould's porosity allows air and gases to escape without risers.

Preparation of a crucible

The Newar word for crucible is 'bhancha'. This is a Newar recipe which I have not yet tried, and therefore may not be completely accurate.

Black clay and rice husk are used in equal parts. They are kneaded together into a paste. To this, ground-up Nepali paper is added (this is paper made from vegetable material, not rag paper; Nepali paper makers use bark digested in an alkali solution, straw, bamboo, sugar cane or leaves). When the paste is the consistency of modelling clay, a crucible is formed by hand. The account does not say by what method, but it is probably coil or pinch. The crucible is then dried in the sun. Finally the crucible is coated inside with borax and fired in the kiln, raising the temperature to red heat.

B. Bamoum lost-wax casting, western Cameroon

West Africa is one of the few areas where the metal casting process known as lost wax, or *cire perdu*, has not been changed by the introduction of advanced technology. Traditionally this is a precise technique based on a combination of skill and local knowledge, using simple, low-cost technology. This makes the method ideally suited to poor countries, or those whose economies have been destroyed by war.

In the search for 'intermediate' foundry technology, one cannot overstate the importance of West African casting. In West Africa the first name that comes to mind is Benin. The fine bronze sculptures of Benin are aclaimed in museums and galleries all over the world.

There is a major problem facing the student of Nigerian sculpture. In studying the technology of Benin and Ife, the ethnographer, sculptor or engineer discovers a break, like a deep ravine, in the path of his search. Nigerian casting today is not the direct descendant of the work of smiths and casters of Benin and Ife. They, like their craft, were destroyed by the punitive British colonial expedition of 1897. For over fifty years the practice of bronze sculpture ceased in Benin and the skills withered away. The Nigerian bronze casting trade that we see today was set up in the mid twentieth century by well-meaning foreign teachers and ethnographers. No one can say for certain how much it relates to the original technique.

The craft in western Cameroon, by contrast, has an unbroken line. This is why the small town of Foumban, former capital of Bamoum, is so important.

Foumban is a delightful, relatively simple town which makes few concessions to tourists or foreign travellers. It was founded in the seventeenth century by a Tikar prince who took it from the Bamileke who ruled the area from Bafousam. Disentangling myth from fact is never easy, but the town's origins are confirmed from various sources, as is the foundation of the artisans' village in a valley on the edge of the town, known as the Njinka quarter.

Whether the Tikar smiths and metal smelters learnt their skills from Benin, or earlier from the civilization around the Cross River, no one knows, but there seems little doubt that the founders of the Njinka quarter were Tikar in origin. I spent a little over one week in Foumban, walking to the village of artisans early each morning.

The Shell company in Douala gave me a letter of introduction which worked wonders, enabling me to meet the antiquary and patron of artisans, El Hadj Moustapha Rengou. Without his help I would have seen no more than a tourist would. As it was, once I had shown him and the artisans' photographs of my foundry and proved that I understood their business, two of the artisans, Abdou Ngou and Monta Oumarou, acted as guides, escort and friends, and let me watch any of the processes that I wanted to see, take photographs and make sketches.

The process of making a West African casting starts with the core. This is true of Ghana, Nigeria and western Cameroon. This is the one major factor which is different from Nepalese and north Indian casting.

The Bamoum method (in order of processes)

The core

The core is always made first, never poured into the wax, as with the Italian method, or modelled into the wax (Newar method). The core is often very elaborate, sometimes even two-layered (see description of wax technique). Unique among the methods I have seen, the Bamoum craftsmen do not vary the constituents of the investment. Core, first coat, second and subsequent coats all use the same mixture: clay 50%; dung 50%.

The clay is a special red clay which has a high percentage of silica sand in it. This makes it a natural casting sand; in texture it resembles heavily-grogged potters' clay. The dung used is horse dung almost always, except rare occasions when there is a shortage, when cow is used as a substitute. Cow dung, Abdou and Monta told me, was not as good because the cow's second stomach chopped the grass fibre too fine. (This is precisely the reason that the Newar use it for the first coat, because of its finely-ground texture.)

When I examined horse dung closely (for the first time, I must admit) I saw that the fibre was indeed much coarser. Monta told me that the investment 'breathes' and so does not need a riser system to allow air and gas to escape. Once again, like the Newar, this is a major advantage over the Italian method.

The wax

The wax is built up on the core in wax sheets or small threads of wax. Sometimes the mould is built up in layers: for example, an ornamental lamp base shaped like a solid bowl inside a fretted bowl. This surprised me because the basketwork technique used in overlaying the wax threads resembled the classic village castings found in India.

The wax is beeswax without any additions. I asked about rosin or microcrystalline. The latter meant nothing to them, but they had heard of the use of rosin. When I mentioned the Nigerian habit of using latex instead of wax they were amused, and quite clearly thought someone had been joking with me. (I discovered later in the Pitt Rivers Museum in Oxford, UK, that in parts of Nigeria casters use latex from the plant *Euphorbia camerounica pax.* Source: Willet, 1967.)

The beeswax was of an excellent quality, a perfect modelling wax. For slush casting one would add rosin to the wax, but none of the casters I met used moulds, all the work was hand-made. On the other hand their knowledge was quite sophisticated; they knew all about rubber moulds though none had used one.

The modellers warm the wax in the sun or over a fire in a clay pot fuelled by ordinary charcoal. Both Monta and Abdou were interested in pictures that I showed them of a 'machan', a small stove used by Newar wax workers. This was also a pot made of clay, but had a small rotary hand-powered blower attached. The Bamoum do not roll the threads as they do in other countries, but model them between their fingers. These threads are remarkably even, and the artisans produce hundreds of metres each day.

Traditional patterns recur, though each artisan has his own way of working and variants to traditional designs. The Bamoum craftsmen are eclectic: within the same atelier I saw copies of Benin, Asante and Yoruba art, as well as styles adapted from local wood carvings. One odd example is the casting of Bamoum, Bamende and Bamileke style dance masks. The traditional masks were made of light wood, for obvious reasons. There are many excellent copies for sale in Yaounde and Douala, all made of the same light wood. Brass copies are, of course, far too heavy to hang on the face, but the craftsmen discovered that there is a tourist demand for metal masks. So a new art form is produced to hang on walls in Dusseldorf, Chicago, Lyons and Birmingham.

The source of basic materials is always important, so I asked them where the wax came from. Monta was deliberately vague. Clearly, wax sources came under the heading of 'trade secrets'.

The investment

Unlike either Nigerian or Newar casting, the Bamoum make no distinction between core mixture, first and second coat. They do not use either powdered charcoal or rice husk ash. The mixture is always the same: sandy clay and horse dung (see core). The mixture would be immediately recognizable to a traditional bell-caster, who would call it 'loom' or loam.

The first and subsequent coats are prepared in the same way, by hand. Moist dung is taken from a damp sack and spread on the ground; the clay is then folded and kneaded over it to make a sandwich, in exactly the same way that a potter would knead clay to an even consistency. The fibre in the mixture prevents the investment from being too sticky or unpleasant to handle. Monta conceded that some casters added other fibrous material such as palm nut fibres, but that he found their mixture satisfactory and saw no reason to change it. Looking at the castings no one could quarrel with that.

The soft mixture is modelled onto the wax surface, like applying putty to a window frame. Pellets of the investment are applied with great care and pushed firmly into place, driving out the air. I had never before seen any method that did not paint or dip the first coat.

The position of the main runner was left exposed. Very occasionally in large moulds the casters leave wax buttons for risers too. I guessed that these risers were more to assist the escape of the molten wax than to allow air to escape. The mould is left to dry in the shade (unlike the cores which are dried rapidly in the sun). The second coat is added in exactly the same way. Either during the first or the second coat, the cup is modelled on.

Judged by European standards, both cup and sprue system are small. This, I suppose, is prompted by the difficulty of melting large quantities of metal. Bamoum crucibles are always small and the problems of the metal melt great. Western foundry practice will always melt more rather than less, using a large cup and a thick section main runner to provide a good head of metal and thus aid progressive solidification. The Bamoum skimp on the amount of metal used in sprue and cup. Sometimes they get away with this, often they do not. Judging by the fake Benin head I have on the desk in front of me, the Bamoum are highly skilled at repair welding (described on page 169).

After each layer has dried, cracks and irregularities are filled and plastered over before the next coat is added. The mould maker sprays on a fine layer of water from his mouth or else damps the surface lightly with a wet cloth. The complete mould, with its small wax cup, is given the final coat, and the inside of the cup coated over (this is the same as both the Newar and the Nigerian practice). Thus the mould is completely enclosed.

The completed mould is dried thoroughly in the shade. Once again any cracks are filled. I pointed out to the casters, when they asked why we used the Roman process with such large plaster moulds, that the sun is an essential ingredient in their process. Like the Newar, they found the Northern European lack of sun during the greater part of the year hard to believe.

Kiln firing

When the moulds are sun dried they are placed near the kiln to warm. The caster makes a small hole in the cup and then heats the mould over the charcoal fire pot, tilting the mould and turning it, to let the wax run out into a calabash. Most of the wax is saved in this way – yet another advantage of the Bamoum method. One has to add, however, that this will only work with moulds small enough to handle without danger of dropping or cracking them. Finally, the moulds are stacked in the kiln which is built up for each firing.

Illustrations of old Newar kilns show that they too were of this two-tier pattern. These died out in Kathmandu years ago, and have been replaced by a less beautiful but simpler kiln, which is almost an exact twin of the Roman design. Though I have seen the two-tier kiln in books, and even found a disused one in an old foundry in Nepal, I had never before seen one used.

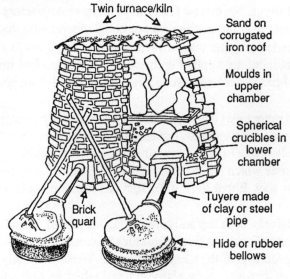

Figure 136. Bamoum two-tier kiln or furnace: upper chamber for moulds, bottom chamber for melting bronze in spherical crucibles

166

The Bamoum two-tier kiln (or furnace, for it serves both purposes) is divided by fire bars about a third of the way up. The kiln I saw was over one and a half metres high. Fire bars are steel reinforcing bars about 40mm or 1.5in thick (cast iron bars would be better but these are hard to find anywhere in the world, and probably unobtainable altogether in Cameroon). There are no fire bricks, so the bricks used in kiln construction are the local adobe kind.

The kiln is double chambered, sometimes built square and sometimes taking the form of elegant double cylinders, inclined inwards in either case. I guessed that the kiln was double chambered for strength, but no one could actually explain why, except to say that they had always been like that. The two bottom chambers contain the crucibles or 'marmites'. These are surrounded by good quality charcoal. This was hardwood charcoal and came from a special place, which was kept secret.

An experienced caster like Monta judges the quantity of charcoal needed by eye because no extra fuel was added once the furnace was alight. I guessed that a certain amount of charcoal would be needed to melt a given number of crucibles, but there must be other factors such as ambient temperature and wind direction which would affect the quantities used.

When the marmites are in place the fire bars are secured and the bottom part of the kiln bricked up. Next, the moulds are placed on the firebars, largest moulds on the bottom, smallest on the top, and the rest of the kiln bricked up.

The blowers or bellows are of a type found in many parts of Africa: two cylinders with goatskin, canvas (or, more often, rubber tyre) diaphragms stretched over them. Older frames are carved from solid wood. The more modern are less elegant but practical, using the wheel hubs of derelict trucks. From the base of each cylinder a steel pipe travels under the floor to each chamber of the furnace. Each diaphragm has a wooden pole attached to push it up and down, and foundrymen take turns in keeping this basic blower going until the metal is melted. In one aluminium foundry in Douala,

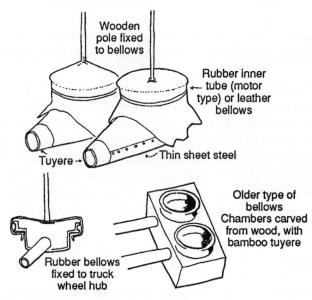

Figure 137. Bellows and tuyere, Foumban, Cameroon

some ingenious soul, tiring of this labour, had made a fan out of tin cans, and a propulsion unit out of an old cycle wheel. A small boy turned this using only half the effort expended by the pole pushers.

The ceramic mixture for the crucibles is not sophisticated and the marmites rarely last for more than one firing. They are made from the same mixture as the moulds (there is room for experiment, and a great deal of room for improvement here). The crucibles are filled with scrap brass and sealed with a clay lid. I saw no bronze used. Monta added a small quantity of aluminium to the brass, and a slightly larger quantity of zinc. I saw no borax or other flux.

Despite criticism of these dangerous and unreliable crucibles, they do have one major advantage, the molten metal was remarkably clean and free from slag. This lack of oxides is caused, obviously enough, by the sealing of the lid.

The Bamoum gauge the temperature of the metal by the smoke. Some cracking in the crucible lids is inevitable, and the cracks allow the fumes to escape. As the zinc vaporizes the white smoke is obvious. The kiln shed was open at the sides so the danger to the lungs from the zinc fumes is not great.

The top half of one side of the kiln is dismantled, small moulds are leant against bricks outside, larger moulds are buried to the neck in dry soil, exactly as with the Roman/European method. These are lowered into the pit and then soft sandy earth tamped round them. This process was done with more enthusiasm than science, if judged by Italian standards, endangering the moulds with much too much vibration.

Metal pouring

The closed crucible has the advantage of excluding oxygen. Once the brass has reached temperature, the crucibles are removed from the fire by two men using wet green sticks (i.e. four sticks holding one crucible). A small hole is punched in the side of the crucible at the top edge. The metal is poured through this hole and it flows out remarkably pure. That is the good news; the bad news is the danger. The marmites are lifted and the metal poured using bare hands with only wet sacking for protection. I saw not a leather glove or boot in the workshop. Had I not actually seen this for myself, I would not have believed it.

Abdou did the lifting and pouring. He appeared to revel in my disapproval at the lack of safety clothing. I asked Monta if there were many accidents; he admitted that there were some. Neither Abdou nor Monta, nor those close to them, wore any form of eye, hand or foot protection. Unlike the Newar, the Bamoum disdain the use of gloves, and several of the casters carried evil ridged scars on hands and forearms to prove it. Abdou showed me a long scar on the inside of his right arm and told me that this was made by a marmite. When I remarked on this later to Monta he was scornful. '*Il ment*' he said ('he lies'). Monta then added that Abdou had been bitten by an animal. Looking at the size of the scar I was no less impressed.

The quality of the metal

Unlike bronze, which is golden as it flows, the brass used by the Bamoum is pale yellow. As it cools it turns silver. Broken out of the mould the metal looks like aluminium. This coating (one might almost call it a flux) is easily removed with a wire brush. What it does to the alloy is less predictable. Like the Newar, the Bamoum care little for the quality of the metal that they cast, let alone keeping to a specific alloy. They use the words 'cuivre', 'bronze', and 'laiton', but I doubt whether it is understood what alloys are, or how the various alloys behave. The castings are purely decorative. Originally for the court of the Sultan of Bamoum, now for wealthy tourists, who they believe will buy any old rubbish. For visiting professors and collectors with time to pick and choose and haggle, they have some special, well-finished pieces, but once again the quality of the metal does not affect the price.

Good quality metal is easier to buy in Cameroon than in Nepal, because the latter is landlocked. I have no doubt that one could buy gun-metal or phosphor bronze from the repair yards in Douala, but inland, in Foumban, I saw only brass.

Flow welding

Art historians tell us that the classical bronze casters of Benin and Ife used a repair technique called 'flow welding'. I was fascinated and excited to come across this in Foumban. Like most of their craft practices, the Bamoum artisans did not make a great mystery of it, neither hiding nor displaying the technique.

Every lost-wax foundry in the world has dud castings, though the Italians usually hide this fact. Some castings are beyond repair and melted down, but others have small faults that we would repair with a gas or arc welder. Small holes caused by gassing can usually be pinned, but holes where the metal has not flowed completely, or where the core has slipped, closing the cavity between the core and the investment, need a patch.

The Bamoum repair a fault by the traditional and very ancient method (one particularly appropriate for poor countries where artisans cannot afford such luxuries as cylinders of compressed oxygen and acetylene). The fired core is kept in place after the outer investment is removed and the bronze cleaned. The missing piece is replaced in wax, and this wax is modelled and incised in every detail. To this wax piece are attached two runners which act as an inlet and an outlet, and a cup is attached to the inlet runner. The whole casting is invested in the usual way and fired in the kiln.

While the piece is very hot, it is removed from the kiln and molten metal poured into the cup. The metal is allowed to flow through the system until the craftsman judges that the flowing metal has partially melted the edges of the original piece, then he stops pouring and allows the entire piece to cool slowly. Once it is completely cool the investment is removed and the surplus metal sawn or chiselled off. This method achieves a true weld – fusion rather than adhesion. To see this ancient process carried out was a rare privilege.

Metal work

The quality of the metal finishing varied. Some pieces were sensitively and skilfully finished, others only crudely fettled. The workshops I saw had no power tools, so all work was chiselled or sawn. The artisans used files only rarely. This is not a bad thing as chiselling gives the work a better quality than indiscriminate filing.

169

Patination

Though the Bamoum try to fake age, just as Benin craftsmen do, their patination is neither subtle nor successful. As a present, to show my appreciation, I left them an old Roman patination formula, so the quality of fakes may well improve dramatically in this area, to the puzzlement of art historians.

Other casting techniques

I asked about a technique used in other parts of West Africa, the enclosed mould and crucible. Yes, Monta agreed, they did use it but only for small pieces, or when they wanted to make just a few pieces in a hurry for a special order. Generally, they used the open cup mould and the marmite type of crucible, because this was more practicable for a whole batch of moulds.

This confirmed the suspicion I had when I read accounts by art historians. Despite these accounts I had felt that the enclosed mould and crucible were far too heavy to be practicable on a large scale. Monta laughed at the idea of casting a large section by this method. No one but an imbecile would believe that, he said.

C. The Dedza crucible

In 1988 IT commissioned an experimental crucible to be made at Christopher Stevens' pottery in Dedza, Malawi. The purpose of the crucible was to melt bronze and brass, and the crucible was to be tested and proved at Frank Soko's foundry in Lilongwe. Until then the foundry had melted only aluminium. They had no crucible to melt bronze, nor were they certain that the furnace would reach a high enough temperature. For aluminium a welded steel pot lined with fireclay was sufficient. This would not stand the extra temperature needed to melt brass.

No handbooks or foundry technology textbooks in current use gave any information on crucibles. It was quite obvious that foundries like this one (and similar small businesses all over the developing world) could not afford the high cost of an imported crucible. Added to this was the hazard of transport; the chance of the imported article arriving in usable condition is slim to the point of invisibility.

Research in the UK at this time, and attempts to pick the brains or appeal to the good nature of the foundry suppliers and crucible manufacturers in the UK, achieved nothing. This was not, I suspect, through ill will, or guarding trade secrets, but quite simply that crucible making has now become a highly technical, specialized and competitive industry. Technicians that I spoke to at the International Foundry Exhibition could not imagine how a crucible could be made outside a sophisticated factory, or why anyone should want to make one. The comment that metal casters had made crucibles for hundreds of years, or paid the local potter to make them, was received with incomprehension. No one could tell me how to make a crucible, regarding the question as frivolous or just plain mad.

Late nineteenth and early twentieth century books on iron and brass founding reveal little about the composition of the crucible, but describe the two types then in common use. One example comes from the 1912 volume of Cassel's *Metalworking:*

> Crucibles are of two descriptions. Those commonly used formerly were composed of fireclay, mixed with burnt clay (grog), cement, pipeclay, etc. Fireclay crucibles are being very generally superseded by plumbago crucibles: while a clay pot cannot be used for more than four or five heats, a plumbago crucible may be used for as many as thirty-two heats. Plumbago crucibles are usually made from varying proportions of fireclay mixed with powdered graphite and coke dust.

The author goes on to say that the crucible should be annealed 'mouth downwards in the fire, after which it is ready for use', and adds 'these cost one penny per pound calculated on the weight of metal the pots hold'.

Early crucibles were 'annealed' (warmed and dried) for several days before using in the furnace. Modern crucibles are less sensitive to thermal shock. *But one cannot emphasize too strongly the danger of damp, or rough handling.* If, by some accident, or by neglect, a crucible becomes damp, it must be dried out very slowly before being placed in the furnace. A damp crucible will explode with a report like a cannon.

Locally-made crucibles, such as the Dedza crucible, need more care and a slower drying time than the expensive, specialized European or American crucible.

The prototype Dedza crucible was composed of graphite clay and kyonite, with a liquefier. It was fired up to a temperature of 1280°C. When it was tested, it demonstrated excellent resistance to thermal shock, but poor resistance to abrasion. The crucible, which was made using traditional African pottery-forming techniques by an experienced lady potter who specialized in the larger range of cooking pots produced at Dedza Pottery, was too elegant for its purpose. We recommended that the next one should be thicker, and fired to only 1180°C, thus reducing the fuel cost, which was a major part of the manufacturing cost.

One of the problems was the supply of graphite, which came from nearby Mozambique, then in a state of civil war. Obtaining graphite was extremely dangerous because of the unpredictable movements of the warring factions and the ruthlessness of Renamo guerillas. By good fortune, a supply of graphite was discovered in Malawi by the time the second and third Dedza crucibles were planned.

The Dedza crucible

Proportions
5 parts graphite
4 parts clay
1 part kyonite
To this was added 10% liquefier.

Dedza is very close to the border with Mozambique, where the graphite came from. The clay was a fine and very sticky grey kaolin type, from the bed of the Linthipe river. The liquefier was a mixture of gum arabic and cow dung.

Care of crucibles
Crucibles rarely, if ever, last as long as the makers claim. On the other hand it is true that care and attention to the handling and storage of a crucible will make all the difference to its longevity.

- Anneal the crucible before use (warm it to drive off any moisture). It is a wise precaution to warm up any furnace or kiln *slowly* and increase the heat after about twenty minutes. Heating too rapidly causes spurling of the brickwork.

- The tongs and shank for lifting and pouring the crucible must be a good fit. If they only grip in a few places this puts a strain on the crucible.

- Do not overfill the crucible when it is cold, or jam or wedge ingots into the crucible, hot or cold. The metal expands as it heats. If the ingots are jammed tight in the crucible they will crack it. The correct practice is to place one ingot, or some scrap, in the pot, and add more metal as this melts.

- Store the crucibles in a warm dry place, mouth downwards, on wooden battens. Never leave a crucible touching an earth or cement floor, or anywhere else where it could take in moisture.

○ *Examine with care the condition of the crucible before placing it in the furnace.* If it shows any sign of cracking or spurling it should be rejected. Anyone who has seen a crucible crack open as it is lifted will agree that a damaged crucible is not worth the risk. Spoiling the moulds is the best result you can hope for in such an accident, at worst the uncontrolled flow of molten metal could cause severe injury to the casters.

Filling a mould with aluminium to cast a small part for an agricultural machine, using the green sand moulding technique in Malawi

D. Sand conditioning and testing

Conditioning

The essential qualities for a good moulding sand are as follows:

- Flowability
- Green strength
- Dry strength
- Refractoriness
- Permeability
- Friability
- Durability.

Flowability

The sand must flow easily into the mould. If it does not it will make the work of the moulder harder and take more time.

Green strength

The mould must retain its shape and not crumble or distort when the pattern is removed. The most usual cause of poor green or dry strength is a low clay content.

Dry strength

The mould must retain its shape as the sand dries out and stay in place as the metal flows into it.

Refractoriness

The sand must not change its nature as the molten metal flows into it. Obviously this is an ideal rarely attainable. Under the intense heat of iron or bronze, the surface layer *will* change and will probably need to be discarded when the sand is removed from the casting. This is less obvious with aluminium alloys which melt at a lower temperature. Therefore, the desirable sand should change *as little as possible* when heated.

Permeability

Air and gases must pass through the sand as the metal enters. If they do not they will cause blow holes or porosity in the metal. Too great a clay content restricts permeability.

175

Friability

Sand must be easily removed from the mould and, more critically, the core. The sand must not be so rigid and hard that it is impossible to remove, or can only be removed with difficulty. This seems to contradict the need for toughness in the sand, and some compromise has to be reached. The ideal sand should be tough and resistant to temperature increase until the casting has cooled in the mould and then break away easily.

Durability

Sand should retain the above essential qualities for as many castings as possible.

This list of essential properties is true for both natural and artificial sands. The last, durability, is not strictly an essential, but it is a highly desirable quality. Changing the stock of sand frequently adds to labour and cost.

Even if you are fortunate enough to build your foundry close to a supply of natural sand and can dig it up without paying for it, transport is an expensive addition to costs involved in moving the burnt sand out of the foundry.

Sand must be worked (or tempered) before use to return it to mouldable condition. It must be rolled to remove lumps and even out the texture; it must be riddled (sieved) to remove impurities, including core nails and fragments of metal or hard slag; it must be aerated by turning over with a shovel, or mechanical blade, to separate the grains so that the sand flows well and recovers permeability. A good quality moulding sand which has been thoroughly processed, is described as 'silky'.

The task of reconditioning the used sand can be done by a foundry worker with a shovel, a riddle and a roller. On the other hand, a machine can do the work quicker and more efficiently. Sand reworked through a muller (see below) tends to be more even and silkier than that worked by hand.

The muller

The most useful (almost essential) machine is the muller. 'Muller' is the German word for mill. The simplest form of crushing mill has always been powered by water or by oxen, and such mills can still be found all over the world. Today the more common muller is powered by an electric or petrol motor.

Natural sand needs a heavier muller while silica sand one with lighter rollers, to avoid crushing the grains.

The traditional muller has a vertical shaft driven by gearing so that it rotates slowly within a drum. Two heavy, cast iron rollers on a horizontal axle are fixed to the shaft with hinges. Two ploughs scrape the sand off the floor and wall of the cylinder. The hinges, or rockers, on the axle allow the rollers to ride over lumps, and the occasional metal fragment. These should be sieved out or removed with a magnetic separator, or by hand. A chute with a door in the side of the drum allows the sand to flow out into a barrow or buckets. Sometimes the chute drops the sand onto a riddle (sieve).

Mechanical riddle

This can be of the compressed air type where a piston forces the sand through a screen, or the type operated by an electric motor where the sieve is agitated by an eccentric cam. A moving belt carries the sand to the riddle which vibrates, or shuttles backwards and forwards to sieve the sand into a hopper.

Aerator

There are several types of aerator, some use impellers or rapidly rotating paddles, the simplest works on the Archimedean screw principle. A very coarse screw turns the sand over, 'fluffs it up', and extrudes it through a wide nozzle.

Sand testing equipment

Accurate testing is essential in a large modern foundry. Clearly, test equipment is a more accurate gauge than hand and eye, especially where large batches of sand are moulded, processed and reprocessed. On the other hand, most experienced moulders believe that apprentices and trainees should get the feel of the sand and learn to judge its quality before relying on test equipment, no matter how useful this equipment is.

Sand testing equipment is rarely found in a small family business where experienced moulders judge the condition of the sand by touch. The oldest test is to squeeze the sand in the hand. Even the newest apprentice learns rapidly to tell sand in mouldable condition from sand which is burnt out, or will not hold together – or the opposite: sand which is 'fat', meaning that it has too much clay in it, making it impermeable.

Routine testing

Sand is tested for the following qualities:

- Moisture content
- Permeability
- Green compression strength
- Total clay content
- Sieve analysis
- Combustibles

For cores:

- Sand grain shape and size
- Permeability
- Shear strength.

Moisture content

There are two methods. The first and most cumbersome is to bake out the water and measure the difference. The second, and more usual, is a small testing kit using an aluminium flask with a chamber containing calcium carbide. A measured quantity of sand is placed inside the chamber, the water in the sand combines with the calcium carbide to produce acetylene gas, which is measured on a gas pressure meter and thereby indicates the water content in the test specimen of sand.

177

Permeability

This measures how much air can flow through the sand and how fast.

Green compression strength

Measuring the toughness of the sand is more complicated and involves various different instruments. In each test a sample of sand is prepared in a standard sand rammer. For strength testing the sample is placed in a holder and squeezed mechanically until it breaks. The force applied to it registers on an indicator. By changing the holder, the same tester may be used for testing shear and tensile strengths.

The shatter test is another way of measuring sand toughness, particularly the capacity of the sand to withstand rough handling and strain during pattern withdrawal. The test machine is a simple gallows-like structure of a measured height which releases the prepared, rammed sample onto a steel plate (called the anvil). The broken pieces are placed on a 12mm mesh sieve. The shatter index is the ratio of the percentage of the weight retained on the sieve to the total weight. Too low or too high a value on the shatter index indicates poor moulding sand.

Clay content

The clay content tester works on the principle that sand grains sink and settle faster than the very fine particles of clay. Moulding sand (which is, of course, a mixture of sand and clay) is dried, ground down, sieved and weighed.

A measured quantity is placed in a jar which is filled with water and the jar placed in the testing machine – a shaker, or agitator. Jar and contents are agitated for a definite time, then allowed to settle for a definite time. Then the water is syphoned off. The clay, which is still suspended in the water is syphoned with it. Finally the sand is removed from the jar, dried and weighed. The difference between the first and the second weight is the clay content.

Sieve analysis

Grain size is measured using a standard sieve set. This consists of a set of sieves with a varying, but known, number of meshes, coarse mesh at the top, fine at the bottom.

After the clay and moisture have been separated from the sand, the sand is placed in the top sieve and shaken in a sieve shaker machine for a definite period. The quantity of sand remaining in each sieve is weighed and expressed as a percentage of the whole.

The grain fineness number can be used to compare fineness of different sands. More important is the distribution of different grain sizes. For good compaction of sand the amount retained in three or four consecutive sieves should be in the range of 75 to 80 per cent of the total quantity.

Combustibles

The percentage of organic combustible material should be as low as possible. These impurities reduce the refractoriness of the sand and cause gas evolution.

The amount of combustible matter is estimated by heating a weighed sand sample for one hour at 875°C, cooling and then weighing to find the percentage lost. This value is called 'loss on ignition'.

Conclusion

Permeability and strength are the two most important properties to look for when testing a moulding sand. These depend on the size and shape of the grains and on the clay content. However, these qualities cannot reach their potential unless the sand is mixed with the correct quantity of water and rammed to the correct degree of hardness.

The Bamoum foundries use a mixture of green sand and floor moulding methods to produce large cooking pots in aluminium, which is plentiful and cheap in Cameroon; this picture shows a smaller, French-type 'marmite' with lid and spoon

E. Other sand processes

Processes based on sodium silicate

Sodium silicate added to dry silica sand makes moulds in which drying, baking, and in some cases, even ramming, are unnecessary. The differences in processes lie in the type of chemical reaction which causes hardening, the quality of the hardener, and the nature of the catalyst.

Regarding pattern making: wood, resin or metal patterns are all suitable for these processes, though certain paints used on wooden patterns will not release easily from the sand (e.g. synthetic enamels). Shellac or varnish show better results on wood. If a paint is essential, use aluminium paint with a nitro-cellulose base.

The carbon dioxide–silica sand process

Of the three sodium silicate processes, this is the most widely, one could almost say universally, used in large and small foundries for both ferrous and non-ferrous castings.

The principle

If CO_2 gas is passed through a sand mixture containing sodium silicate binder, the mixture hardens by a chemical reaction between sodium silicate and CO_2. The bonding strength eliminates the need for drying or baking the mould and metal can be poured into the mould immediately.

The sand must be dry, cold, and free from clay. Usually the sand is mixed in a sand mixer with between 3% and 5% by volume of sodium silicate. The quantity of binder depends on the grain size of the sand. As the fineness grade increases, increase the percentage of binder.

The hardened sand mix has great compressive strength, which is one of its advantages. This virtue can cause problems with collapsibility (meaning the removal of the sand from the casting). For this reason one of several additives can be used to promote collapsibility after metal pouring. Dextrine, coal dust and wood flour are all popular.

The duration of the gassing process is important and can be determined by test gassing specimen batches of sand. Gassing is carried out for a predetermined time. The binder setting begins rapidly, but full strength is only reached after a certain amount of gas has passed through the sand.

Over-gassing should be avoided because it makes the mixture friable. The evidence of over-gassing is the appearance of white sodium bicarbonate crystals in the mixture. Practical experience shows that it is better to under-gas than over-gas, and that a low pressure of gas over a long period is preferable to a high pressure over a short period.

The most common form of gassing in small foundries is by a single cylinder of CO_2 using a pressure reducing valve. Too rapid a draw of gas will make the gas in the cylinder freeze. Larger foundries use either a battery of cylinders with a gas manifold, or a bulk storage tank.

There are various techniques for introducing the gas into the sand. The most common in a small foundry is a probe. This is a metal pipe (approximately 12mm diameter) attached to the reducing valve by a hose. The probe has several holes drilled in the end. Sometimes several probes are connected to one tube. The favourite method is to gas the sand flask from underneath using a cover board with a rubber seal and a tube connected to it. This can also be placed on top of the flask.

Advantages of the CO_2–silica sand process

The advantages of the process are:

o   Accuracy and good surface finish

o   Less moulding skill needed, therefore lower labour costs

o   Versatility. The process is used in large and small foundries, for ferrous and non-ferrous casting, jobbing and production foundries.

The materials are indigenous to most countries. The process is widely used in the Indian sub-continent, in southern and central America, and in most African countries.

The ferro-silicon (Fe–Si) process

This is also known as the 'Nishiyama' process. Silica sand is hardened and bonded during the reaction produced by exothermic action between sodium silicate and ferro-silicon powder. At room temperature the reaction is slow, but the reaction accelerates as the temperature is increased.

The process may be modified by adding a foaming agent to turn the sand mix into a flowable slurry.

Advantages

o   A versatile process used widely in foundries large and small, particularly in Japan and Russia

o   The slurry is poured into the flask and over the pattern, eliminating the need for ramming.

Disadvantages

o   The heat generated

o   The hydrogen gas generated.

Thorough ventilation is important in the Nishiyama process to allow the hydrogen by-product to escape. The combination of heat and a volatile gas makes an explosion possible, even likely, in a confined space.

The dicalcium silicate process

This is also called the 'fluid sand' process. The bonding principle here is the chemical reaction between sodium silicate and dicalcium silicate. Unlike the Fe-Si process described above, the chemical change involves a negligible amount of heat.

Dicalcium silicate can be produced from slags from various melting and reduction processes.

The most usual application is in large iron and steel-casting foundries. The process was widely used in Russia and Japan and is now also used in India.

Loam (or loom) moulding

The great advantage of loam moulding is its versatility, the disadvantage is its rarity. As heavy industry declines and demand for large one-off castings decreases, so loam moulders become a rarer and rarer breed.

In shipyards, such as Harland and Wolfe in Belfast, for example, massive castings were produced by this method without the expense of large patterns, using instead the simplest equipment and materials. A spindle, steel straps and a striking board were the necessary tools, the materials being loam, bricks and cinders, and the key ingredient is the skill and ingenuity of the moulder.

Loam sand mixture is very similar to green sand, but with one important difference: added moisture makes the mixture soft and pliable. The usual mixture consists of a light (or 'open') sand blended with a heavy, or clay-rich sand (known as 'fat' sand).

In the technique of bell-casting, fibrous material is added in the form of horsehair, horse dung, chopped straw or fine wood chippings. Though the technique does not exclude other forms, it is most suited to cylindrical, conical, or dome shapes of large size. Bells are the most common and obvious example, but in the past many large castings in iron were made for the cylinders of ships, locomotives, for large industrial pumps and electric motor housings.

The following description refers to bell-casting at the Fonderie des Cloches, Val de Poelles, Normandy, France. (As far as I know, loam moulding survives in Europe only in bell foundries, but the technique is the same for any other large cylindrical casting.)

The core is built up of brick on a cast iron plate. The brick armature has a centre of cinders which will absorb any air or gases which vent through the core. The plate has lugs on its circumference for attachment to a crane or hoist. Loam is built up over the brick armature, oversize.

The true shape of the core is refined by a strickle, made up of a striking board, the edge of which is sheet steel, cut to a template the exact size of the inside of the bell. The strickle hinges on a spindle revolving in a socket. The socket is cemented into the floor so that the spindle is set at a true vertical. As the striking plate turns it strickles (scrapes and polishes) the inside of the loam surface, which will form the inside surface of the casting.

The outer surface of the casting, named the cope, is formed in the same way, but the strickle forms the inside of the brick–loam construction instead of the outside. For smaller castings the cope is built up and strickled upside-down, inside a pre-formed

183

case (often metal but sometimes built of timber). An alternative, used for large castings, is to build the cope out of brick. This is done in sections or layers, each layer being divided from the one underneath by a ring-shaped iron plate.

In the former technique the case is lined with brick and then coated with a lining of loam. Once again, a strickle is cut to a template. The strickle edge cuts the shape of the outside of the bell. The mould is vented through pipes in the brickwork or sometimes straw set into the loam between the bricks.

Both the cope and the core are finished by hand, polished with wood ash and then baked in a kiln to remove all moisture. Finally, chains are attached to the iron plate, connected to the hoist, and the core is lowered into the pit.

Next the cope is turned over and lowered over the core. Great care is taken not to brush the surface of the core with the cope as it is lowered. The cope is located onto the iron base plate carefully to make sure that the space between core and cope is regular (it is obvious that an even thickness of metal is crucial to the sound of the bell).

In the case of a large bell, the brickwork is too heavy and fragile to be turned over, so the top section is built the right way up, the cap of the mould being turned over. Each section is lifted by lugs on its iron base plate and placed in the kiln to be dried. Then each section is lowered onto the core. Finally, the cap is lowered into place, and a gate and pouring basin modelled in sand around metal plugs which temporarily close off the runners.

Finally, the furnace opening is tapped and the molten bronze flows into the mould. A large bell is left to cool in the loam for several days.

F. Summary of ceramic shell investment process

Key elements

Waxes

o The wax should be strong and flexible

o Check waxes and sprues for strength before dipping

o Degrease in alcohol

o Dry in moving air current, moderate temperature

o Allow enough time for the wax to return to normal temperature

Building the shell

First coat (slurry)

o Colloidal silica (Syton X 30)

o Distilled water

o Molochite – fine 200 grade, or zircon flour (Zircosil 300)

The slurry is formed by a mixture of colloidal silica and Molochite 200. Many casters dilute the Syton with 50% distilled water for the first two coats. (If the coat is still difficult to remove from the finished casting, some casters recommend the addition of 30% fused silica flour.) Add extra Molochite 200 to the first coat slurry. Add a very small quantity of detergent. Mix thoroughly then let the slurry stand for an hour to release the air bubbles. Remix slowly and carefully.

First coat (stucco)

o Molochite 30/80

Drying

The first coat must be dried completely in moving air (at least 15°C) before the second coat can be added. Make sure that corners and blind ends are dried by using air tubes. The drying time is lengthy, preferably overnight. *The need for thorough drying of the first coat cannot be overstressed.*

185

Second coat (slurry)

o Syton diluted with distilled water

o Smaller quantity of Molochite 200 (thinner mixture).

Second coat (stucco)
Repeat as first stucco.

Third and subsequent coats

o Use Syton full strength

o Third, fourth and fifth stucco – Molochite 16/30

o Thorough drying is very important.

De-waxing
Flash de-wax.

Back-up coat

o One coat of slurry (full strength)

o For larger moulds use glass fibre to reinforce

o Be careful not to drop slurry or fibre into the mould.

Timetable for the investment process

This is a suggested timetable suitable for the water-based type of slurry. Alcohol based or ammonia setting slurries are much faster. In time you will work out your own timetable based on temperature and drying time.

Mixing the slurry

o Mix up a thick slurry (like double cream)

o Let it stand for two or three hours to let the air escape

o Stir very gently and thin down to a usable consistency, using a mixture of silica suspension and distilled water (if first or second coat, full strength for later coats).

Dip and stucco

Day one
About 11.00am: first coat
3.00pm (1500 hours): second coat
Dry overnight.

Day two

10.00am: third coat

12.15pm: fourth coat

3.15pm (1515 hours): fifth coat (this coat is not necessary for small shells).

Day three

9.30am: de-wax (this process takes most of the morning)

2.00pm (1400 hours): back-up coat, reinforce with glass fibre. Dry immediately with gas torch

3.00pm (1500 hours): light furnace and holding kiln. Warm fired shells up to dull red heat in holding kiln. Use an oxidizing flame to remove all the carbon remaining in the shells.

Cored shells

These take longer in order to remove the last traces of wax gas from the core. Cores need a slow gentle bake at a moderate heat.

Timing the metal melt

The time the metal takes to melt depends on the metal and the type of furnace. For bronze allow one to two hours (according to quantity of metal). The ceramic shells will not be harmed by heat-soak. For thin sections pour the metal when the moulds are red hot. For thicker sections the moulds should be 'cool' (meaning pink-hot). For very thin sections, or when using a high conductivity metal like silver, it is worth considering building a heat trough where the shells are heated by a flame as the silver is poured into them. Silver is notorious for rapid freezing.

Summary of common problems and safety precautions

Waxes

Waxes used for the ceramic shell method need to be tougher and more flexible than those used for the block method. The wax should not be brittle, neither should it sag or be too soft.

The core

There are two methods for producing the core:

1. A conventional Roman core (grog and plaster)
2. Cut and weld (Benin method). Invest wax in the form of a tube. Make sure that the air circulates inside to dry thoroughly.

Wax welding

Take care that the welds are strong and well fused.

The sprue system

The main runner and cup are often larger than in other methods to aid progressive solidification. The sprue has several functions:

As a support. The sprue system must be strong enough to support the wax during investing. During drying it must either stand up or be hooked up to allow air to circulate.

It flows the molten metal to every part of the casting as quickly as possible.

As well as aiding progressive solidification, the sprue prevents shrinkage on the casting by feeding more metal to the thicker sections.

Though Roman style risers are not necessary (air escapes through the porous shell) one or two open or blind vents at the top of the wax prevent dirt or inclusions becoming trapped in the casting.

Degreasing

Add a very small quantity of liquid detergent to alcohol (either isoproponol or methylated spirits). Allow sufficient drying time for the wax to return to normal temperature.

Building the shell

Materials

- Binder (liquid) 1030 (coloidal silica)
- Slurry – binder with molochite 200 (or zircon flour)
- Fine stucco – molochite 30/80
- Coarse stucco – molochite 16/30

First coat

Add an equal amount of distilled water to colloidal silica, then add Molochite 200 to make a creamy slurry. This must be thick enough to coat the wax well. Test the covering quality of the slurry by dipping a wax test strip. Let the slurry settle for about two hours to remove bubbles. Remix gently, adding a teaspoon of detergent (wetting agent).

Dip wax in the slurry, then stucco with Molochite 30/80. Dry thoroughly in a moving air current (at least 15°C). Allow enough time for the first coat to dry, paying attention to the inside forms, or any deep crevices or hollows. The first coat will take between one to two hours to dry.

Second coat

This consists of the same slurry mixture thinned down with more of the liquid (50% colloidal silica and 50% water). This time the cream must be thin enough to coat the dried first coat. Stucco with Molochite 30/80. This coat needs more drying time than the first – about six hours. Leaving it overnight is a good plan.

Third and subsequent coats

For the third coat use the binder at full strength. Mix colloidal silica with Molochite 200 to make a thin cream. Use the coarser stucco – Molochite 16/30. Dry for two hours.

Apply fourth and fifth coat in the same way. Dry between coats.

De-waxing

Flash de-wax. Shell is plunged into preheated furnace. The outer layer of wax melts too fast, to expand and crack the wax.

Final or back-up coat

After de-waxing apply one full-strength coat to the shell. Take care not to drop any inside the mould. Where needed this can be reinforced with glass fibre. As the wax has gone there is no danger of wax expansion, so the shell can be dried rapidly near a flame.

Baking

De-waxing removes the wax; however, the moulds need a period in an oven at a lower temperature (pink heat) to remove all traces of carbon and wax gas. Maintain an oxidizing flame. Do not overheat because this weakens the glass fibre reinforcement. The moulds will need extra time if using a conventional core. This needs to be heat-soaked to remove any wax gas. The bigger the core, the longer the baking time.

Metal pouring – filling the moulds

The ceramic shell moulds must be very hot. Keep in the holding kiln until the last moment before filling the moulds.

Removing the shell

Use a matting chisel and wire brush. Sand and water blast. To remove really stubborn or deep seated traces of shell, use caustic soda or an acid pickle (hazardous – see notes on safety, below).

Hydrofluoric acid

This is used for removing stubborn traces of shell. Dilute with water, and observe safety precautions.

Note: It is vital to always take safety precautions when using hydrofluoric acid. Even diluted acid can be extremely dangerous because the water content evaporates (for example, on clothing) and the acid eventually returns to full strength.

Diluting

The acid is usually supplied in 2.5 litre plastic containers at 60% strength. Dilute the acid to 1 part acid to 6 parts water. I use a large blue plastic drum with 15 litres of water, using full safety clothing, immerse the bottle of acid in the water, then remove the cap. Nothing happens with the bottle in this position. When you invert the bottle the acid flows out leaving a colourless, oily looking trace in the water. The water becomes cloudy and fumes. Cover the drum, lock it and let the mixture settle. For larger quantities, dilute 40 litres of water to 3 bottles of acid.

Acid cleaning

To clean, for example, a bronze with texture and deep undercuts which trap the shell:

1. Place in acid for two hours.

2. Dip in alkaline liquid (lime in water) to neutralize acid.

3. If traces of shell remain, wire-brush out as much of the shell as possible (remember to wear a dust mask). Re-immerse the bronze in the acid for four and a half hours. This will soften the last of the shell. Limewash again and brush off the last traces of shell.

Safety precautions

Use an acid container with a lockable lid, and place it inside another container filled with lime, which will neutralize any spillage. Have a bucket of lime water nearby to neutralize the acid on the castings and, no less important, any spills on the floor, on your clothing or boots. *Always* use a full set of safety clothing – chemical protection suit, face mask, gas mask with anti-acid filter, anti-acid rubber gloves and rubber boots. Periodically test the gloves by filling them with air and placing them up to the wrists in water. Tiny bubbles will show up punctures invisible to your eye. Have an alkaline solution handy to neutralize the hydrofluoric acid.

Remember: unlike most acids, you will not feel the effects of hydrofluoric acid until the damage is done. You cannot smell it, and it looks like a harmless colourless liquid. If you do spill some on your skin, immediately neutralize with alkaline solution. Wash

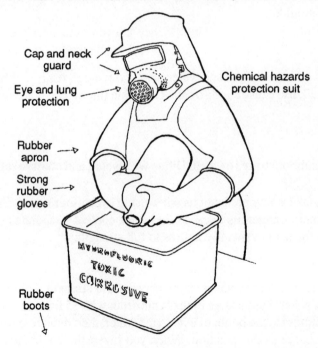

Cap and neck guard

Eye and lung protection

Chemical hazards protection suit

Rubber apron

Strong rubber gloves

HYDROFLUORIC
TOXIC
CORROSIVE

Rubber boots

Figure 138. Full protection is essential when handling hydrofluoric acid

skin with soap and water and then apply calcium glutonate gel. This is sold in a tube as a 2.5 solution. If you suspect that your skin has been seriously contaminated, take calcium tablets ('Sandocal' tablets, made by Sandoz).

Alternative method of removing the shell

Silica can be dissolved by caustic alkalis. There are three methods in use in industry:

1. Molten caustic bath

2. Boiling caustic solution (atmospheric pressure)

3. Boiling caustic solution in an autoclave (raised pressure). This method is not practical in a small workshop.

Caustic soda (NaOH or sodium hydroxide) and caustic potash (KOH or potassium hydroxide) are both used to remove the last traces of ceramic shell, or to leach out ceramic cores. The former is more usual.

Most refractories are inert, meaning not affected by chemical attack. The main exception is silica. The bond between the refractory grains in the ceramic shell is silica, but in such a form that the chemical attack is very slow. However, if you add from 20% to 30% fine fused silica, the caustic dissolves this first, allowing the non-siliceous refractory fines and stucco particles to wash out. Experiment has proved that frequent washing in water between periods of immersion in the caustic bath speeds up this leaching process.

Caustic alkalis are dangerous. You must, for your own protection, study and observe the safety precautions.

Molten caustic bath

Caustic soda can be melted in a cast iron pot, or a stress relieved mild steel pot (this must contain a sludge tray). The pot can be heated either externally or using an immersion heater. An exhaust hood must be placed over the pot to remove the fumes. The minimum temperature is 400°C and the maximum 500°C. The caustic fumes badly above 500°C and the pot deteriorates rapidly.

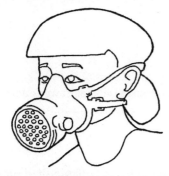

Figure 139. Acid vapour, solvents and many other chemical fumes can damage the lungs: when degreasing, patinating, or using concentrated acid, protect lungs against fumes

Figure 140. When investing, protect lungs against silica, molochite, grog and plaster

Pre-heated castings are lowered into the caustic in a basket. Agitating the pot, or raising and lowering the basket, speeds the rate of leaching out (do not wash the casting between dippings). *Caustic solution is dangerous. Wear eye protection and full chemical safety clothing.*

Boiling caustic solution

This should be 20% to 25% caustic by weight. This concentration boils at 121°C. Maintain the solution at boiling point in a mild steel container which has an inner lining of stabilized austenitic stainless steel. As the water evaporates, add de-mineralized water.

Washing the castings in water for one minute for every five of immersion in caustic increases the speed of leaching.

Caustic solution is dangerous. Wear eye protection and full chemical safety clothing (as recommended for hydrofluoric acid).

o Agitate the bath or basket during leaching.

o Do not use too high a concentration of caustic; this causes a low solubility phase which will be difficult to remove. Check the concentration by titration against standard acid solutions.

o Position the castings with the areas you want to clean (or cored holes) uppermost. If these holes face down, gas becomes trapped, shielding the refractory from the caustic, and this slows down the process.

o Do not allow leached castings to dry while some of the refractory remains. If you do, the residues will be extremely difficult to remove.

o When the process is complete, wash the castings in dilute acid and then rinse well in water. *Wear eye protection and protective clothing.*

Figure 141. When pickling castings, protect eyes, hands and skin against weak acid

Troubleshooting

The following is a list of common problems encountered in the ceramic shell process:

o *Wax or sprue breaks when handled during investment.* Either the welds are not secure (not well fused) or the wax is too brittle. Add beeswax or soft micro-crystalline. If the wax is too soft and sags, add tree resin.

192

- *First coat sloughs off the wax.* The mixture is too thin. Add more fine refractory powder to the slurry.

- *First coat will not stick, or sticks in places and the wax rejects it in others.* There are two possible reasons for this: either the wax is not properly degreased (wash it in water, dry it and then repeat the degreasing process), or there was no wetting agent in the slurry (add a small quantity of liquid detergent). A third reason is that the slurry may be too thin. Or it could be a combination of all three reasons.

- *Second coat 'balls up' on the first.* This usually means that the second coat is too thick. Thin it down. Some casters recommend dipping the dried first coat into liquid colloidal silica before dipping in the second coat slurry.

- *Second coat removes patches of the first coat.* This is a sure sign that the first coat has not dried properly. The places where it is likely to happen are the sharp crevices or blind caves where air has not reached and circulated as it should. It is essential that air circulates. Use the hair dryer and tubes trick. To patch the faulty mould, paint in some slurry onto the exposed patch of wax, stucco and dry it, then continue as normal.

- *The shell comes off in patches on the cup.* This cannot be avoided if you are handling the sprue system by the cup. You must patch the cup as you go, and make sure that it is properly reinforced after the wax burn-out. The only alternative is to build in a stainless steel hook from which wax and sprue systems are suspended during drying. Many small industrial investment foundries prefer this method.

- *Shell collapses during de-waxing.* This will only happen during cold weather. The temperature is so low that the ceramic shell has not bonded together as it should. I am sorry to say that the whole batch is wasted, there is no way of retrieving it. Check the colloidal silica for signs that it is separating out, it will do this if the temperature drops below freezing. The only cure for this problem is to keep the foundry above freezing point. Shell will not dry and bond below 20°C (70°F).

- *Shell cracks and metal weeps out of the mould during metal filling.* These cracks are usually tiny (I have never seen a large one). Either the first coat was put on while the wax was chilled (during degrease) or the wax has expanded during the de-wax process, probably because the heat was not intense enough, or the wax heated slowly, or the shell and wax were stored somewhere with an uneven temperature. If, for example, the wax was stored in a cool place in the morning and a shaft of sunlight moved round and warmed it in the afternoon, this could expand the wax and crack the shell. The immediate cure is a wad of glass fibre, or ceramic fibre blanket dipped in slurry and plastered over the weep. This poultice will harden on contact with the hot metal and staunch the flow. Long term prevention entails keeping your waxes stored in an even temperature. Avoid sudden temperature changes and flash de-wax (plunge the shell into a pre-heated furnace chamber).

193

○ *Shell is difficult to remove after the metal casting has cooled.* This is rare, or even impossible, on smooth surfaces because the metal shrinks as it cools and the shell detaches itself. However, it is a notorious problem with art casting because the shell clings into fine detail (such as hair, texture and deep crevices in the form). These white deposits are unsightly and also blunt metal chasing tools. There are several ways of removing the last traces of shell and these are described on pages 187 to 190.

Further reading

Four books which are useful when setting up a small foundry business

Aspin, B.T. *Foundrywork for the Amateur*. Model and Allied Publications Ltd, UK (1969).
   An excellent short handbook, not solely for amateurs. Highly recommended.

Brown, J. *The FOSECO Foundrymen's Handbook*. Butterworth-Heinemann, UK (Revised edition, 1994).
   Very clear and extremely useful reference book.

Jain, P.L. *Principles of Foundry Technology*. Tata McGraw-Hill Publishing, New Delhi (Second edition, 1991).
   An excellent, highly practical reference book, especially suitable for the Indian subcontinent and S.E. Asia. Highly recommended.

Titov, N. and Stepanov, Y.A. *Foundry Practice*. Mir Publications, Moscow, USSR. (English translation, 1981).
   Old-fashioned, but practical, and thoroughly sound book. Includes sections on how to make fluxes and other foundry chemicals which I have not found anywhere else. Highly recommended.

Useful books for the small foundry

Alexander, W.O., Davies, G.J., Reynolds, K.A. and Bradbury, E.J. *Essential Metallurgy for Engineers*. Van Nostrand Reinhold Publications, UK (1985).
   As the title indicates, essential information for any caster who wants to understand what metal does when it changes from its liquid to its solid state.

Alexander, W. and Street, A. *Metals in the Service of Man*. Penguin Books Ltd, UK (Ninth edition, 1989).
   Interesting and enlightening introduction to the behaviour of metals.

American Foundry Society. *Metal Casting Dictionary* (1968), *Casting Copper Base Alloys* (1980), *Aluminium Casting Technology* (1980), *Report on the Conference on Green Sand Technology* (1980), *Pattern Makers' Manual* (1980).
   Published by the American Foundrymen's Society, USA.

Ammen, C.W. *Sand Casting*. TAB Books, USA (1979).
   Apart from the introduction, a thoroughly practical and useful handbook.

Ammen, C.W. *Lost-wax Investment Casting*. TAB Books, USA (1977).

Written for a wealthy society; the author assumes that any material can be bought easily and cheaply. Poor on waxes and alternative methods, but it does contain much useful information.

Hudson, R.F. *Non Ferrous Castings*. Chapman and Hall, London (1948).

Very good on problem solving, particularly sand problems, furnaces and oil burners.

Hudson, F.D. *Gun-metal Castings*, MacDonald, UK (1967).

Laing, J. and Rolfe, R.T. *A Manual of Foundry Practice*. Chapman and Hall, UK. (Second edition 1938. Third edition 1960).

Highly recommended if you can get hold of a copy. Unfortunately now out of print.

Laing, J. and Rolfe, R.T. *Non-ferrous Foundry Practice*. Chapman and Hall (1939).

Libouton, J.M. 'Precision Foundry: The ceramic shell process'. *Monsanto Technical Bulletin*. Monsanto Europe SA, Belgium (1984).

Investment Precision Casting. Machinery Yellow Book, Series No.35. The Machinery Publishing Co. Ltd, USA (Approx 1950, reprinted 1966).

Useful summary of alternative methods of lost-wax casting in industry rather than art casting.

Midland Foundry Industries Training Centre. Course Handbook. Foundry Industries Training Board, UK (1977).

NALCO. *Investment Casting*. NALCO Chemical Co., USA (1970).

Nelson, E. *Course Handbook, Foundry Processes and Techniques*. Belfast College of Technology (1980).

Rusinoff, S.E. *Foundry Practices*. American Technical Association, USA (1955).

Excellent. University level.

Salmon and Simons. *Foundry Practice*. Pitman, UK (1960).

Simons, E.N. *A Dictionary of Foundry Work*. Crosbie Lockwood, UK (1972).

Webster, P.D. *Fundamentals of Foundry Technology*. Portcullis Press, UK (1980).

Specialized books

Colson, F.A. *Kiln Building with Space-age Materials*. Van Nostrand Reinhold Co., USA (1975).

Written for an American market. Most of the materials will be too expensive (or unobtainable) for developing countries, nevertheless contains much useful practical advice.

Davis, H. *The Potter's Alternative*. Methuen, Australia.

Although this impressive book is concerned with equipping a pottery, some of the equipment for which he gives construction details is also useful for a foundry, for example a pug mill.

Davies and Delman. *Metallurgical Processes and Production Technology*. Pitman, UK (1985).

Dunn, R.J. *Appropriate Technology*. MacMillan, UK (1978).

Gettens. *The Freer Chinese Bronzes*. Smithsonian Institute, USA (1969).

Gingery, D.J. *Build your own Metalworking Shop from Scrap: The Charcoal Foundry*. D.J. Gingery, 2045 Boonville, Springfield, Mo 65803, USA (1983).
   A useful do-it-yourself book by an American backyard enthusiast, dealing with small-scale sand casting in aluminium (the first in a series concerned with the house-building of machine tools using car parts).

Harper, J.D. *Small Scale Foundries in Developing Countries*. IT Publications (1981).
   Excellent general book for foundry managers. Does not attempt to be a 'do-it-yourself' book.

Herbert, E.W. *Red Gold of Africa: Copper in pre-colonial history and culture*. University of Wisconsin Press, USA (1984).

Rhodes, D. *Kilns: Design, Construction and Operation*. Chilton Books, USA (1974).
   Highly recommended. Covers design of kilns from all over the world. Practical, useful diagrams and photographs.

UNECE. *Engineering Equipment for Foundries*. Pergamon, UK (1979).

Untract, O. *Metal Techniques for the Craftsman*. Doubleday, USA (1968).

Webster, P.D. (ed.) *Fundamentals of Foundry Technology*. Portcullis Press, UK (1980).

Willet, F. *Ife in the History of West African Sculpture*. Thames and Hudson, UK (1967).

Modern translations

Agricola, G. *De Re Metallica*. Basle 1556. Trans: Hoover and Hoover. Dover Publications, USA (1950).

Biringuccio. *De La Pyrotechnia*. Venice 1559. Trans: Smith and Gaudi. Aimme, USA (1965).

Brossand, M. *The Casting of the Equestrian Figure of Louis XIV*. Paris 1699. Trans: Helen Tullenberg. Picton Publishing, UK (1974).

Taking technology off the back shelf

The following are examples of a great many books of the period 1900-60. All those that I have seen have been obsolete for the modern foundry industry but well-written, practical and useful to someone setting up from scratch with little capital and some general practical common sense. Books of this period do not assume that you can go out and buy the parts or chemicals you need. In many cases they tell you how to improvise or make them. Although they are out of print, there are many copies about, and a library may be able to obtain one.

Buchanan, J.F. *Brassfounders' Alloys*. E. & F.N. Spon Ltd, UK (1901).

FOSECO Technical Publications. *FOSECO Foundrymen's Handbook*. UK (Seventh edition, 1964); Pergamon Press, UK (Eighth edition, 1975).

This handbook has been produced by different publishers in Britain and the USA over a period of forty years. The most recent edition (Butterworth-Heinemann, 1994) is excellent but, for the small foundry, earlier editions are as useful.

FOSECO produced a large number of technical leaflets as well as a quarterly magazine, *Foundry Practice*. Old copies contain much valuable information. They are well worth collecting.

Horner, J.G. *Practical Iron Founding*. Whittaker & Co., UK (1914).

Laing, J. and Rolf, R.T. *A Manual of Foundry Practice*. Chapman and Hall, UK (1938).

Laing, J. and Rolf, R.T. *Non-ferrous Foundry Practice*. Chapman and Hall, UK (1939).

Laing, J. and Rolf, R.T. *A Manual of Foundry Practice for Cast Iron*. Chapman and Hall, UK (1960).

McWilliam, A. and Longmuir, P. *General Foundry Practice*. Chas. Griffin, London (1912).

Richards, W.H. *Principles of Pattern and Foundry Practice*. McGraw-Hill Publications, USA (1930).

Good design patterns for feeding and venting. Much useful advice on woodwork and pattern making.

Spon's Workshop Receipts. E. & F.N. Spon Ltd, UK (1909).

Spon's technical books were published in four volumes and a supplement printed in 1930. It is rare, but if you can get hold of a set it will prove invaluable. Spon's contains every formula you can imagine, from how to build an acetylene gas plant to making soap; from dyeing cloth to building pumps. Several different publishers printed similar technical encyclopaediae at the turn of the century.

The International Correspondence Schools Library

Malleable Casting, Brass Founding, Smithing and Forging. ICS, UK (1901, reprinted 1903, 1905, 1906); *Woodworking, Pattern-making, Core-moulding, Cast Iron*. ICS, Scranton Textbook Co., USA (1901, reprinted 1903, 1905); *Foundry Appliances, Malleable Casting, Brass Founding*. ICS Reference Library. Vol 11B. ICS, UK (1922).

These books (among others) were designed for foundry apprentices and engineering students, and printed between 1900 and 1940 in both london and New York. Consequently, they are found in second-hand bookshops all over the English-speaking areas, the USA, the Commonwealth and former colonies.

Glossary

Note: Sand casting and lost-wax casting terms vary slightly. Where appropriate, or where there is danger of confusion, lost-wax terms are marked 'LW' (see note at end of glossary).

ADOBE Sun-dried brick.

AGGREGATE Large particles or grains, usually of sand or other refractory. In concrete or plaster, larger particles are introduced to add strength to the mixture.

AGITATE To shake or move rapidly.

ALUM A chemical used in solution to harden the surface of gelatine used in a flexible mould.

ALUMINIUM Pure aluminium is valuable as a conductor of heat or electricity; it is too soft to have an engineering use. The term 'aluminium' covers a wide range of alloys. An extremely useful metal, it is not as easy to cast as might at first appear. For best results, special fluxes and de-gassers are needed, while certain alloys need grain refinement (usually by a sodium modifier – q.v.). Aluminium was first made from the ore bauxite by Sainte Claire Delville in 1854, but was too expensive for commercial use. In 1886 the discovery of the electrolytic process (coincidentally by both Hall in the USA and Heroult in France) led to the evolution of the aluminium industry. In the early twentieth century, German metallurgists discovered the advantage of adding a small quantity of copper (less than 5%) to make a light, very strong alloy. The result possessed a mysterious property called age hardening. Named 'duralumin' it was first used to build zeppelins during the 1914-18 war, later for every type of aircraft.

ALUMINIUM BRONZE A copper-aluminium alloy, with between 8% and 11% copper, used widely in shipbuilding, aircraft and defence industries; for pump impellers, bearings and hydro-electric turbines. Because it picks up oxide easily it is not an easy metal to cast, but it is exceptionally strong and corrosion-resistant.

AMBIENT TEMPERATURE Surrounding temperature: usually refers to the outside air temperature.

AMORPHOUS SILICA (see also silica). Takes many forms. One of them is calcined china clay, used as a stucco for the ceramic shell process (q.v.). Amorphous silica can be dissolved by caustic alkalis, a common way to remove the last traces of the shell on the casting.

ANNEAL, ANNEALING The process of heating metal or alloy to a temperature below its melting point, maintaining the temperature for a time, and then cooling

199

slowly. The process of annealing generally confers softness. In reference to crucibles it is the process of slow heating to drive out moisture.

ARMATURE The strengthened centre of a pattern. Usually refers to a metal or wooden skeleton inside a clay model.

ASHLAND PROCESS Silica sand is mixed with a resin binder. A catalyst, in the form of a gas or liquid, is added to and cures the resin–sand mixture and makes a rigid, durable mould.

ASPIRATION The tendency of molten metal to draw in air as it is poured into the mould (see turbulence).

AUTOCLAVE A pressure chamber where a combination of dry heat and pressure evacuates the wax from the mould. Used in the aircraft industry for de-waxing ceramic shell moulds without the use of fire.

BACKING SAND (also floor sand; black sand). Sand, generally from used moulds, for filling in the mould between the facing sand layers.

BAG WALLS Walls inside a kiln to separate the moulds from the direct flame.

BALL CLAY A special class of natural refractory plastic clay, sometimes used for bonding synthetic sand mixtures.

BANK SAND (see silica sand).

BENTONITE A colloidal clay, essentially of the mineral known as montmorillonite, which swells and becomes plastic on wetting. Used as a bonding agent for silica sand.

BINARY ALLOY An alloy composed of only two major ingredients, such as copper and zinc. An alloy with three ingredients is known as a 'ternary alloy'.

BINDER, BONDING AGENT Any material which holds together a refractory or inert material. Cereal, vegetable oil, molasses, resin, etc. For example, plaster is the binder used to hold silica sand together in the lost-wax process. In green sand casting, clay is used as the binder.

BLACK SCALE (LW) Hard, rough skin on casting, caused by metal–mould reaction when the metal is poured too hot.

BLACKING or BLACKWASH A powdered carbonacious material applied in a spirit or water suspension to the surface of moulds and cores (usually plumbago in alcohol).

BLAST Air driven into a cupola or other furnace for the combustion of fuel.

BLAST CLEANING A process using air or water under pressure to direct an abrasive onto the casting being cleaned.

BLEMISHES Faults, small holes or depressions in a casting.

BLIND FEEDER (also called blind riser). A feeder which is not directly open to the atmosphere, which forms part of the running and gating system.

BLOCK INVESTMENT (LW) See also Italian method. The Romans altered the casting process developed in the eastern Mediterranean to suit a northern climate. They used plaster instead of clay as a binder, and it is probable that they invented the first flexible moulds. These developments put lost-wax foundries into a form of mass production.

BLOW HOLES Major faults. Holes in the casting caused by gas or steam trapped in the metal (see also wax gas).

BOTT or BOD A conical plug of refractory clay in the tapping hole of the furnace to stop the flow of metal.

BOTTOM BOARD A board of wood or metal to carry moulds or cores.

BOX Container for part of the sand mould (see also cope and drag and flask).

BRASS A general description of a range of copper-zinc alloys. Red brass (10-20% zinc) was the first brass to be worked because it could be easily cold-worked, beaten and formed. The addition of zinc makes brass both harder and more difficult to work. Brass casting as an industry started in Europe in the middle of the sevententh century using standard yellow brass (35% zinc). In 1840, Munz discovered that a brass could be hot rolled and worked with 40% zinc, hence its name, Munz metal.

BRAZING The joining of metal using an alloy of lower melting point.

BRICK MUFFLE Simple, improvised furnace used for slow heating or cooling a casting either for heat treatment or welding (see muffle).

BRONZE General term to describe a copper-based alloy which contains zinc, tin and sometimes lead (see also gun-metal). All tin bronzes flow and cast well, but unlike the brasses, cannot be either hot, or cold formed. They are not suitable either for rolling or hammering. A soft, easy flowing bronze, LG2, is described as a leaded gunmetal (copper 85%, tin, zinc and lead 5% each). Applied to early sculptures, or used in ethnography, the term 'bronze' means almost any copper-based alloy. Phosphor bronze was discovered in 1870 and was used principally for electrical applications. It can be cold worked and is excellent for springs and electrical contacts. More recently it has been used for bushes and bearings.

BUCKLING A fault similar to a scab. Describes the effect on a casting of the movement of the sand mould surface under the combined heat and pressure of a quantity of molten metal, allowing the metal to leak under the surface.

BURNER A device which mixes fuel with air and can be regulated to provide a good combustion when the mixture is burned.

BURNING ON 1. A fusion of the sand at the pouring temperature, causing it to react chemically with the surface of the casting to form an adherent slag skin which is rough and difficult to remove; 2. A method of repairing a defective casting common in ancient times, and still used where there is no gas or arc welding available.

BURNISHING Polishing by friction or pressure.

BURN-OUT (LW) Slang term describing the de-waxing process, particularly with reference to ceramic shell (see de-waxing and flash de-waxing).

CALCINING (see also amorphous silica). The heat treatment of gypsum in its chalk-like state to return it to its dry state. This is particularly valuable in traditional lost-wax casting as a by-product of the kiln burn-out of the wax. The refractory plaster mixture can be ground down and re-used (see ludo).

CARBON DIOXIDE–SILICA SAND A sand in which the bonding agent is based on sodium silicate, hardened by the passage of carbon dioxide (CO_2) gas.

CASE The retaining shell of a flexible mould, usually made of plaster, sometimes glass fibre resin.

CASTING An object produced by the process of introducing molten metal into a cavity of the required shape by gravity, centrifugal force or pressure.

CASTING STRESS The latent stress left in a casting as a direct result of the production process.

CATALYST A substance that precipitates or accelerates a chemical reaction. In casting this refers in particular to the hardening of synthetic resins or rubbers for mould making, or for the making of patterns in synthetic resins.

CATENARY KILN A kiln built as an arch with no division between wall and roof.

CEMENT SAND (Randupson process). A process in which moulds and cores are made from a mixture of silica sand, cement and water.

CENTRE LINE SHRINKAGE Shrinkage cavities found near the centres of castings of uniform section. Due to insufficient feeding and poor directional solidification.

CENTRIFUGAL CASTING Casting molten metal into a rotating mould. The axis of rotation may be horizontal, inclined or vertical. Very common in jewellery casting.

CENTRIFUGE Casting machine which uses centrifugal force, rather than gravity, to introduce metal into the mould.

CERAMIC FIBRE An advanced, and exceptionally efficient, lightweight refractory which resembles cotton wool.

CERAMIC SHELL A form of precision investment casting, the ceramic shell process is the great-grandchild of the clay slurry (q.v.) method (see chapter 7 describing this process).

CEREAL BINDER An addition which imparts cohesiveness or bond strength to foundry sands. The addition can be of wheat or rye flour. Most modern binders are starches and dextrins which are produced from cereals.

CHAMOTTE A bonded, calcined, crushed and graded refractory clay. Used extensively on the continent as a substitute for compo (q.v.) in the making of large moulds.

CHAPLETS Stainless steel pins used to hold the core (q.v.) in its correct position.

CHARGE A specific quantity of materials charged into the melting furnace to produce molten metal of the composition required.

CHASE To refine the surface of a casting by grinding, filing, or chiselling.

CHEMICAL CHANGE A change in the properties of a material, always accompanied by heat. For example, the addition of water to a plaster makes it first into a slurry (q.v.), secondly into a solid. The plaster becomes perceptibly warmer as it solidifies. This can be a problem in the catalytic action of a synthetic resin, where the chemical change produces heat, and the heat accelerates change, each speeding up the other.

CHILL A material or component of high thermal conductivity used in moulds or cores to accelerate cooling and to control structure in the casting.

CHINA CLAY (kaolin). A hydrated aluminium agent, in general of low plasticity, used as a bonding agent. It includes ball clay (q.v.) and fireclay (q.v.).

CHUCKING SPIGOT An extra piece on the pattern, similar to a core print (q.v.) which, in the casting, is held in the lathe chuck for turning (q.v.).

CINDERS Burnt remnants of coke after combustion.

CIRE PERDU (LW) See lost wax.

CLAY A finely-divided mineral substance containing hydrated aluminium silicate. It is the common binding agent in foundry sands.

CLAY SLURRY (LW) General term for the traditional Indian and West African method of lost-wax casting. There are local variations, but the principle remains the same. The wax is coated with a slurry of clay, dung and silica sand; then dried and re-coated. The final coats consist of slurry mixed with vegetable fibre such as rice husk, palm fibre, or coconut husk, to make a porridge-like mixture. Fired out, the shell mould is much thinner than the block-like Italian mould. Its lack of bulk allows a shorter kiln-firing time, thus making a considerable saving in fuel.

CLAY WASH Clay diluted with water to a creamy consistency.

CMC American term 'cold moulding compound' (see RTV).

CO_2 Carbon dioxide gas. Commonly used in the carbon dioxide–silica sand (q.v.) process.

COD A projection of the sand mould, off the cope (q.v.) or drag (q.v.), to form a cavity in the casting.

COKE Coal from which gas has been extracted. Furnace coke is coke with the physical and chemical properties for use in a blast furnace. High carbon coke is a slow-burning coke with low ash content. Often used in cupola (q.v.) furnaces.

COLD SHUT (or cold lap). A casting defect which is caused when two streams of molten metal meet and do not unite.

COLLAPSIBILITY The quality in a casting sand which allows it to be easily removed after casting. Applies in particular to core sand.

COLLOID An uncrystallizable, semi-solid substance capable of only very slow diffusion or penetration. A chemical which aids the suspension of solids in a liquid, e.g. fine molochite (q.v.) suspended in colloidal silica (q.v.) in the ceramic shell (q.v.) process.

COLLOIDAL SILICA (also called silica gel when used for absorption). Minute grains of silica in suspension in water. Alkaline in character. The liquid part of the silica slurry used in the ceramic shell (q.v.) process.

COMPO (Sheffield composition). A moulding material composed of a mixture of crushed and graded firebrick and a refractory clay, used to produce heavy steel castings but also useful for general kiln and furnace repair (see also grog).

COMPRESSION STRENGTH Resistance to pressure. For example, cast iron has great strength under compression, but little tensile strength (q.v.).

CONDUCTIVITY (electrical or thermal). The measure of the ability of a substance to allow the passage of electricity or heat. Copper is an example of a good conductor; rubber a bad one.

CONDUIT A channel, canal or pipe. It carries molten metal into the mould.

CONTRACT To draw into a smaller space.

CONTRACTION Shrinkage, metal expands as it melts, and contracts as it solidifies.

CONTRACTION ALLOWANCE The amount by which a pattern or corebox is made oversize to compensate for the shrinkage of the casting after solidification. Also known as pattern maker's allowance, or shrinkage.

CONTRACTION RULE (also known as pattern maker's rule). A ruler which allows for contraction. Rules are available for different metals and alloys.

COPE The top half of the mould flask (q.v.), the other being the drag (q.v.).

CORE Sand compacted into a given shape and inserted into the mould before it is closed. The core forms an internal cavity in the casting which cannot be shaped by the mould.

CORE BAR A metal former or bar around which cores are constructed. Its function is to stiffen the core and often to assist in its handling.

CORE BOX Mould, usually made of wood, for forming the sand core. Also known as core mould.

CORE NAIL Nail or chaplet (q.v.) for retaining the core in place.

CORE PIN Small core nail.

CORE PLATE Plates onto which cores are turned out and transported to the oven and which are used to support them during baking.

CORE PRINT The extra piece on a core which allows the core to be held in place in a mould.

CORE OVEN or CORE STOVE A simple kiln in which cores are dried by heat.

CORE VENT Wax, inflammable plastic or similar material which forms a pipe (or vent) in the core when burnt off.

COVER FLUX Powder which, when heated, turns to a glassy material on the top of the molten metal, excluding the gases present in the atmosphere. Also acts as a slag coagulant (q.v.).

CRUCIBLE Refractory container or pot used to melt metal. Crucibles were usually made of a clay, graphite, silica sand mixture. Now silicon carbide is a common ingredient. Modern crucibles are mechanically strong as well as having extreme resistance to thermal shock.

CUP A funnel into which the metal is poured and which directs the metal into the sprue system (q.v.). Also called a pouring basin.

CUPOLA A vertical shaft furnace in which the metal charge, mixed with fuel (usually coke) is melted by burning, in a blast of hot or cold air.

CUPOLETTE A small cupola with a short shaft, for outputs up to one tonne per hour.

CURE In casting terms, this means to set or harden, particularly in the case of cements, rubbers and resins.

CYLINDER A straight roller-shaped body, solid or hollow, and of uniform circumference.

DE-GAS To liberate or remove the gases which have penetrated the molten metal.

DE-GASSER Unfortunately, both oxygen and hydrogen have an affinity for copper, while aluminium tends to pick up hydrogen. A de-gasser is a chemical, e.g. phosphorus, which scours gas and impurities from the molten metal. The earliest form of de-gassing was to bubble nitrogen through the melt. Nitrogen removes both the hydrogen and oxygen. This technique is complicated and difficult in a foundry. Today it has been superseded by the oxidation-deoxidation process (q.v.). Charcoal is the simplest form of de-gasser because it removes the oxygen before it reaches the melt (see also deoxidization).

DEGREASING (LW) Preparing the wax pattern to receive the investment slurry. Any liquid which removes the greasy surface of the wax. Alcohol, detergent or washing soda are the most common. Isopropanol alcohol with about 0.05% liquid detergent works well as a degreaser.

DENSENER An insertion in the mould or core face, or a protrusion into the mould cavity, to promote localized solidification.

DEOXIDANT A material used to remove oxygen or oxides from molten metals.

DEOXIDIZATION Removal of oxygen from the molten metal by plunging a tube into it containing chemicals with a great affinity for oxygen.

DEOXIDIZING TUBE Some deoxidizers contain lithium or calcium boride. These are normally only used for high-conductivity copper. The tubes used for brasses and gunmetals contain phosphorus. When plunged into the liquid bronze the de-oxidizer both removes the oxygen and increases the fluidity of the melt (see also poling).

DE-WAXING (LW) (also called burn-out). This is the essence of the lost-wax process. Removal of the wax from the refractory mould leaves a void. This remains the basic principle regardless of the variations in the process. The void is an exact negative of the original object. Metal poured into the void makes a replica (or translation) of the soft wax into hard metal. Apart from the change of material, the only difference is a small amount of shrinkage as the metal cools (see contraction). According to the type of process, de-waxing can take place in various ways: flash de-waxing (q.v.), melted out in an autoclave, burnt out in a kiln, or even melted out with boiling water and then kiln fired.

DEXTRINE A bonding agent used in foundry sands, derived from starches produced from maize, potato, sago or wheat.

DIE CASTING 1. The process of introducing molten metal into metal moulds, as distinct from sand moulds; 2. The object produced by this process.

DILATION Outward movement of the mould wall during solidification of the casting.

DIP COAT (LW) Term used in the ceramic shell (q.v.) process for immersion of the wax pattern in slurry, referring in particular to the first coat.

DIRECTIONAL SOLIDIFICATION The progressive solidification of a casting from its remote parts towards a feeder head.

DIRT TRAP (also called dross or slag-trap, among other names) A device incorporated in the running and gating system to prevent dirt entering the mould with the metal stream.

DISTILLED WATER Water processed through a still, therefore containing no impurities.

DOUBLE BOILER A vessel within another vessel which contains a liquid to prevent the inner substance from burning. This liquid is usually water. Most commonly used for gelatine (q.v.) or wax.

DOWEL A cylindrical piece of wood, used for holding different pieces of wood together. Also the name for the metal pin which locates the cope (q.v.) in position on the drag (q.v.).

DOWEL PLATE A plate drilled to match a dowel to register the two halves of a moulding box.

DOWN-GATE The main passage, running vertically, which allows metal to enter the mould from the ladle or crucible, via the pouring basin or cup.

DRAUGHT ALLOWANCE A measured amount of extra material on a pattern to allow for drawing, or shrinkage.

DRAG The bottom part of a mould (see flask and cope).

DRAW LIFT The removal of the pattern from a mould.

DRAWBACK The section of a mould which is removed on a suitable carrier or lifting plate to facilitate pattern withdrawal. The section is then replaced.

DROP CORE Removable sand piece fitted into the mould.

DROSS Oxides and impurities floating on the molten metal (see slag).

DRY SAND MOULDING Moulding in a sand containing more moisture than is used with normal green sand, the mould being dried in an oven before it is cast.

DRY STRENGTH A measure of the property of cohesion of the grains of sand containing no free moisture.

DUCTILE When applied to metal, it means that it may be drawn out like wire. Malleable, not brittle.

DUCTILITY The property of a metal which enables it to be given a considerable amount of mechanical deformation (especially stretching) without cracking.

EPOXY A synthetic resin. Epoxy resin is a hard and durable material particularly well-suited for cast patterns. Mixed with a catalyst it sets hard within an hour.

ETCH To treat the surface of the metal with acid. Etching is used in metallurgy to show up the grain structure and any irregularities or faults.

EVAPORATIVE CASTING (also called the lost foam, the full mould, or the lost expanded polystyrene process). A fast-growing part of the iron and steel casting industry. Expanded polystyrene patterns are formed in dies. The patterns are coated with a ceramic dip-coat and then rammed in silica sand flasks and cast on an automatic, or robot production line (see also lost expanded polystyrene process).

EXOTHERM A mixture of chemicals which give off heat. A chemical reaction (as in exothermic (q.v.) feeder-head). See also thermite.

EXOTHERMIC Any substance which generates heat.

EXOTHERMIC SLEEVE Material built into the cup (q.v.) or feeder-head (q.v.) to keep the metal hot, thus aiding directional solidification (see also thermite).

EXPANSION SCAB A casting defect in the form of a thin layer of metal separated by a thin layer of sand from the casting, held to the latter at one or more points.

FACING SAND A sand which is sometimes placed against the face of the pattern or corebox, thus forming the face of the mould or core cavity.

FALSE PART An additional piece or part constructed on a pattern, possibly to accommodate a drawback (q.v.).

FAT SAND Foundry sand having a high clay content.

FEEDER-HEAD A funnel or cylindrical cavity similar to a cup (q.v.) but placed on a riser (q.v.) to act as a reservoir of molten metal, as required during contraction of a mould, and to aid directional solidification.

FEEDING The supply of additional metal to the casting to compensate for the contraction of that metal already in the mould during cooling and solidification of the liquid metal.

FEEDING COMPOUND An insulating or exothermic (q.v.) material placed on or around feeding-heads to facilitate feeding by keeping the metal in the mould liquid for a longer period.

FETTLING (dressing, trimming). The cleaning of castings, removal of fins (q.v.), in-gates (q.v.) etc. by chipping, chiselling or grinding.

FILLET The radiused corner piece on a pattern or core box, used with the purpose of rounding out sharp corners at intersections.

FINS Wafers of metal projecting from the metal, caused by metal entering parting lines or cracks.

FIRE BARS Bars of cast iron used to hold a coke fire in a kiln above the air passages.

FIRECLAY A refractory clay consisting of hydrated aluminium silicate.

FLANGE A projecting rib or rim used either to strengthen the casting, or to attach it to another piece.

FLASH (or fin, or feather). A wafer of metal projecting from a casting, caused by the metal entering parting lines at the junctions of moulds (q.v.) and of cores (q.v.).

FLASH DE-WAXING Part of the ceramic shell (q.v.) process where the wax must be 'skimmed' (q.v.) to prevent it expanding and cracking the shell.

FLASK Two halves, or boxes, containing the sand mould when locked or bolted together (see cope and drag).

FLEXIBLE INSERT (see insert).

FLEXIBLE MOULD The preliminary mould for forming the wax pattern (see also gelatine, hot-melt rubber, silicone rubber and RTV). A flexible layer is necessary for moulding a complex wax part which has undercuts or protruberances. The flexible mould can then be peeled away without breaking the wax. To keep the shape of this flexible skin, a backing, or case (q.v.) is constructed, usually in two halves (see case). The wax is poured or painted into this mould. Once the wax is rigid, the case is removed and the flexible mould peeled away.

FLOWABILITY The property of sand grains to move easily among themselves and reproduce the contour of the core box or pattern.

FLUIDIZING BED A machine which uses a rapid upward current of air through a screen to aerate a fine powder, e.g. molochite (q.v.), and make it appear to behave like a fluid. The machine is used in large investment casting foundries for the stucco (q.v.) part of the investment process.

FLUX A substance which has a 'scavenging' action by promoting the fusion of impurities to form a slag (q.v.). See also cover flux.

FORMALIN A solution of formaldehyde (HCHO or methanol) used as an antiseptic for the destruction of germs and as a food preservative. *Do not breathe the fumes.*

FREEZING (metal). Metals become liquid when heated above their melting point, and solid when they cool. The moment when the metal recovers its solid state is called the freezing point. Different pure metals and alloys form different structures during the freezing period.

FRIABLE Easily reduced to powder. A useful quality in a moulding sand after the mould has been filled.

FUNNEL A cylindrical cavity through which metal is introduced into the mould. More usually called the cup (q.v.) or pouring cup (q.v.).

GATE Specifically that part of the running system through which molten metal enters the casting cavity. Sometimes used as a general term for the entire running or gating system which conveys the molten metal from the cup (q.v.) at the top of the mould to the mould cavity.

GEL (solidify). The semi-solid state of a colloid (q.v.) when it has been left standing. More usually this refers to the setting of a synthetic resin after it has been mixed with a catalyst (q.v.).

GEL COAT The first and most detailed and time-consuming coat when laying synthetic resin into a mould.

GELATINE A semi-transparent substance which forms a jelly (semi-solid state) in water. Obtained from connective animal tissue such as skin, horns, tendons and bones.

GELATINE MOULD (LW) The first flexible mould (q.v.) used from Roman times up until the early 1970s, and still used under certain circumstances. Gelatine is a very ancient form of glue. In this case it is used not as a glue, but for its viscous and flexible qualities, its ability to seek out cavities, details or texture on the pattern. After the case (q.v.) is constructed, the liquid gelatine is poured into the cavity between the case and the pattern. Once it has set and been chemically treated to harden the surface, the process is repeated on the other side. The gelatine has to be chemically toughened with alum before the hot wax is painted into it.

GLOVES Hand protection, usually against cold, but in foundry work they protect against heat and molten metal. Foundry gloves are usually made of leather or asbestos, or an asbestos substitute. Welding gloves protect against both metal burns and flash burns. Ceramic fibre (q.v.) blanket protects the gloves from direct contact with red hot steel or hot moulds. Because gloves are always expensive, the use of ceramic fibre blanket cannot be too highly recommended.

GRAPHITE A crystalline form of carbon used in the making of crucibles. Also known as black lead, plumbago (q.v.).

GREEN SAND Sand containing free moisture, as distinct from sand which has been dried.

GREEN STRENGTH (or green bond). A measure of the cohesion of sand grains containing free moisture at atmospheric temperature. Usually determined by a compression test.

GROG This is either fireclay (q.v.) after calcination, or crushed firebricks. The main constituent of compo (q.v.). Grog is also a common refractory used for investing lost-wax moulds by the block method.

GYPSUM Basic raw material of plaster of Paris (see plaster).

HEADER A riser (q.v.), often quite large in section, which acts as a reservoir and feeds extra metal to the casting, not to be confused with the in-gate or runner system.

HEMISPHERE The half of a sphere or globe divided by a plane passing through its centre.

HOLDING KILN Low-temperature oven used to keep moulds warm after flash de-waxing (see ceramic shell process).

HORNGATE A variation of the running and gating system.

HOT-MELT RUBBER (see also thermoplastic). Successor to gelatine (q.v.). An intermediate solution to the problem of flexible moulding, before the invention of RTV (q.v.) rubbers. Banned from English schools and colleges in the 1970s for fear of carcinogens, later the makers improved it and removed the dangerous toxins. Hot melts are not as accurate as RTVs, nor as a well-made gelatine mould. However, they are extremely useful as an intermediate process for making and then re-moulding the pattern. Hot melts do not penetrate like RTVs, and so are useful for taking impressions off clay. The second advantage is cheapness: hot melts have a good shelf-life and can be used, remelted and used again many times.

HOT SHORTNESS An undesirable property of certain metals whereby they are brittle at some elevated temperature ranges (e.g. bronze).

HOT SPOT An area of heat concentration usually found at positions of joining sections in a casting, or due to the impingement of a stream of metal from the gate causing localized heating. Hot spots can be avoided by improving the sprue design.

HYDROFLUORIC ACID One of two ways of removing the last traces of ceramic shell from a casting. The other is caustic soda. An efficient but exceptionally dangerous acid, chemists and safety officers advise against using hydrofluoric acid because of the danger to health. Despite this, it has the great advantage that it removes exceptionally hard ceramic material. It is also used to etch plate glass.

IGNEOUS Literally 'of the nature of fire'. Generally refers to volcanic rocks or minerals produced by extreme heat.

INCLUSION A non-metallic particle of slag (q.v.), oxide or other chemical compound which has become entangled in the metal during its manufacture. (Most frequently found either as a sand or slag inclusion).

INDIAN METHOD (LW) See clay slurry.

INDUCTION FURNACE The metal is held in a refractory container surrounded by a coil through which an alternating current passes. This induces currents in the metal, causing it to be heated and, if required, to melt by internal resistance.

IN-GATE The horizontal part of the running and gating system closest to the casting.

INGOT MOULD Cast iron open mould for re-forming metal surplus to casting requirements, or for making ingots (q.v.) during the alloying process.

INGOTS Blocks of metal made by casting the liquid metallic contents of a furnace or crucible into open moulds.

INOCULATION A process of introducing relatively small additions of elements or alloys to the molten metal for the purpose of improving the structure and mechanical properties of the finished casting (see sodium modifier).

INSERT (also called 'flexible insert'). A flexible section set into a plaster piece mould. For example, this could be used to cast a small complex form within a larger smooth area.

INVEST Literally, to beseige or surround. In lost-wax casting it means to cover or coat the wax with a refractory cover or mantle (see also lost wax and ceramic shell).

INVESTING (LW) The technique of applying the investment. In the Italian process this demands a high degree of experience and craft skill. Starting as apprentices, the artisans progress to improvers and then to journeymen before becoming maestros of their craft. Until 1970 this was a male preserve, but recently a small number of women have entered the craft. In the mechanized ceramic shell (q.v.) process, the investing is usually done by robots.

INVESTMENT The refractory coat or mantle enclosing the wax.

ITALIAN METHOD (LW) Also called the 'Roman method'. The process favoured in Northern Europe for around 2000 years because it can be continued in winter as well as summer, no matter how severe the temperature changes. The refractory investment (q.v.) depends on plaster (q.v.) as its binder, and so does not depend on warmth and sunshine as does the clay slurry (q.v.) method. The plaster binds together a fine refractory, which is usually grog (q.v.) or silica sand (q.v.). Fine powdered brick dust was the favoured refractory from Roman times up to 1960, when it was banned as a health hazard. The investment is built up methodically, first painted and flicked or poured on, then smoothed on in blocks, rather than layers (which the Italians deride as 'onion skins'). The result is a thick, block-like mould, unlike the elegant, thin, Indian slurry shell mould.

JELLATONG Pattern makers' wood. Technically a hardwood because of its close grain, in fact this Malay wood is soft and even-textured, rather similar to balsa wood.

JOINT FACE See parting line.

KEYS Wedge-shaped pieces on the edge of a flexible mould, used to retain the mould in its proper position in the case (q.v.).

KEYWAYS Negative spaces in the case to hold the keys.

KILN, BURN-OUT (LW) Describes any form of kiln, oven or furnace used to remove the wax from the moulds. These can range from a simple can lined with ceramic fibre (q.v.) blanket for flash de-waxing (q.v.), or a Roman wood-burning or coke kiln, of simple construction, to a modern electric, gas or oil-fired kiln.

KNOCKING OUT The separation of sand from casting.

KYANITE Refractory mineral of the sillimanite (q.v.) family.

KYONITE Colloquial term for the ash of rice husk, rich in silica. Used in the Newar (q.v.) lost-wax process.

LADLE A vessel of steel, lined with a refractory material, used to carry molten metal.

LEAN SAND Foundry moulding sand with a low clay content.

LIFTING IRON A rod which screws into the pattern, used to lift the pattern from the moulding sand.

LIFTING PLATE Steel plate threaded to accept the lifting iron.

LIQUID TO SOLID CONTRACTION The amount of volume contraction that occurs during solidification.

LOAM A strong sand of high clay and very high moisture content, containing additions of fibrous materials (horse hair and horse dung are common ingredients). Used for producing moulds and cores for heavy castings from skeleton patterns or strickle boards (loam, or 'loom' is used in bell foundries).

LOAM MOULDING (also called strip block). A system of moulding, common in pipe foundries, employing a pattern strickled in loam around a barrel. Such a pattern can, and often does, incorporate a thickness of loam equivalent to the section of the casting. After moulding and removing this thickness, the block is then used as the core (a system very similar in principle to this one is often used with CO_2 moulding).

LOOSE PATTERN A pattern, either solid or split, which is not mounted on a moulding or pattern plate.

LOOSE PIECE A loose piece of pattern equipment so designed that it can be removed from the mould (q.v.) or core (q.v.) after the withdrawal of the main pattern or core box (q.v.).

LOST MERCURY (see mercast process).

LOST EXPANDED POLYSTYRENE PROCESS In the 1950s and 1960s this was seen as a useful method of producing a rough, one-off casting in aluminium, particularly in schools and colleges as an introduction to casting principles. The sculptor, Geofrey Clarke, produced some large pieces, using a combination of pit moulding and lost polystyrene. Later there were worries regarding the fumes given off, and the process was abandoned in schools. Many artists and engineers still find it a useful way to make a one-off sculpture or prototype. Lost polystyrene has now been adapted to make precise iron and steel castings (see evaporative casting). Expanded polystyrene foam is found on rubbish dumps all over the world, so there is usually no problem about a supply of materials.

LOST WAX (LW) Also known as 'cire perdu' or 'cira perdida'). A general name for several variants of the same process. The technique is so old that no one can be precise about where it first started, or when. Castings, bronze scrap and remains of foundries have been excavated in China, the Near East, India and South America, dating from 4000 years ago. In ancient times, an object was made in wax, coated with a refractory mixture of clay, dung and silica sand, and then allowed to dry (all the early foundries were located in warm climates). The moulds were then baked until the wax ran out, and further baked until the refractory was red hot. By this time the bronze or brass alloy was melted. The moulds and crucibles were removed from the heat, and the molten metal poured into the moulds. Once the metal had cooled, the investment was broken off, and the sprue and any flashing chiselled off. This process can still be seen in parts of West Africa, India and China to this day. Unfortunately the craft, which reached a high art form in pre-Colombian South America, was destroyed by the Spanish Conquistadors (see also Italian method).

LUDO or LUTO In lost-wax casting, it refers to the investment (q.v.) after it has been fired and removed from the casting. Because the plaster content has been recalcined (see recalcination), the ludo can be recycled, ground down, sieved and reused. Ludo is used on the back-up coats in the Italian lost-wax process. It has excellent refractory and mechanical strength and costs the caster nothing except his labour. In Italian foundries ludo is ground up and sieved by the youngest apprentice.

LUGS Attachments on a casting for fitting or bolting onto another part.

MACHINING The process of refining the casting by using lathes or milling machines.

MACHINING ALLOWANCE Extra thickness on the pattern (and therefore on the casting) to allow for machining.

MAKING GOOD A pattern rarely leaves (is extracted from) the sand leaving a perfect impression. 'Making good' is the process where the moulder cleans up the surface of the mould and replaces missing pieces, such as corners, that were displaced as the pattern was withdrawn.

MALLEABILITY A property of some metals enabling, them to be hammered and beaten into forms, such as thin sheets, without cracking. Gold is the most malleable of all metals.

MANTLE (LW) See investment.

MATRIX The major structural constituent of a metal.

MATTING Blending in the surface of the casting after a positive irregularity or a runner has been cut off, using a matting punch (see below).

MATTING PUNCH Flat or pitted-ended punch, large or small, for matting (see above).

MELT 1. To pass from solid to liquid state by heating. The melting points of different metals and their alloys vary widely; 2. A general term describing a complete crucible of metal as it passes through the melting process, from cold ingots to pouring.

MELTING LOSS The difference between the amount of metal charged into a melting furnace and the amount of metal removed.

MERCAST Mercury patterns have been used instead of wax for many years. The patterns are produced by submerging the master dies filled with mercury in refrigerated acetone at –60°C. After ten minutes the frozen mercury patterns are removed from the dies. Investment (q.v.) then follows standard procedure (see ceramic shell). When the shell has hardened, the temperature is allowed to return to normal and the mercury melts and runs out. The rest of the process is the same as any other casting process. The advantages of 'mercast' is said to be the greater accuracy of the patterns. *Note: mercury is extremely poisonous.*

METALLURGY The science of metals. The study of the way metals are refined and alloyed, and how they behave; in particular during the melting, cooling, cold forming, work hardening or heat treatment processes. The science of metallurgy is vital to the advancement and efficiency of the foundry industry.

METALLOGRAPHY The microscopic study of the internal structure of metals.

MID PART The intermediate section of a moulding box (q.v.), inserted between the cope (q.v.) and the drag (q.v.). Necessary where more than one parting line (q.v.) is used (for example, in casting a pulley wheel with a grooved edge).

MOLASSES A bonding agent used in foundry sands. A by-product of sugar refining.

MOLOCHITE (LW) A refined refractory, calcined china clay, used in both the slurry (q.v.) and stucco (q.v.) in the ceramic shell (q.v.) process. (From 'Moloch' a fiery god of the Phoenicians to whom burnt human sacrificial victims were offered.)

MOULD The form which contains the cavity into which metal is poured to make castings.

MOULD CAVITY The impression left in the sand after the withdrawal of the pattern.

MOULD COATINGS Paints having a refractory base which, applied to moulds or cores (q.v.), prevent metal penetration and give a good surface finish to the castings.

MOULDING BOX A container, made of steel or wood, into which sand is rammed around a pattern to form a mould (also called a flask).

MUFFLE A temporary kiln or furnace to retain heat, usually during welding repairs or heat treatment, to heat the casting evenly and slowly, and to reverse the same process.

MULLER A mill. Generally, a sand mill or sand-processing machine.

MULLITE A refractory sometimes used in the ceramic shell (q.v.) process.

NATCHES Negative and positive register holes or protruberances in a plaster mould to locate the two sides together.

NATURALLY-BONDED SAND Sands quarried from geological deposits, containing natural clay as a bonding agent.

NEWAR The original inhabitants of the Kathmandu valley in Nepal, famed for their craft skills.

NEWAR CASTERS Traditional casters in copper and brass using their own variant of the lost-wax method, which has changed very little over several hundred years.

NEWAR KILN (LW) Used in Nepal, the Newar kiln is similar to traditional West African kilns. It is fired by hard charcoal (sometimes coke nowadays). The Newar kiln consists of two chambers: the bottom contains the crucibles, the top the moulds. Tuyeres (q.v.) create a draught and increase the heat in the bottom chamber. As the metal in the crucibles melts, the moulds fire out. The white zinc fumes are the only guide to the temperature of the bronze. When the metal is molten, the moulds are removed and placed, partially buried, ready to receive the metal. The crucibles are taken out and the moulds filled. In the Kathmandu valley most of these traditional kilns are disused. They have been superseded by Roman kilns (q.v.) and simple pit furnaces using coke fanned by electric blowers.

NICK (the shell) Before de-waxing (q.v.) in the ceramic shell (q.v.) method, parts of the shell where wax might be trapped are cut (nicked) with a fine saw. These nicks allow the wax to escape rapidly without cracking the shell.

NITROGEN PROCESS The gas nitrogen, when passed through the melt (q.v.) under pressure, removes oxygen and hydrogen. A difficult and expensive process, now superseded by the oxidation–deoxidation process (q.v.).

ODD SIDE Foundry term for the throwaway piece of the green-sand (q.v.) moulding process. A one-piece pattern is placed in a roughly rammed bed of sand in the cope (q.v.) half of the flask (q.v.). This is called the 'odd side' and it provides a temporary surface against which the drag (q.v.) may be rammed, when separated by a parting agent. The odd side is removed and the sand removed from the drag. The drag is then refilled and rammed in the usual manner. Finally, the cope is refilled and rammed in the same way as the drag.

OIL-BONDED SAND A synthetic sand mixture, based on silica sand (q.v.), bonded with a drying oil such as linseed oil. Other substances are often added to give green strength (q.v.).

OLIVINE SAND A sand, the grains of which are formed from a group of silicate minerals, consisting of orthosilicates of magnesium and iron. It is relatively free from scabs and other such troubles.

OXIDATION–DEOXIDATION PROCESS This has superseded the nitrogen process (q.v.) for removing gases from the melt (q.v.). Using a cover flux (q.v.), adjust the furnace flame to a slightly oxidizing atmosphere. The presence of the oxygen in the melt excludes hydrogen. Once removed from the furnace, the melt is deoxidized.

OXIDE A chemical compound formed when an element unites with oxygen, as by the action of burning. Water is hydrogen oxide; sand, silicon oxide and quicklime, calcium oxide.

OXIDIZING FLAME Also called a 'lean flame'. A flame where there is a bias towards air rather than fuel in the combustible mixture. A 'fat' or reducing flame includes more fuel and less oxygen. An oxidizing flame is preferred in the melting of copper alloys to prevent the entry of hydrogen. This is followed by deoxidation (q.v.).

OXIDIZING OIL Vegetable oils oxidize (harden when exposed to the oxygen in the air) with greater or lesser efficiency. This makes them useful as sand binders, particularly in the forming of cores (q.v.), usually with the use of low heat in a core oven (q.v.).

PARTING LINE The plane where sections of a mould are separated (also called a 'split line').

PARTING POWDER Finely-ground material dusted onto a pattern, core box (q.v.) or mould (q.v.) to reduce the adherence of the sand.

PATTERN A model of wood, metal, plaster, resin, or any suitable material, around which the mould cavity (q.v.) is formed. In lost-wax (q.v.) casting, it is also applied to the wax model, or replica, of the original pattern before it is invested. The pattern should be made oversized to allow for contraction.

PATTERN DRAUGHT (also called delivery, draught draw, taper) The taper on vertical elements in a pattern which allows easy withdrawal of the pattern from the sand mould.

PEANING Reducing and compacting metal with a round hammer or punch (see also matting and work hardening).

PEAT Vegetable matter, partly carbonized, used for fuel.

PERMEABLE Can be penetrated, allows gases or liquid to pass through. The permeability of a given sand can be measured. It is the useful quality which allows gases to 'vent' (q.v.) or pass through the sand during the casting process.

pH A measure of acidity or alkalinity, used in the preparation of the slurry (q.v.) in the ceramic shell (q.v.) process.

PHENOLIC RESIN A thermosetting resin used with silica sand (q.v.) in the automated shell sand process.

PHOSPHOR BRONZE A modification of copper–tin bronze. One type of alloy contains 4.5% to 6.0% tin and less than 0.3% phosphorus. This is used for springs and other electrical components because it is resilient and non-magnetic. Another alloy is tough and hard-wearing and so is used for bearings.

PIECE MOULD (LW) In lost-wax, as opposed to sand casting, this refers to a plaster mould used as an alternative to a flexible mould. A pattern with no undercuts and a smooth surface can be moulded in plaster and the wax taken from this plaster. This saves both time and expensive material (see also insert). Ceramic shell piece moulds save on wax and part of the firing process.

PINNED, PINNING Usually refers to the retaining of a mould (q.v.) in the correct position by the use of pins, nails or chaplets (q.v.).

PINHOLE A casting defect in the shape of a small hole, generally found under the surface of the casting after machining.

PINHOLE POROSITY A casting defect caused by the evolution of gases, and appearing as dispersed small cavities less than approximately $1/16$in (2mm) across.

216

PINS, BOX Locating pins used on moulding boxes to ensure proper register of the cope (q.v.) and drag (q.v.) halves of the mould.

PLASTER Powdered and calcined alabaster (see also gypsum) related to cement. A material with many uses in mould making, for moulds, patterns and models of all kinds. Plaster is also used as a binder for the Italian method (q.v.). In Europe there are many grades of plaster, from those used on walls (on the whole not suitable because of the additives) through to coarse and fine casting plasters, refined dental, to extra hard (and extra expensive) plasters such as Herculite and Crystocal. Experience in India and South America proved that their ordinary domestic plaster, used on houses, worked well. It had no additives, was coarsely ground and had good refractory qualities. The plaster sold as 'dental' or 'medical', on the other hand, was useless.

PLASTIC Capable of being moulded.

PLUMBAGO Graphite or blacklead. Used in the making of crucibles.

POLING De-gassing method used with copper and its alloys. Molten copper contains both oxygen and hydrogen in solution. When copper solidifies these combine to form steam. Up until the use of deoxidizing tubes (q.v.) copper was 'reduced' (deoxidized to remove the excess oxygen) by 'poling', or plunging a stout greenwood pole into the melt.

POLYESTER Synthetic resin which sets hard when mixed with a catalyst (q.v.). Its most common use is as a bond for glass fibre. It can be used to form cases for flexible moulds or to make patterns.

POLYSULPHIDE RUBBER (LW; see also RTV). One of several cold-setting rubbers on the market. Cheaper than silicone rubber (q.v.) but not as easy or as pleasant to use. The lead-based catalyst is toxic and sometimes difficult to mix in. The rubber has a good viscosity and makes a strong mould, but cannot compare with the silicone range.

POROSITY The quality of being porous (full of pores). Usually refers to a casting defect caused by liquid metal shrinkage or gas evolution.

POTATO (LW) Rounded, surplus piece of bronze attached to the casting at one or more points. Potatoes are casting faults caused by air bubbles trapped in the investment, which fill with metal.

POURING BASIN or CUP (see cup). The receptacle on the mould top into which the molten metal is poured and which directs the molten metal to the running and gating systems.

PRESS MOULD A plastic material (e.g. clay) is formed by pressing or squeezing between strong negative shapes.

PROGRESSIVE SOLIDIFICATION The controlled change of the metal from liquid to solid state by the skilful planning of the sprue system (q.v.) and the use of chills (q.v.) or denseners (q.v.) or reservoirs or thixotropic feeder-heads (q.v.). The process makes the casting solidify first and the runners and reservoirs solidify later, thereby preventing contraction or 'drawing' (see draught allowance).

PYROMETERS Instruments for measuring high temperatures, particularly in kilns or furnaces.

QUARL The refractory element of the burner head through which the flame enters the kiln or furnace.

RAM To pack sand in a mould or core box (q.v.).

RAIN MACHINE (LW) A device used in the ceramic shell (q.v.) process as an alternative to the fluidizing bed (q.v.). The machine consists of a box, rather like a small shower cabinet, and a riddle on top which is filled with stucco (q.v.) and shaken by a small agitator or electric motor (an old electric sander does the job well). At the bottom of the cabinet is a chute or funnel to catch the falling stucco. This is either recycled by suction or, in a home made version, collected in a bucket. When full, the bucket is emptied into the hopper at the top. Instead of dipping the slurry-covered wax into the floating stucco, the wax is placed in the box and the stucco rained down on it. The operator turns the wax to make sure that the stucco falls evenly on every part and hollow. (Always wear a dust-protection mask.)

RAPPING The act of loosening a pattern from the moulding sand to permit easy removal.

RAT-TAIL A casting defect appearing as a scab (q.v.), a narrow irregular indentation.

RECALCINATION The recycling of plaster, particularly in ludo (q.v.) where the hardened plaster (gypsum) returns to its powder state. Gypsum is calcined, that is, turned to plaster, using heat. Recalcination, therefore, merely repeats the process.

REDUCING ATMOSPHERE A 'fat' or fuel rich atmosphere, much used for certain glazes in the colouring of domestic ceramics. The opposite to an oxidizing atmosphere (q.v.).

REFRACTORY In foundry terms, a material which will not change its state (or changes little) when heated. A refractory brick is one that can be used in a kiln or furnace without fear that it will crumble or crack when heated.

REFRACTORY QUALITIES The qualities of a material, extremely valuable in the foundry industry, which keep a material stable when baked, or when molten metal is poured into it (refractory strength to an extraordinary degree is found in the modern silicon carbide crucible).

REGISTER See natch.

REPRODUCTIVE CASTING (LW) Term used in lost-wax casting where many identical objects are cast. This form of statue casting first became possible when the Romans invented gelatine (q.v.) moulds for forming the waxes.

RESERVOIR (see also progressive solidification) Allowing for shrinkage is as important in lost wax as it is in sand moulding. Any place on the pattern that is liable to suffer from contraction as the metal cools needs a reservoir on the runner or riser (q.v.). A spherical form retains its heat best, so in lost-wax casting, reservoirs usually take the form of a ball of wax (see also sprue system).

REVERBERATORY FURNACE (also known as a rotary furnace). A horizontal blast furnace where heat is reflected off the roof and walls onto the metal charge. A common type still found in Africa and India is the oil-fired, drum-shaped furnace which can be rotated to draw off the molten metal.

RHEOLOGY From the Greek *rheo*, to flow. 1. The study of both plastic and non-recoverable deformations; 2. In metallurgy it is applied to the plasticity, work hardening, annealing and fatigue of metals; 3. applied to ceramics, rheology covers the behaviour of pastes, doughs, and, more important to the metal caster, the tendency of clays to slide, and their plasticity. Those areas described by clay or sand moulders as 'firmness', 'body', 'springiness', 'tack', 'stickiness', or 'plasticity', are covered by rheology.

RIBS Flanges or extensions on a pattern to strengthen the casting.

RIDDLE A coarse sieve used for sieving sand and also in the recycling of ludo (q.v.).

RISERS Vents (q.v.), conduits or tubes which both vent air and allow the metal to rise out of the mould. Sometimes combined with a reservoir or header (q.v.) to aid progressive solidification (q.v.).

ROASTING The process of heating an ore at medium temperature in contact with air.

ROMAN JOINT A sleeve joint on a bronze statue, usually held in place with rivets. The Newar casters (q.v.) still use this type of joint, preferring it to gas or electric arc welding.

ROMAN KILN (LW) A simple and efficient wood-burning kiln used to burn out wax in most, if not all, lost wax foundries in Europe until recent developments in refractory insulation made them unnecessary. Roman kilns were adapted to burn coke some time in the nineteenth century.

RTV Room Temperature Vulcanizing. A cold-setting moulding compound. In the USA the term CMC (q.v.) is more common.

RUNOUT A casting defect caused by the escape of metal through a fault in the mould construction.

RUNNER (LW) The meaning is slightly different in lost-wax casting from the sand moulding term (see below). Any tube carrying molten metal towards the mould cavity is a runner. Smaller runners connecting the main runner to the mould cavity are sometimes called 'feeds' or 'feeders'. It is normal to place these at right angles to the main runner, or even to incline them upwards, in order to put a brake on the flow of the metal. This is the opposite to normal practice in the running and gating system in sand moulding. During de-waxing the wax flows out of the runners just as readily as the risers.

RUNNERS The conduits or feed tubes in the sprue system (q.v.) that carry the molten metal to the mould cavity (q.v.). Also called the in-gate (q.v.).

RUNNER HEAD The solid metal ultimately formed in the pouring basin or cup on solidification.

SAGGERS Ceramic shields placed around pots to protect them from direct flames in the kiln. Used in the manufacture of crucibles as well as domestic ware.

SAL-DUP (LW) Newar word meaning literally 'tree juice'; tree resin.

SAND HOLE or SAND INCLUSION A casting defect which appears as an irregular hole in the casting, arising from the presence of loose sand in the mould cavity.

SAND MILL or MULLER A machine which kneads and mixes sand to develop its moulding properties. The sand is kneaded by being passed between a rotating roller, or rollers and the mill bottom and sides. The sand is mixed by ploughs or scrapers.

SCAB A defect where the surface of the mould (sand or lost-wax investment) has detached itself from the mould. The metal then forms a positive bulge or scab containing the sand inside it.

SCRAP A generic term to describe all types of metal only suitable for remelting.

SCRIM (LW) Hessian sacking, used for reinforcing plaster and strengthening the exterior of lost-wax moulds after kiln firing.

SEGAR CONES Simple and cheap devices for measuring temperature in the kiln. The cone bends at a given temperature; a sequence of three cones, bracketing the temperature, indicates to the operator when to reduce fuel or turn down the heat source on the kiln. A cheap but efficient alternative to a pyrometer (q.v.).

SHAKING OUT Removing the sand from the casting.

SHANK Also called a ring shank. A metal holder operated by two men, to carry the crucible of molten metal and to pour the metal into the moulds.

SHAW PROCESS (LW) Very similar to the Italian method (q.v.), from which it derives, in the later stages. The difference lies in the investment procedure. A silica sand slurry, bound with plaster, is poured over the wax. When it is set the complete mould is inverted and placed in the kiln, flask and all. After that the technique is the same as the Italian. The Shaw process was invented during World War II to produce precise castings at a time when there was a shortage of skilled labour.

SHELL MOULDING A process in which thin biscuit-like moulds or cores are made, using a sand bonded with a thermosetting resin to set in the form of a thin shell against the faces of hot pattern plate or core box (not to be confused with ceramic shell).

SHELLAC An ancient form of quick-drying varnish made from the excreta of the lac beetle, found in the jungles of South-east Asia.

SHORT RUN A cast which is incomplete because the quantity of molten metal available was insufficient, or had insufficient fluidity.

SHOT BLAST or SAND BLAST A casting cleaning process which utilizes abrasive particles directed through a nozzle under pressure onto the casting being cleaned.

SHRINKAGE, LIQUID CONTRACTION The decrease in volume which occurs in molten metal as its temperature is lowered to the liquidus.

SHRINKAGE CAVITY A fault where the surface of the casting is deformed and drawn inwards, caused either by bad planning in the sprue system (see progressive solidification) or metal poured too hot, causing unnecessary expansion.

SIDE-STEP GATE A modification of the running and gating system, with the purpose of filling the mould cavity progressively with the hottest available metal.

SILICA See also amorphous silica; colloidal silica.

SILICA FLOUR Finely-ground silica, prepared from quartz or quartzite rocks, sufficiently pure to give a product which is minimum 95% pure silica. Now banned by law.

SILICA SAND (also called 'beach sand' or 'dune sand') Pure particles of quartz. Used in investment slurries in both Italian and Indian techniques of lost-wax casting.

SILICA SOL (LW) See colloidal silica.

SILICON (Si) A non-metallic element second only to oxygen in its abundance. Igneous rocks consist mainly of silicates. Silicon dioxide ('free silica', SiO_2) is commonly found as sand or quartz.

SILICONE RUBBER The best, and also the most expensive, of the range of RTV (q.v.). flexible moulding materials. Easy to use, long lasting, and stable, it has no major disadvantage other than high price.

SILICOSIS Fatal disease of the lungs caused by breathing in silica dust over a long period. Silicosis can be prevented by wearing an efficient dust mask.

SILLIMANITE 1. A mineral of composition aluminium silicate (Al_2O_3, SiO_2); 2. The name of a group of minerals, which includes, besides sillimanite, kyanite and andalusite. This group is capable of withstanding high temperatures. When fused, each of them is converted into a mixture of mullite and silica. For this reason they are much in demand as high grade refractories. Large deposits of silimanite and kyanite are found in India. Andalusite is quarried commercially in Nevada and California and in the Transvaal.

SINTER Literally, a calcareous or siliceous rock precipitated from mineral water. In the manufacture of a pot or crucible it means to form a hard glassy crust during the first firing.

SKELETON PATTERN A pattern made by mounting shaped pieces of wood on a base frame, to economize on the cost and quantity of timber used.

SKEWBACKS Tapered bricks used to form an arch, the arched bricks forming the roof of a kiln.

SKIMMER A handtool for removing scum, slag or dross from the surface of the molten metal, and for holding these from the lip of the ladle when casting.

SKIMMING (LW, ceramic shell process) Used to describe rapid heat treatment of the mould to remove the top surface of the wax before it can expand and crack the mould.

SKIMMING (metal). Removing the dross, and any form of cover flux (q.v.) or slag coagulant, from the surface of the melt before pouring.

SKIN BOB A small upward bulge in a runner (q.v.) a short distance from the casting. It acts as a dirt trap (q.v.).

SLAG The non-metallic covering formed from the impurities in the melt, from the refractory lining, fuel ash and flux.

SLAG COAGULANT Molten bottle glass, or a foundry chemical sold in powder or brick form. Floating on molten metal, it becomes a glassy substance which binds the powdery slag together into a crust.

SLAG HOLE A casting defect caused by slag inclusions in the metal.

SLEEK A smoothing operation carried out on the mould face.

SLEEKER Term applied to various moulders tools designed to obtain a smooth surface on the mould face.

SLURRY Powder added to a liquid to form a mixture the consistency of cream, e.g. a clay slurry or a refractory slurry with a plaster binder.

SMELTING The operation by which a metallic ore is converted into metal by the use of heat and chemical energy.

SNAP FLASK A moulding box fitted with diagonally opposed hinges and fasteners so that it can be opened for removal from around the sand mould.

SODIUM MODIFIER Metallic sodium contained in kerosene in an aluminium can. When plunged into the crucible of aluminium alloys such as LM6 it modifies (refines the grain structure (also known as the Paz process).

SODIUM SILICATE (also called waterglass). A strong solution is valuable as a glue or joining agent for refractories, particularly ceramic fibre board and blanket, for the construction of kilns and furnaces.

SOLUTION The liquefaction of a solid or gaseous body by mixture with a liquid. The liquid produced by this process.

SPALLING (also known as spurling). To flake, splinter or chip. More usually refers to the deterioration of refractory bricks when overheated or heated too rapidly.

SPATULA A broad knife or trowel-shaped tool for spreading plaster, liquid wax, etc.

SPIKE A sharp, pointed implement. A pointed piece of metal.

SPLIT LINE See parting line.

SPLIT PATTERN A pattern split for ease in moulding.

SPONGINESS A casting defect exhibiting a system of intercrystalline or interdendritic cavities of a coarse and usually localized form.

SPRUE, SPRUE SYSTEM The system of channels, gates (q.v.) and runners (q.v.) through which metal is poured into the mould. Moulders often include the risers (q.v.) (incorrectly) in reference to the sprue system.

STRESS RELIEF or HEAT TREATMENT STRESS RELIEF A low temperature (generally below red heat) heat treatment used for the relief of casting stresses. Note: the term 'annealing' should not be used for stress relief treatment.

STRICKLE A straight edge to level any granular substance. Used by moulders to level and make regular the face of the sand mould. A shaped strickle is used for loam moulding, particularly in casting bells.

STRICKLING The action of levelling the mould surface.

STRIKING BOARD or STRICKLE BOARD A shaped board used to form the profile outline in a mould or core.

STUCCO (LW) Term used in the ceramic shell (q.v.) process to describe the dry molochite (q.v.) grains applied to the dip coat, or slurry coat, by hand or using a rain machine (q.v.).

SUBANGULAR (SAND GRAINS) Part way between round and sharp grains of sand.

SULPHITE LYE A liquid bonding agent for foundry sand. A by-product of the wood pulp, paper industry, consisting of a solution of lignin.

SUPERFICIAL POROSITY Small pinholes which are found only on the surface of the casting.

SWARF Turnings from a lathe or milling machine. Often this term is used for any fine, clean scrap metal.

SWELL A casting defect appearing as a distortion on the face of the casting caused by the mould face not being strong enough to withstand the pressure of the metal, or not being rammed sufficiently hard.

SYLESTER (LW) Hydrolized ethyl silicate made by Monsanto Chemicals (see ceramic shell).

SYNTHETIC SAND Sand prepared from sharp or unbonded silica sand by the addition of bonding agents such as bentonite, dextrine, molasses, starch, resins, oils and proprietary mineral clays (q.v.). Also silicate bonded sand used in the CO_2 process (see carbon dioxide–silica sand).

SYTON (LW) Colloidal silica (q.v.) made by Monsanto.

TANGENTIAL RUNNER The runner enters the mould to one side and in a curve in order to give a directional flow to the stream of metal.

TANGENTIALLY Entering a circle at a tangent, to one side. Refers to the flame entering a furnace to one side of the crucible so that it passes round and upwards, describing a spiral.

TAPER To become gradually smaller.

TAPER ALLOWANCE The angle of taper on a pattern which allows it to be easily withdrawn from the sand mould.

TEMPERING A warming process intended to alter the hardness of a metal which has already been subjected to heat treatment. The tempering temperature is lower than that at which the first heat treatment was carried out.

TENSILE STRENGTH Resisting tension. For example, a steel bar or girder has tensile strength where a cast iron bar has compression strength but very little tensile strength.

TEXTURE A patterned or rough surface, or one having complex surface detail, particularly one with deep indentations, e.g. a bronze casting of a horse. The metal body is said to be smooth, but the mane of the horse is said to be textured.

THERMAL EXPANSION Metal expands when it is heated, contracts as it cools. For this reason, the pattern is always made larger than the finished casting (see pattern makers' rule, calibrated to allow for thermal expansion). This expansion varies in different metals and alloys.

THERMITE A mixture of aluminium powder and a metal oxide, particularly iron, which produces intense heat on combustion (see also exothermic sleeve).

THERMOCOUPLE A thermo-electric couple is used to measure temperature differences. When two wires of different metals are joined at each end and one junction is heated, a small electric voltage is produced which depends on the temperature and can be measured by a delicate instrument. Thermocouples are used in many kilns and some types of pyrometers.

THERMOPLASTIC (see hot-melt rubber). A material that softens when heated and hardens when it cools without chemical change. As a mould-making material, it is an alternative to the more expensive RTV (q.v.) rubbers.

THIXOTROPIC A chemical similar to a colloid (q.v.) which makes a liquid move sluggishly, therefore used in the preparation of paints.

TIE BARS Part of the sprue system (q.v.). Pipes tying the runners, particularly in large moulds, to prevent distortion during solidification. Often used with reservoirs (q.v.).

TIG WELDING Tungsten inert gas welding. A sophisticated form of gas shielded arc welding.

TONGS Steel tools to lift hot objects. In foundry tems this usually refers to the two-man tongs used to lift the crucible out of the furnace.

TOP-HAT KILN (LW) A drum-shaped lid on a counterweight system, usually made from ceramic fibre (q.v.) blanket to save weight. The 'hat' is separated from the hearth. When the moulds are fired out and ready to fill, the 'top hat' is lifted clear of both hearth and moulds. This is a useful type of kiln for a small precision investment foundry, particularly as a burn-out kiln (q.v.) for ceramic shell (q.v.).

TROLLEY KILN (LW) A type of conventional kiln, usually firebrick, where the door and floor are one, set on a chassis on cast iron wheels, which in turn are on rails. To open the kiln, the entire base and door are pulled out from the main body of the kiln. This has the considerable advantage that you can work on or move the moulds in open space, instead of the constriction, heat and discomfort of shifting moulds inside the kiln. The disadvantage is the tendency of the steelwork to buckle, no matter how well-insulated. Any distortion affects the rails or frame of the trolley.

TRUNNIONS Literally, one of the cylindrical projections from the sides of a cannon or mortar. Generally used to describe any swivel which allows a cylinder to be tilted, e.g. a tilt furnace which is elevated and lowered in a similar way to a cannon.

TUNNEL KILN A kiln, open at both ends, through which pots or moulds pass slowly on a continuous belt or railway, the process being completed by the time the individual pot or mould leaves the kiln.

TURBULENCE In molten metal the unnecessary agitation or distortion of the flow of metal which draws air and gas into the melt. See aspiration.

TURNING (LATHE) The action of reducing and refining a casting with a cutting tool as the casting revolves.

TUYERE French term for pipe or conduit. In a furnace a conductor of air, usually a forced draught of air.

TWO-BUCKET MIXING METHOD (see also ceramic shell) A small quantity of slurry can be re-used by separating the liquid from the solid, chopping the latter into small lumps and then re-mixing. Despite what the makers of expensive slurry mixers tell you, this works.

UNDERCUTS Indentations in a pattern which prevent its smooth withdrawal from the mould. Too many or too complex undercuts make a pattern impossible to reproduce by sand casting, and so the flexible mould, lost-wax casting method must be used.

VASELINE (LW) A petroleum derivative, useful for softening a hard wax mixture.

VENT A pipe, shaft or outlet to allow air or gases to escape from the mould.

VISCOUS The property of liquids, semi-liquids and gases which expresses their resistance to flow, change of shape or rearrangement of molecules. Generally, the stickiness or sluggishness of a liquid. A slurry (q.v.) is measured for its viscosity.

VITRIFICATION To convert into glass by fusion. Silica sand turns to glass under extreme heat. The most dramatic example of this was the glass formed in the Almogordo Desert, California, by the explosion of the first atomic bomb.

VOLATILE Evaporates easily. Sometimes refers to an inflammable or explosive mixture.

WAX A general term for a wide range of thermoplastics (q.v.), natural, vegetable, mineral or man-made. Waxes can be blended to be of hard or soft consistency, they can be slush cast, or modelled, remelted or welded together. Some recent synthetic waxes are so hard and durable that they can be turned on a lathe. Last, but not least, they can be burnt out in a kiln to leave a negative impression, the basis of the lost-wax process.

WAX GAS Petroleum or other gas produced when the wax melts. If the heating or baking process is not carried on long enough, there is a danger that the wax gas will re-enter the refractory, solidify as the latter cools and stay there. This is dangerous because it becomes gas again only when the molten metal is poured into the mould. The result, at best, is a series of gas blows in the casting, at worst an explosion. *The danger of wax gas, and the necessity for thorough baking of lost-wax moulds, cannot be over-stressed.*

WAX VENT A flexible wax taper inserted into intricate cores during production. When the core is dried the wax melts, leaving a vent.

WEST AFRICAN METHOD (LW) See clay slurry.

WHIRLGATE DIRT TRAP A modification of the running and gating system where the metal enters a trap tangentially (q.v.). This creates a whirling motion which prevents the slag or dirt entering the mould cavity.

WHISTLER Similar to a riser (q.v.) or vent (q.v.), but much smaller. Designed to relieve pressure in the mould cavity.

WOOD FLOUR Finely-powdered wood used as an addition to foundry sands to reduce the tendency towards the occurrence of scabs (q.v.), buckling (q.v.) or rat-tails (q.v.).

WORK HARDENING When metals are hammered or compressed by working, the molecules compress and lock together to make the metal harder. The metal can be softened by annealing (q.v.).

ZERO GOVERNOR A device on a gas pipe to reduce the gas pressure to zero. This is used on a proportionating valve on a gas furnace where a second governor introduces gas into the burner in proportion to the pressure of air from the air pipe or tuyere (q.v.).

ZIRCON FLOUR Finely-ground zircon sand used as a refractory base for mould and core paints.

ZIRCON SAND A sand based on zirconium silicate ($ZrSiO_4$).

ZIRCOSIL Also sometimes called zircon flour. Used for the first coat of the ceramic shell process.

Note: Lost-wax investment casting

Terms used in traditional lost-wax foundries vary slightly from those used in sand moulding foundries. The former terms come from two European traditions: French and Italian, particularly the latter because all the nineteenth century foundries in England or the USA were founded by Italian artisans. Thus artisans in traditional lost-wax foundries use a mixture of Italian and English foundry terms. Words such as 'potato' and 'ludo' come directly from the Italian craftsmen. Precision investment foundries set up since 1940 were designed by engineers, mostly aircraft engineers, and they use engineering terms, rather than Italian art casting ones. Though sand and lost-wax foundry areas are usually separate, even within the same company, many of the techniques overlap, particularly with reference to ceramic shell.

Aluminium die for casting propellers for small river boats in Peru